IMAGES
of America

MEDWAY

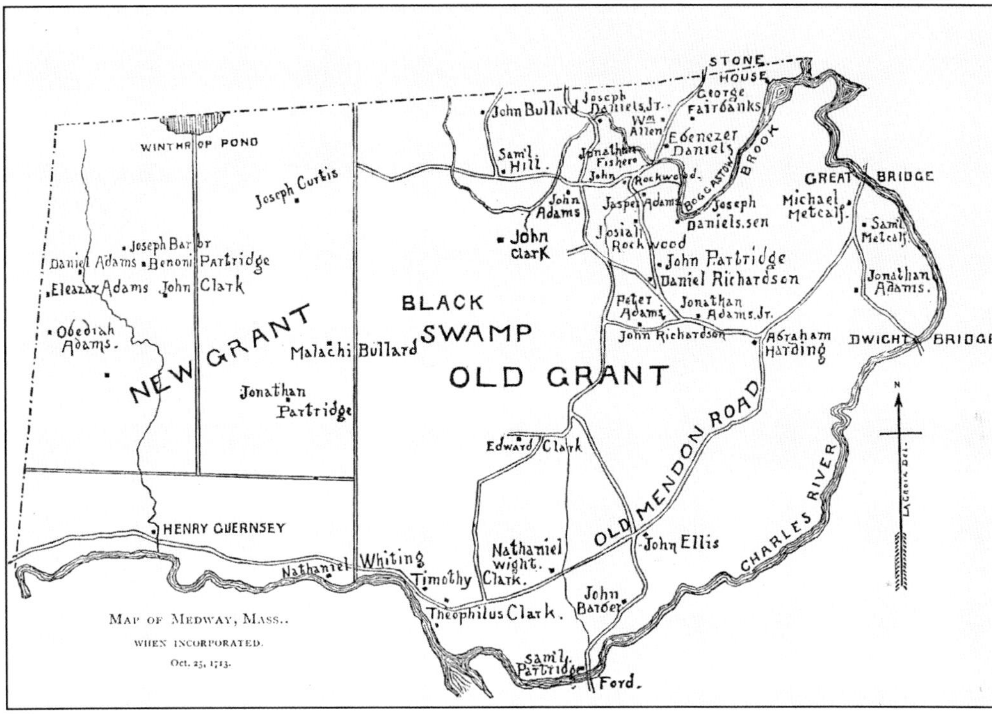

Medway as incorporated in 1713 (above) was bounded on both the east and the south by the Charles River. The map below shows Medway today, after land was added to the west and East Medway separated in 1885 to become the town of Millis.

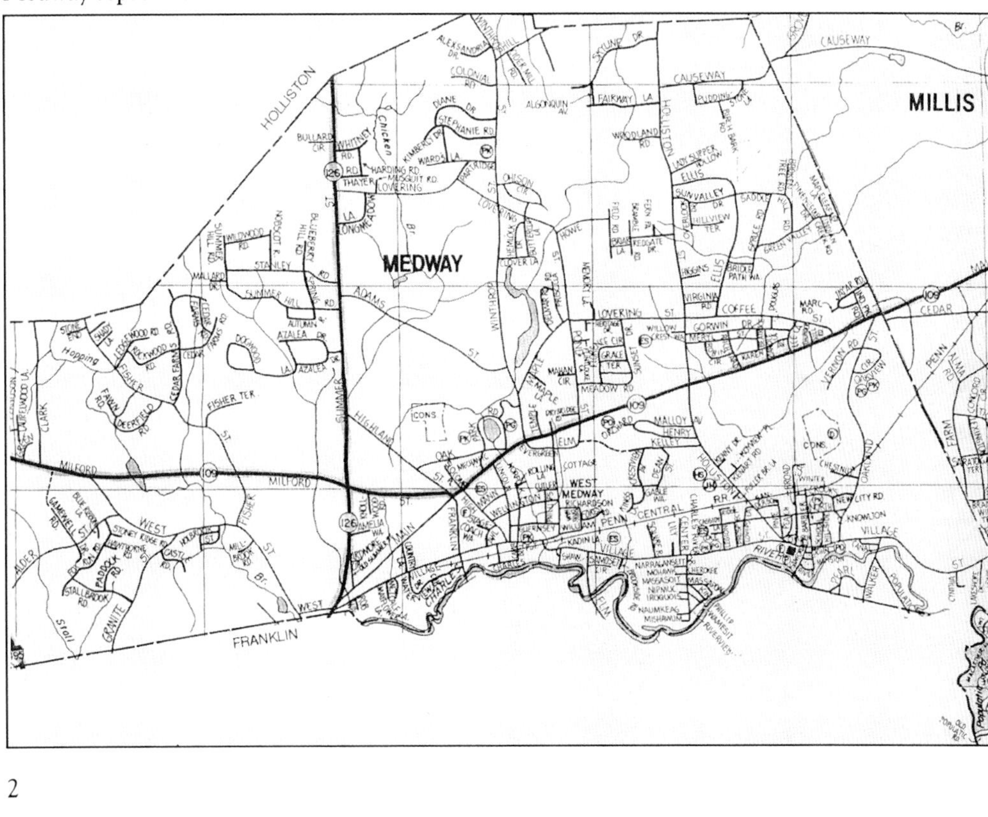

IMAGES
of America

MEDWAY

Grace G. Hoag and Priscilla N. Howker

ISBN 978-0-7385-3581-4

Published by Arcadia Publishing
Charleston, South Carolina

Printed in the United States of America

Library of Congress Control Number: 2004101852

For all general information, please contact Arcadia Publishing:
Telephone 843-853-2070
Fax 843-853-0044
E-mail sales@arcadiapublishing.com
For customer service and orders:
Toll-Free 1-888-313-2665

Visit us on the Internet at www.arcadiapublishing.com

Designed in 1912, the Medway town seal portrays three symbols that are important to Medway's history. The group of trees at the top stands for the grove in which King Philip and his raiding party celebrated after burning Medfield in 1676. The church, or meetinghouse, was central to the founding of a New England town. The boot and bonnet illustrate the two industries that brought growth and prosperity to Medway in the 19th century.

Contents

ACKNOWLEDGMENTS

Most of the photographs in the book come from the collections of Francis Donovan, the Medway Historical Society, and the Medway Public Library. Francis Donovan also filled in historical background for many of the images. Thanks go to Susan Brennan for starting us on our way. We thank the Medway residents who loaned their photographs for use. Lastly, we wish to express our appreciation to Deborah Eastman for her wonderful introduction. Any errors in the text are solely the responsibility of the authors. Proceeds from the sale of the book will go to the Medway Historical Society.

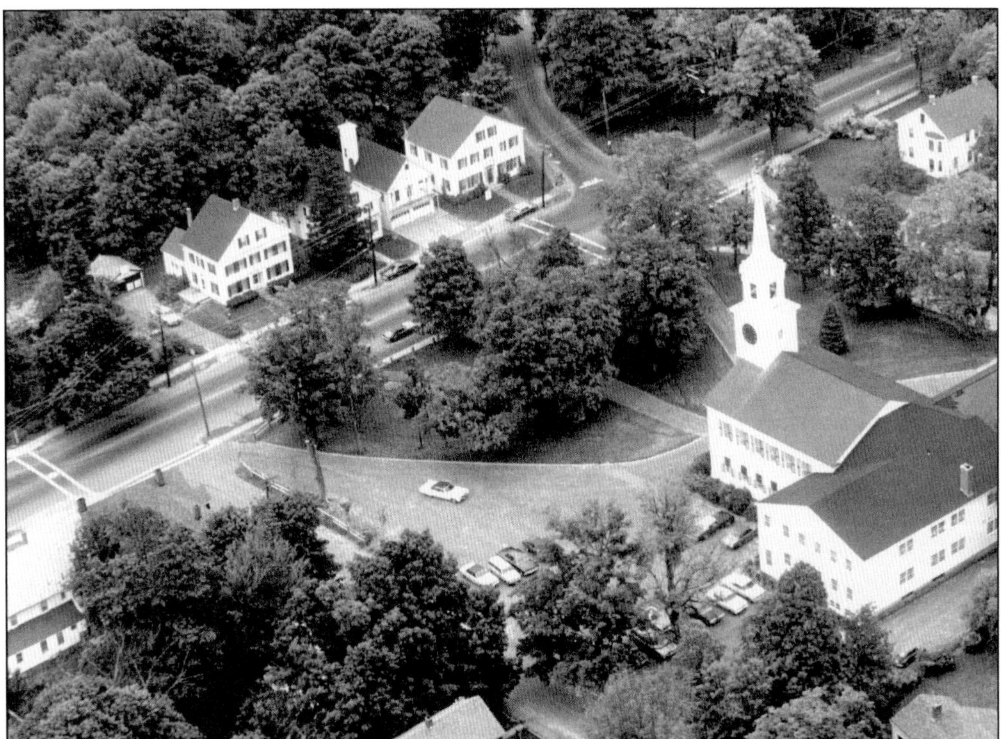

The center of Rabbit Hill Historic District is shown *c.* 1965. After a four-year effort by the Medway Historical Commission, this area of West Medway, comprising 58 buildings, was established as a historic district and was listed on the National Register of Historic Places in 1988.

INTRODUCTION

A community shapes its personality with the lifeblood of its inhabitants. Through generations of effort and pride of place, it is made home. Whether hamlet or metropolis, with laborers or kings, the community shares the need for a sense of belonging and creates its own spirit. In the process, what may have begun as ordinary in detail grows unique.

Medway, in Norfolk County, was established as a town in 1713, at a time when, across the Atlantic, Queen Anne ruled England and George Frideric Handel was composing his *Te Deum* in honor of the Peace of Utrecht. The name Medway originates from the town's location halfway between Providence and Boston and what local historian Rev. E. O. Jameson called "its quiet loveliness of landscape and far-reaching meadow-lands."

After nearby Medfield was established as a town in 1651, an increasing number of newcomers settled on land west of the Charles River. By 1712, this settlement west of the Charles had grown large enough to petition the Massachusetts General Court for a separate new town. That petition was granted, and the town of Medway was incorporated on October 25, 1713. At its founding and for 170 years afterward, the town of Medway included the land that is now Millis. Eventually, the eastern section of town, known as East Medway, separated in 1885 to form the town of Millis and Medway assumed the shape it has today.

As Medway approaches its tercentenary, the town has matured from a humble farming village to a thriving and desirable location of suburban Metrowest.

When the European settlers arrived, a tribe of Algonquin Indians called the Mucksquit camped here as a seasonal community beside the Wennakeening, or "Smile of the Great Spirit," now called Winthrop Pond. The Nipmuck, or Natick, Indians lived by the river they called Quinobequin, or "the circular," the Charles. The advantageous spot at the bottom of the U-curve of the river enhanced the survival of these original inhabitants and all who followed after the lamentable King Philip's War. As a resource for food, irrigation, and, later, energy for the mill town life of the 19th century, the Charles River afforded Medway a comfortable location for families and businesses.

As early as 1806, cotton manufacturing was established and became a vital part of Medway's identity. Straw goods and boot making were successful enterprises. The first awl and needle shop was established in 1869. In addition to river transportation, an extensive railway service moved people and goods from town to town. Hotels opened. Travelers visited. Prosperity flourished.

The residents of Medway responded to the call of duty throughout the years. Many of the earliest settlers, whose names mark many streets today—Cutler, Ellis, Partridge—fought with valor in the French and Indian War. Lt. Moses Adams headed the West Medway Company in the Revolution. Medway men volunteered for Company E, 2nd Regiment, in the Civil War.

Medway can boast of certain famous personages. The author known as Oliver Optic, born William Taylor Adams in Medway on July 30, 1822, edited *Student and Schoolmate* and *Oliver*

Optic's Magazine for Boys and Girls. A teacher in the Boston public schools, Adams wrote more than 100 volumes of adventures for young people, with total sales of one million copies. His simple theme was "to make goodness attractive and vice odious."

The lecturer and author Kate Sanborn, born in New Hampshire, settled in Medway in the 1890s on Breezy Meadows, the farm she immortalized in her book *Adopting an Abandoned Farm*. She created an idyllic spot to which many intellectuals, artists, and alternative religious leaders gathered.

According to local historian Gordon Hopper, another famous Medway man was John "Grizzly" Adams, born in 1812, a bear hunter and wild animal trainer. After losing a fortune in the California's gold rush of 1849, Adams adopted an orphaned grizzly bear cub and launched a new career in Rowe's Pioneer Circus in San Francisco. Later, he worked for Phineas T. Barnum in New York and wrote newspaper articles. In the 1970s, the legend of Grizzly Adams's rugged lifestyle was popularized into a mainstream television series.

An accomplished landscape and portrait painter was reared here in this town of meadows. Anson Daniels, born in 1813, was, as his obituary in 1884 said, "possessed of more than ordinary attainments." He lived in Medway all his life, and his house is still standing.

West Medway's Rabbit Hill Historic District is part of the National Register of Historic Places and features many examples of fine architecture, such as Victorian, Federal, and Greek Revival. The quaint New England churches, picket fences, and stonewalls—these features still remain.

Medway is not just a quiet village, it has in its history the flame of moral code and intellectual activity. The first antislavery vote in Medway was recorded in 1839. The Reverend Charles T. Torrey of Medway was active in aiding slaves to escape to freedom. Public education was established in Medway by 1873, and by 1901, the Medway Historical Society was founded with the intent of conserving historic documents and artifacts. Today an active group, the society works closely with the Medway Historical Commission to preserve older buildings, scenic ways, and open spaces. Until the 21st century, Medway still had cow pastures on Main Street and cold milk in glass bottles could be purchased on the honor system at Briggs's dairy.

This book is the distillation of time caught in the spider's web of an early camera's eye. Painstakingly assembled by Grace G. Hoag and Priscilla N. Howker, longtime residents and devoted members of the Medway Historical Society, it gives us something we forgot we needed: continuity with our contextual environment and duty to its future.

This is our pictorial and collective heritage. These remembrances may be incomplete, but they offer a sense of what has been gained and what has been lost in the course of 290 years of Medway history. This sepia-toned tribute will remain immutable, palpable, and charming. Time and progress is relentless, but within these pages, we pause and appreciate the struggle and triumph of living and thriving in this early American town.

—Deborah DiBisceglia Eastman
Medway, Massachusetts, March 2004

One

Local Scenes

Medway's early settlers cleared their farmland near the Charles River and Chicken Brook and used these streams for powering their mills. The dams soon became the source of power for local industry, employing mill workers living nearby. Farmers gradually moved to available land away from the river.

Villagers also made use of the waterways for swimming and fishing. After Chicken Brook was dammed on the north side of Main Street for the Thayer Mill across the street, a newer dam upstream created Choate Pond. Construction of yet another dam on the Charles, near the police station of today, supplied power for a paper mill.

A traveler on Village Street today, following the Charles along the Old Mendon Road, can still see how these waterways brought settlers and shaped the town's development.

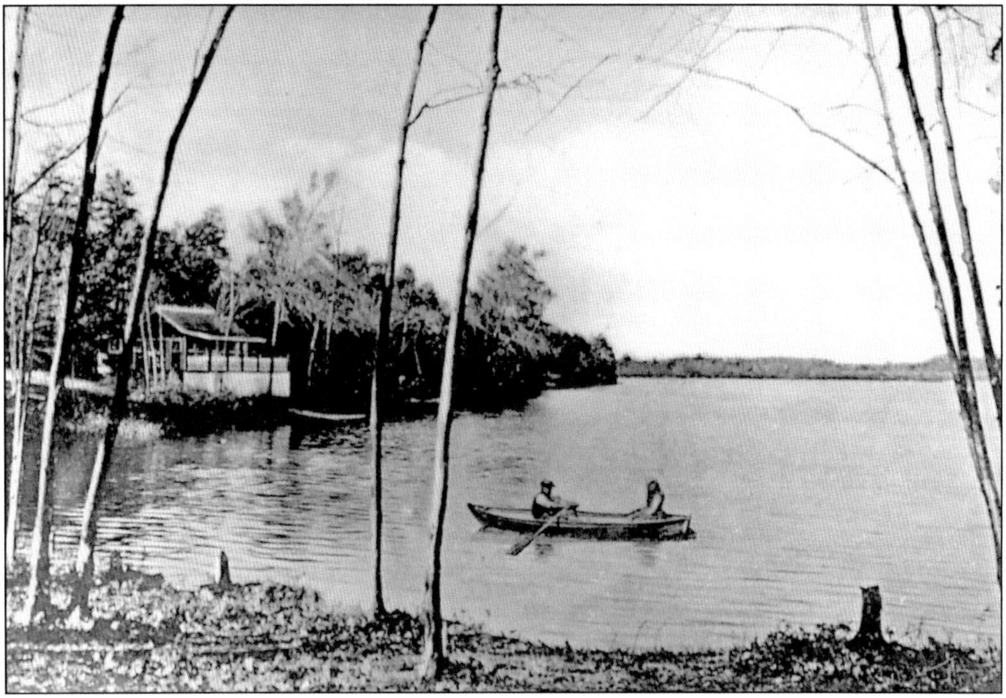

The Charles River broadens out into Lake Populatic at the point where Medway, Franklin, and Norfolk join. The attraction of fishing and boating brought summer cottages to the shore late in the 19th century.

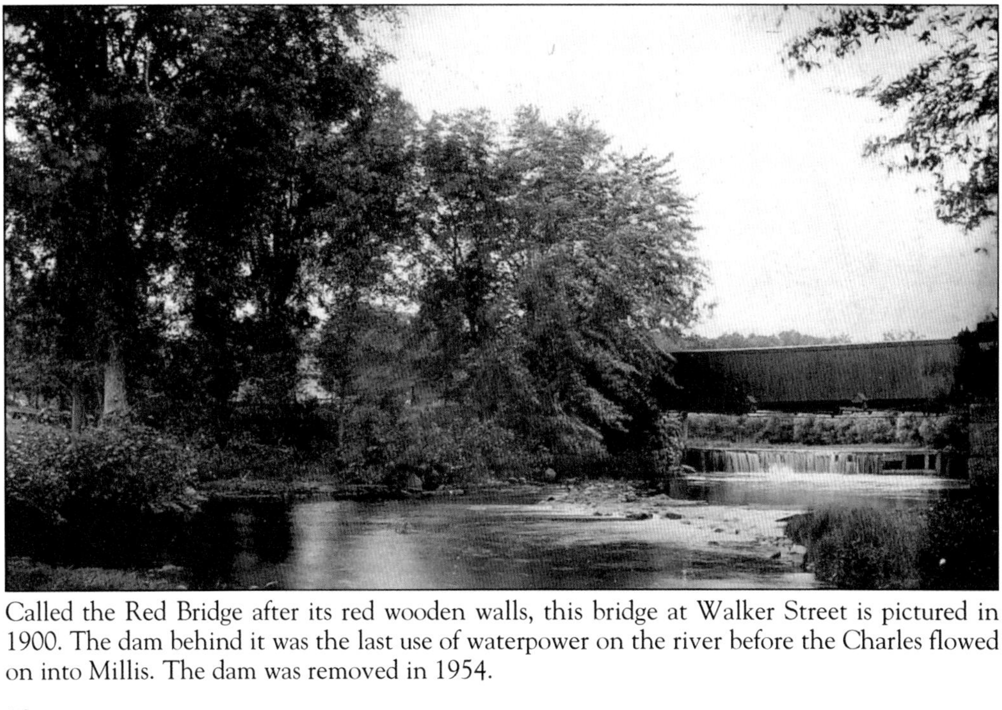

Called the Red Bridge after its red wooden walls, this bridge at Walker Street is pictured in 1900. The dam behind it was the last use of waterpower on the river before the Charles flowed on into Millis. The dam was removed in 1954.

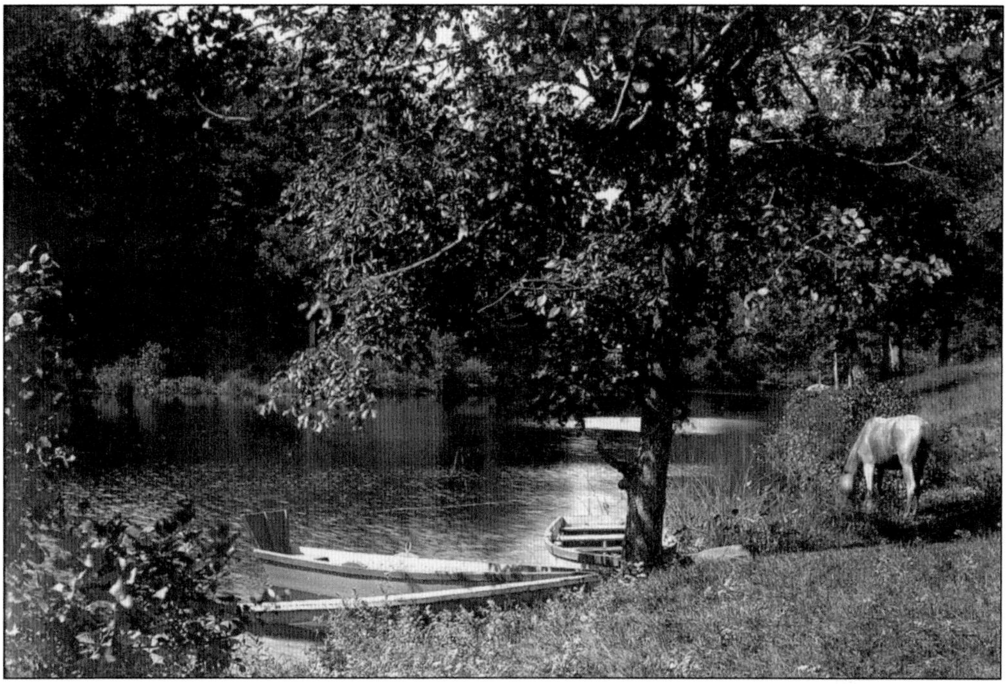

Below the Sanford Street bridge, the Charles was diverted into upper and lower canals, converging at the Walker Street location of Eaton and Wilson's batting mill. These two views along the lower canal in 1895 show the canals were used for recreation as well as waterpower.

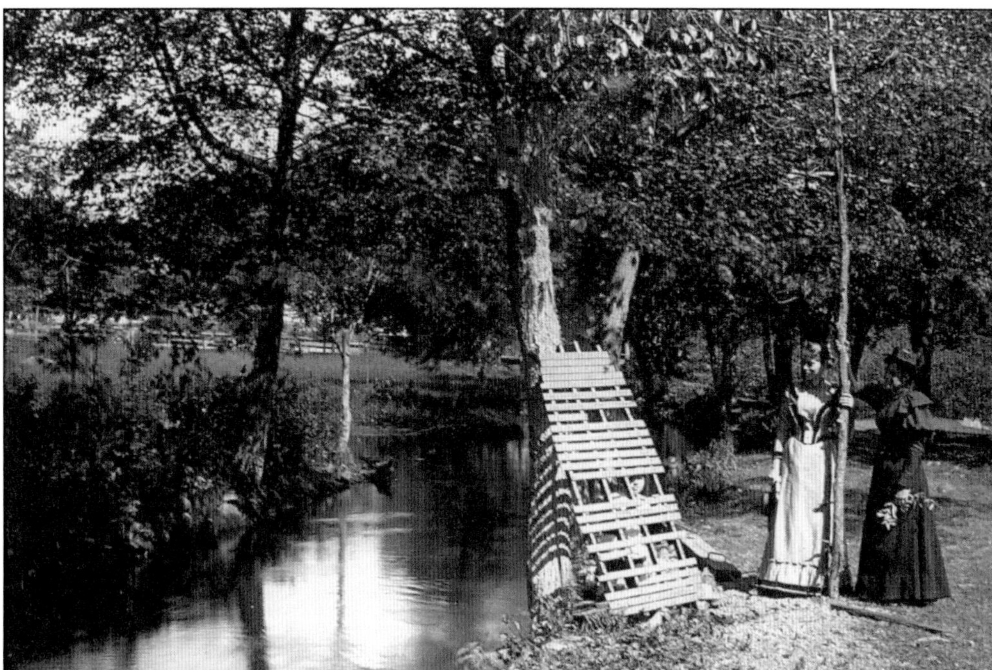

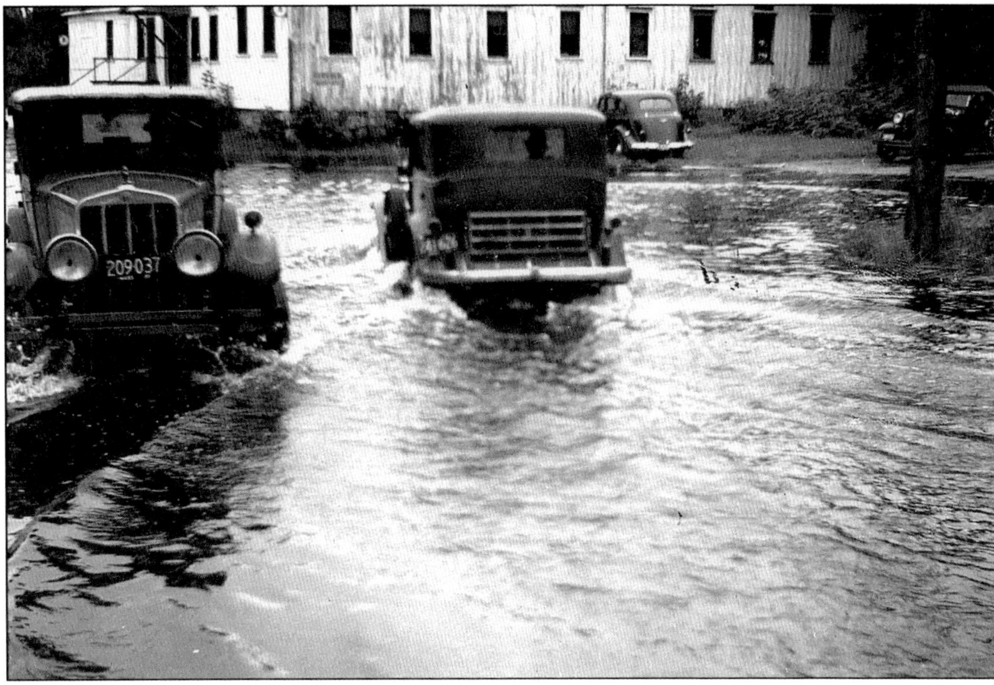

A 1938 storm flooded many sections of Village Street. Seen here are cars making their way along Village Street at the intersection of Walker Street.

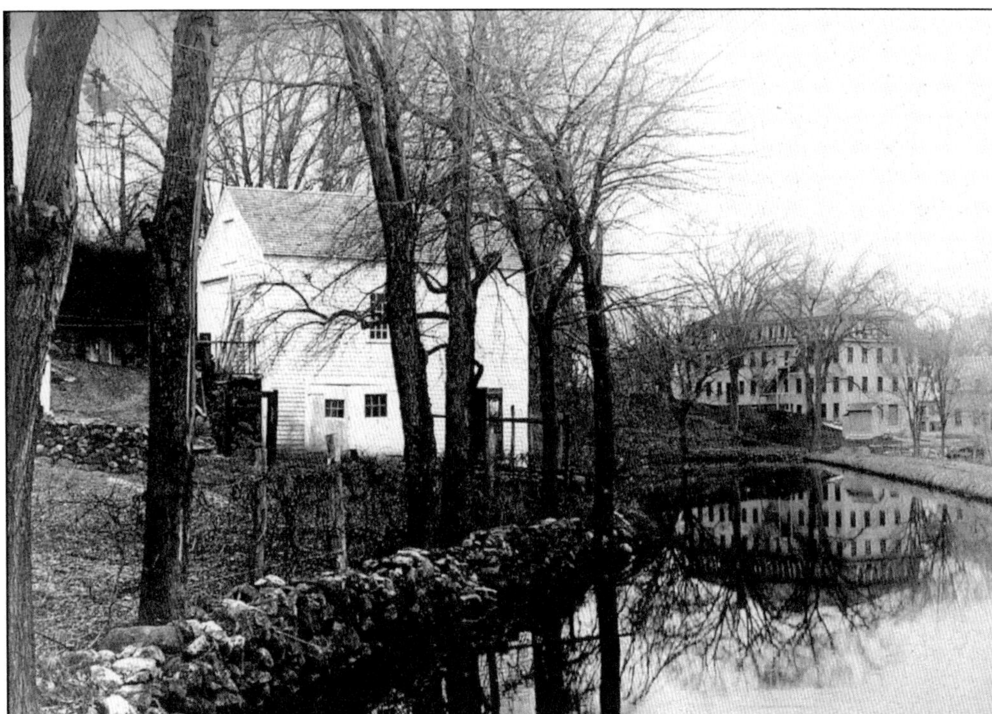

This 1901 view of the upper canal was taken from River Street, looking toward the Thompson Boot factory on Village Street.

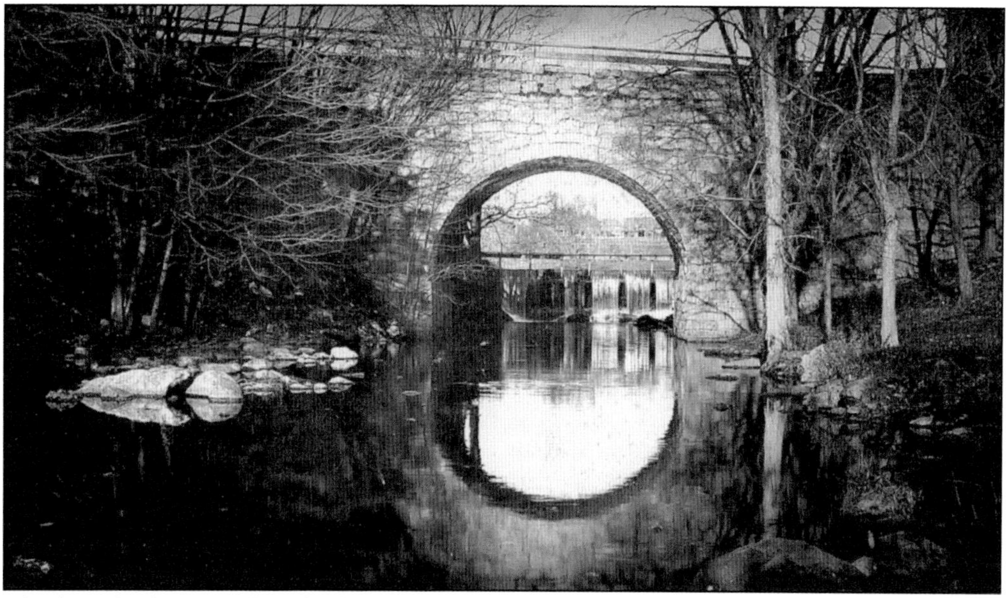

This large bridge over the Charles at Sanford Street was erected to replace a wooden one built in 1806. Through the arch can be seen the milldam and footbridge, with houses on Village Street in the distance. The stone arch bridge was replaced in turn by one of concrete in 1911 to withstand the long span and heavier traffic.

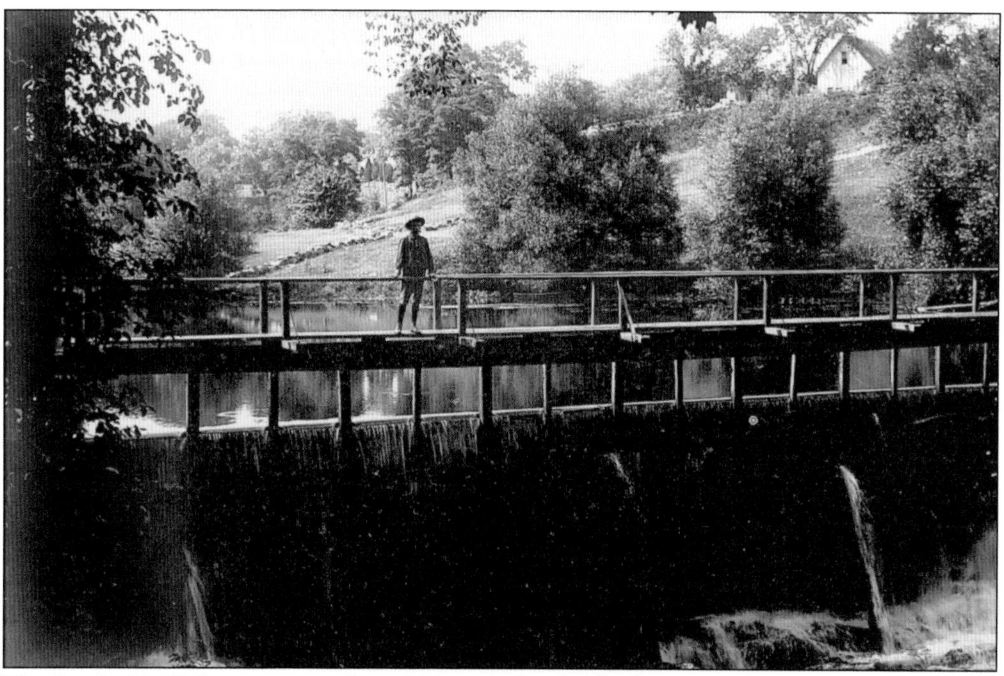

The Sanford Mill dam is pictured in 1910, with the footbridge to Franklin (above). The broad meadow amphitheater (background) is where the 1913 bicentennial pageant was held.

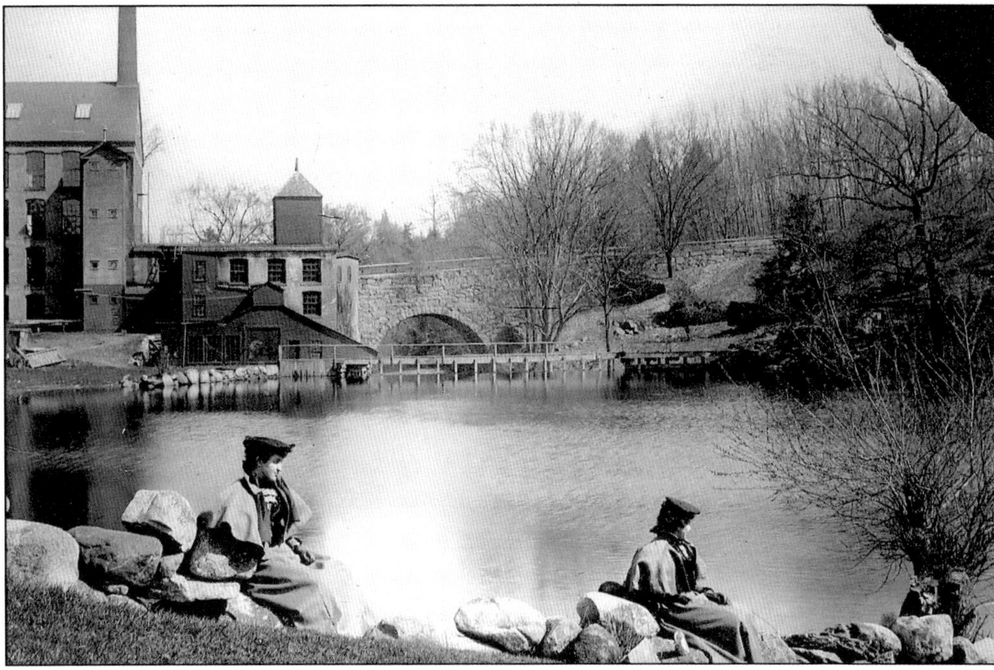

This view shows a sunny day along the Charles River *c.* 1895, with the footbridge to Franklin (background) and Sanford Mill (left).

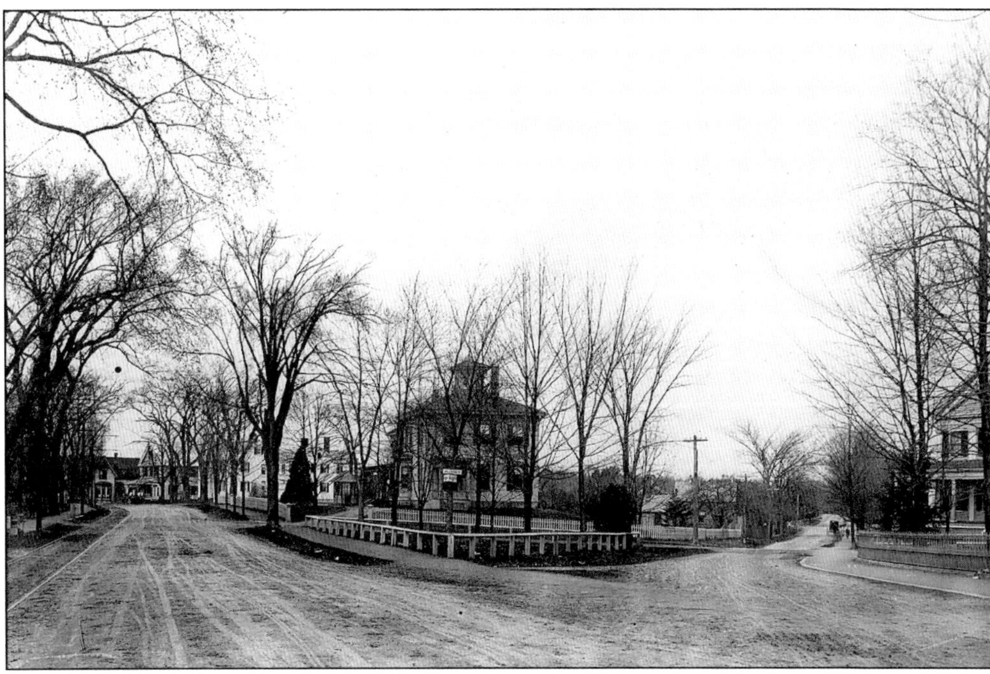

With the exception of the trolley tracks on the left side of Village Street, this 1895 view of the intersection at Holliston and Village Streets looks much the same today.

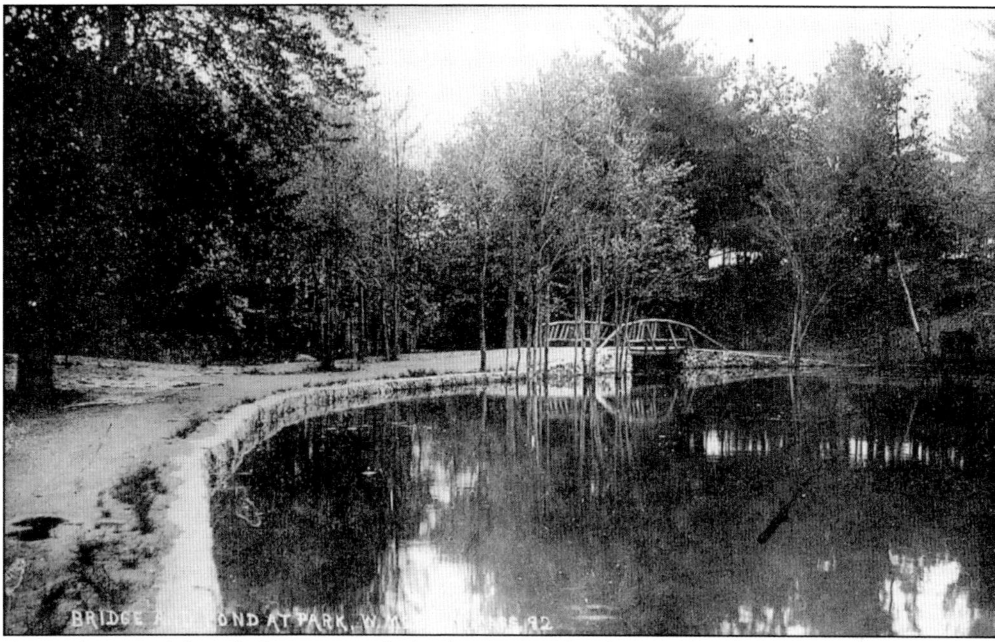

An early view (above) shows a crude bridge across the dam at the Choate Park pond. When the park and pond gained wider use, the bridge was replaced with the ornamental wooden bridge (below). This in turn gave way to the stonework bridge of today.

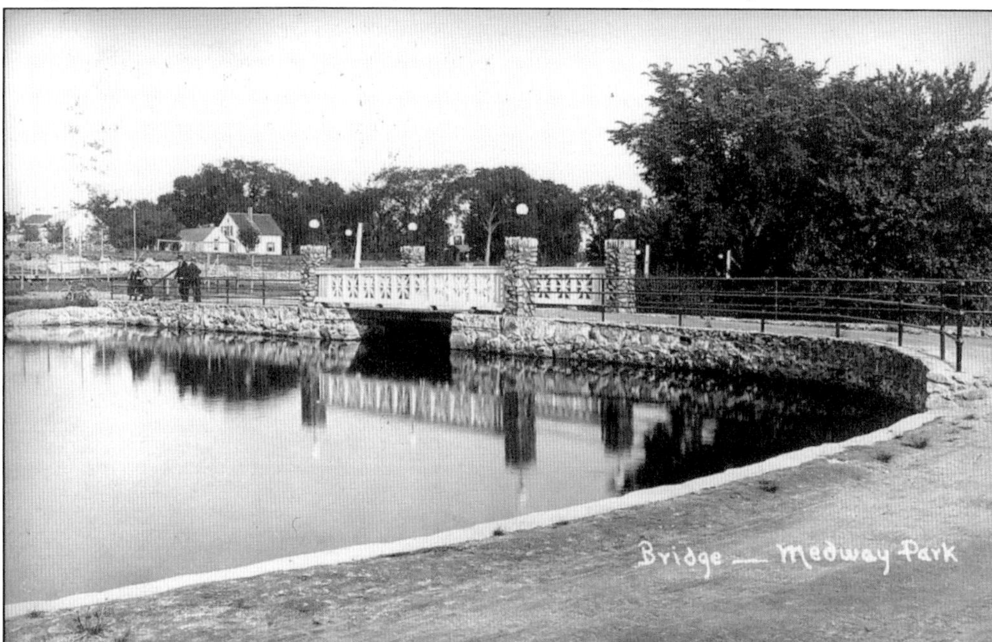

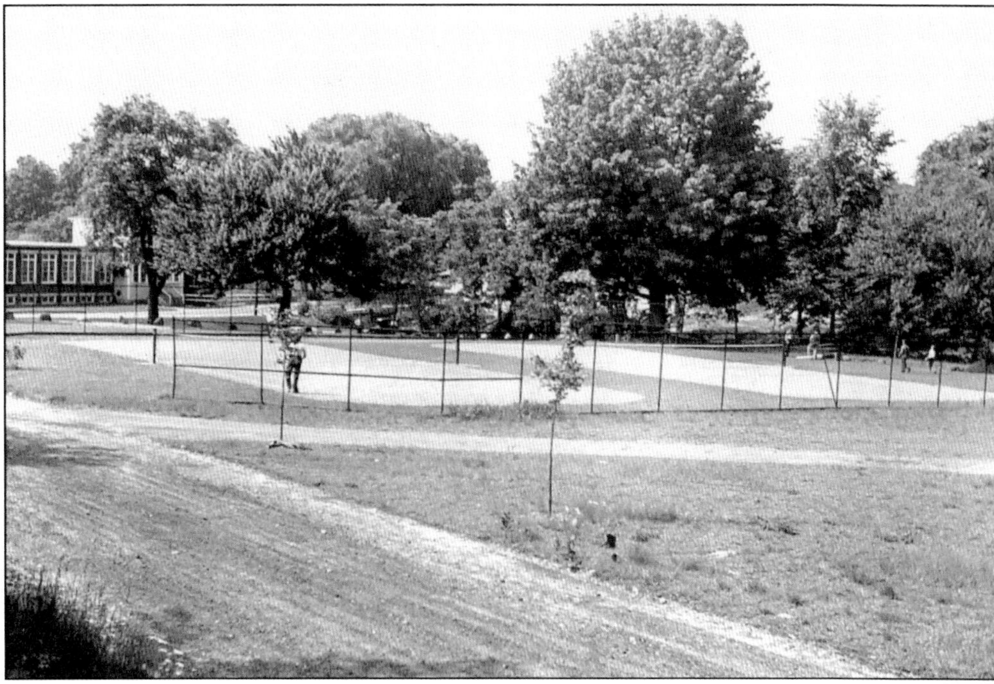

Improvements and additions to the West Medway Park were directed by the selectmen until 1929, when the Medway Park Commission was formed. Shown are the tennis courts in use in 1938. In 1972, the park was named Choate Park in honor of Arthur Choate, a long-serving highway superintendent and park commissioner.

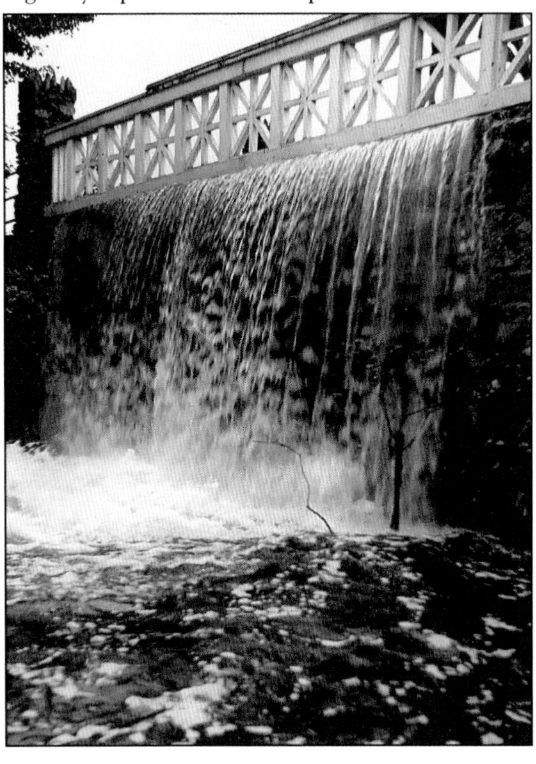

All streams leading into the Charles, as well as the river itself, were flooded by a July 1938 storm. Shown is a view of the small bridge over the dam at Choate Park.

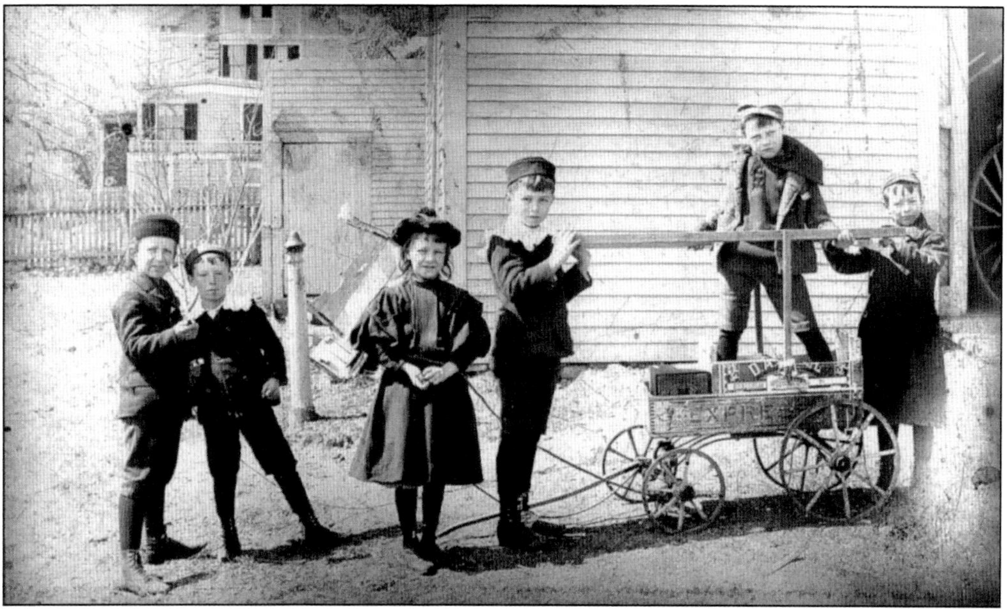

This 1900 image shows "Ownie" Mason, fourth from left, at the hand pumper with his fire department. Mason was the son of well-known town clerk and historian Orion T. Mason.

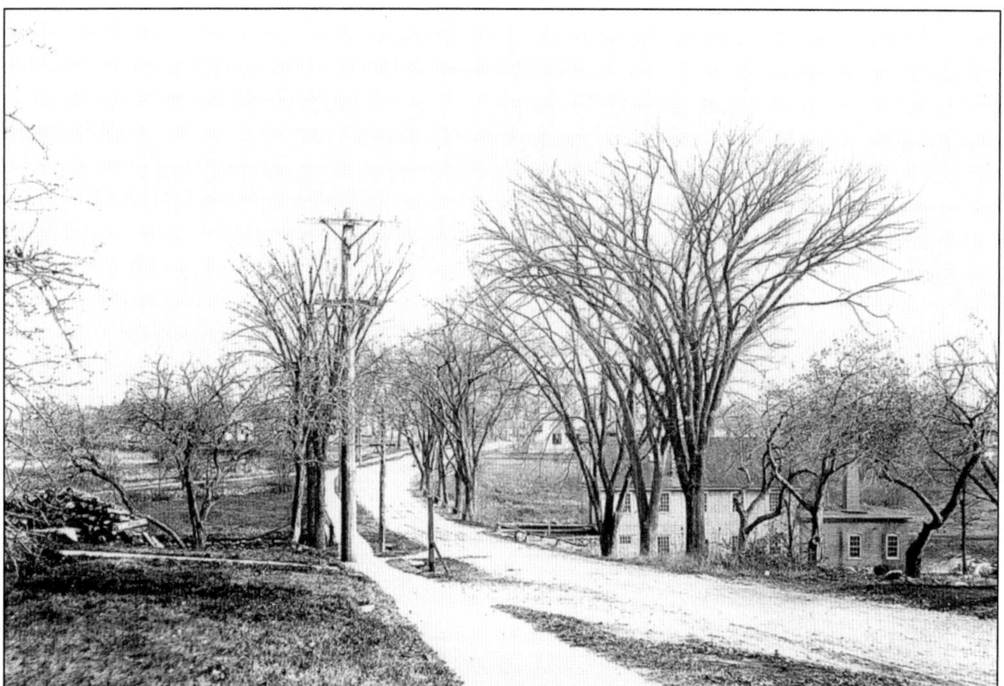

This c. 1900 photograph of Main Street shows the stone mill (right) and the road east uphill past the Jacob Ide house (left).

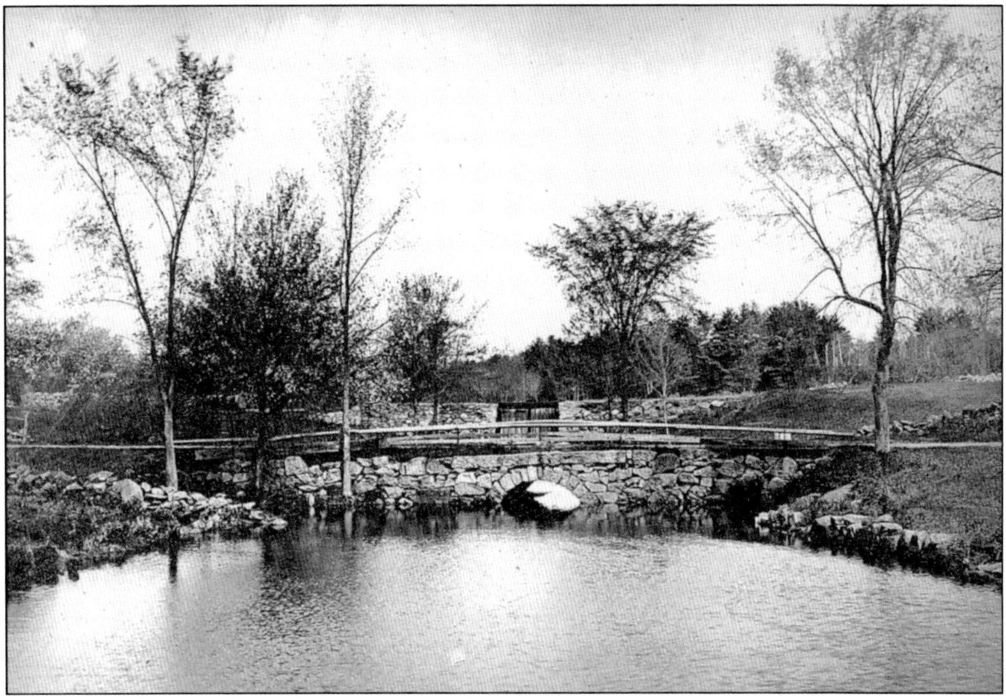

This view of the Thayer Mill pond *c.* 1900 shows the bridge at Oak Street. Pictured from Main Street, the dam in the distance is now the retention dam for Choate Pond.

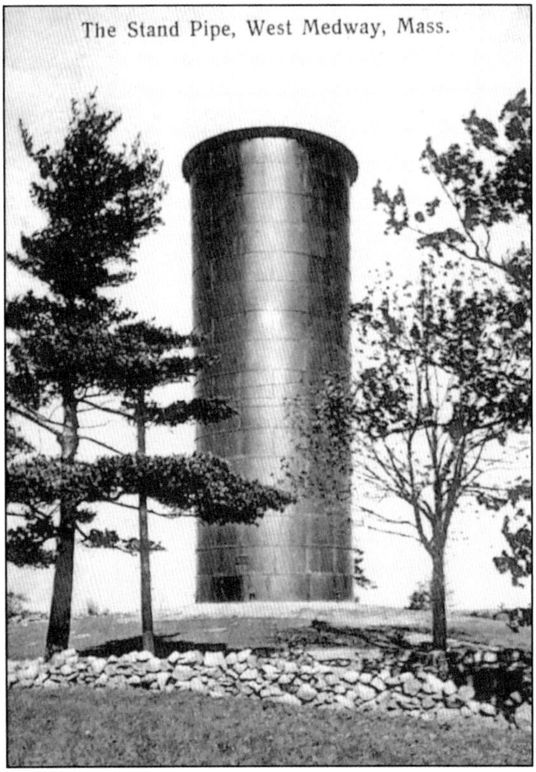

The new standpipe off Highland Street, shown here in 1915, along with the installation of a town water system in 1911, helped cut back dramatically on fire losses.

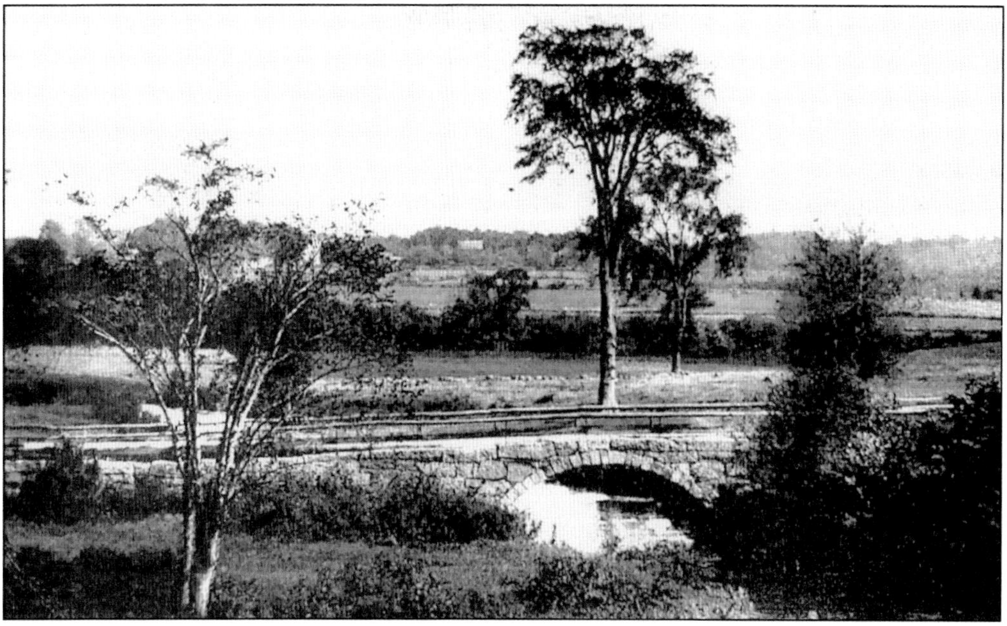

The broad stone arch over the Charles at Shaw Street is the largest surviving stone bridge in town. Smaller stone arch bridges can still be seen at Chicken Brook road crossings.

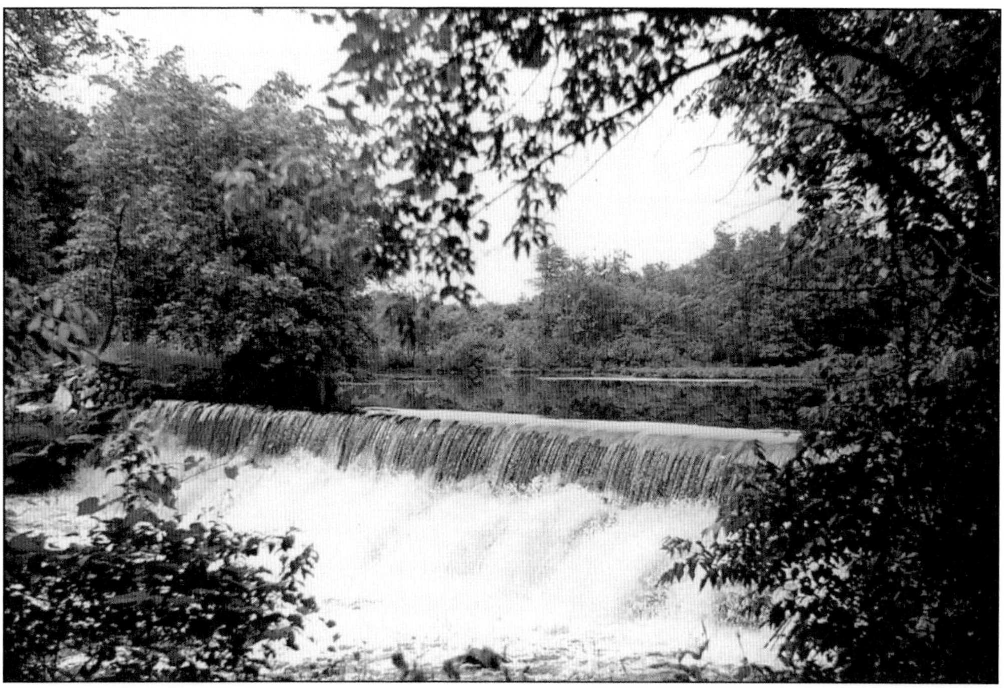

Located at the foot of Cottage Street, this dam supplied power for the Campbell Paper Mill, which operated at this site from the 1850s until the mill burned in 1890. The site is now being restored as a private residence.

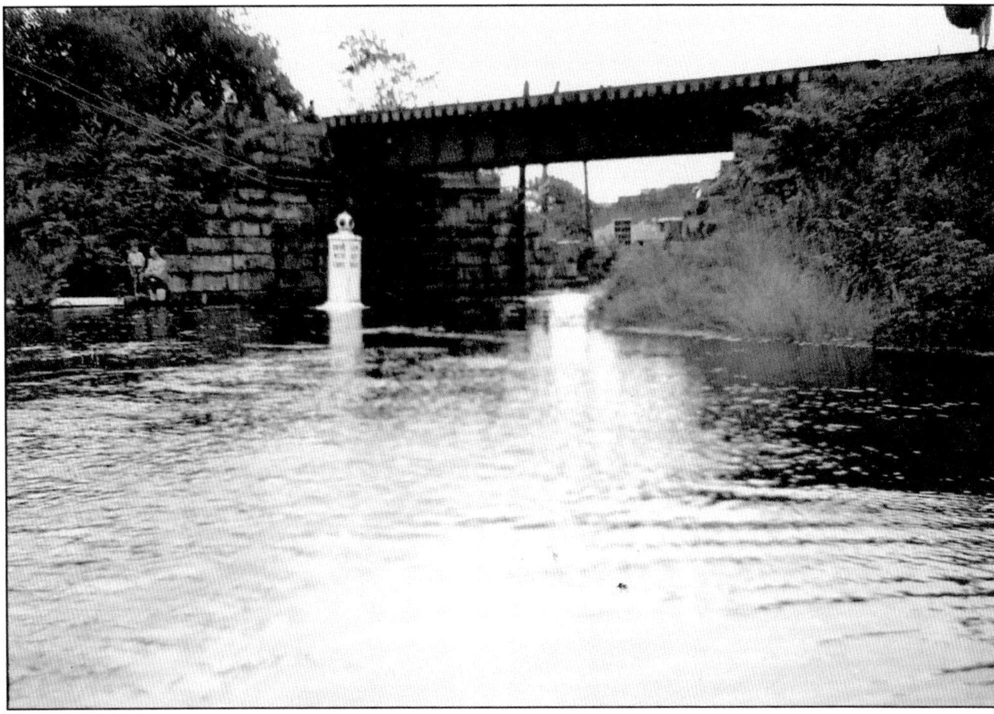

At the "subway" on Village Street near the police station of today, floodwaters from the 1938 storm reached well over a foot. The railroad trestle was taken down in 1968, and the street rerouted. However, the high granite retaining wall (center) remains today.

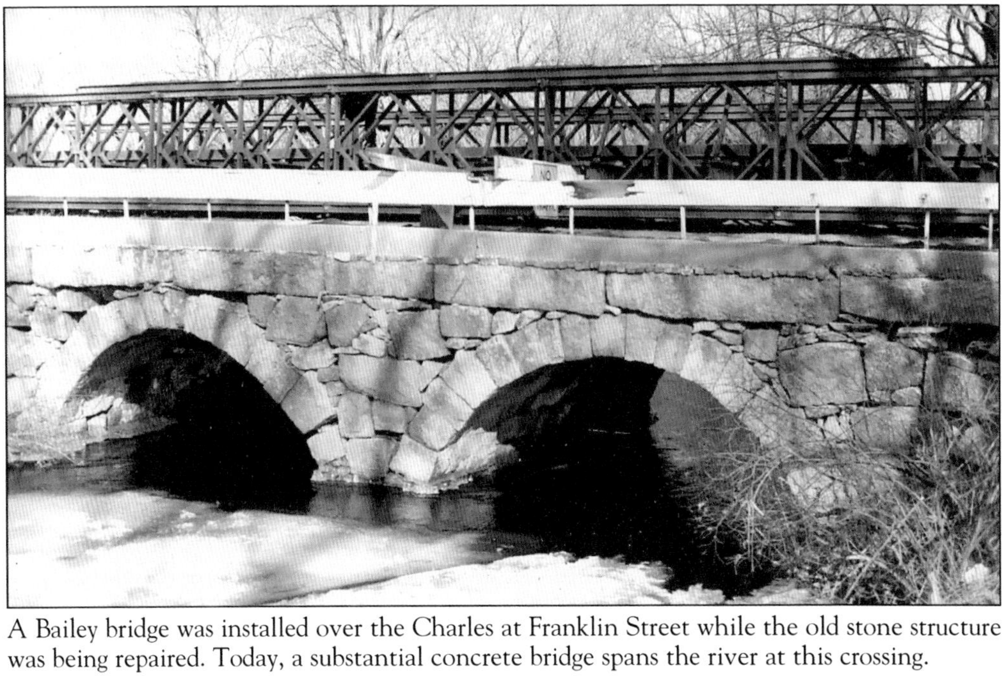

A Bailey bridge was installed over the Charles at Franklin Street while the old stone structure was being repaired. Today, a substantial concrete bridge spans the river at this crossing.

Two

MILLS, FACTORIES, AND BUSINESSES

Medway's first settlers cleared farmland near the Charles River and Chicken Brook and erected dams for powering necessary grist- and sawmills.

Even as some farms moved away from the streams, these settlers employed much of their time providing for subsistence needs. Besides raising hay for their cows and horses, new feed and grain stores, blacksmiths and livery stables further supported self-sufficient family requirements.

But some early citizens with ambition and vision became entrepreneurs and investors, using milldams to power new industry and creating commercial businesses to satisfy local needs. Medway citizens were hired as employees and became customers for the products.

These new enterprises produced shoes and boots, wool and cotton textiles, awls and needles, straw hats, paper, and canned food for local use and for export to other towns.

Doing piecework at home provided families needed income, using available spare time. The boot and shoe factories allocated production and subassembly stages for local men to perform, usually in separate, small sled-like structures in their backyards. Some of these structures survive today in Medway. For some women of the town, the straw factory supplied materials to be woven into straw braid at home, later to be assembled into hats.

Commercial businesses included general stores, grocery stores, dairy farms, hotels and taverns, fish markets, drugstores, dress shops, and eventually restaurants, supermarkets, and discount stores. These businesses provided employment and needed products and services.

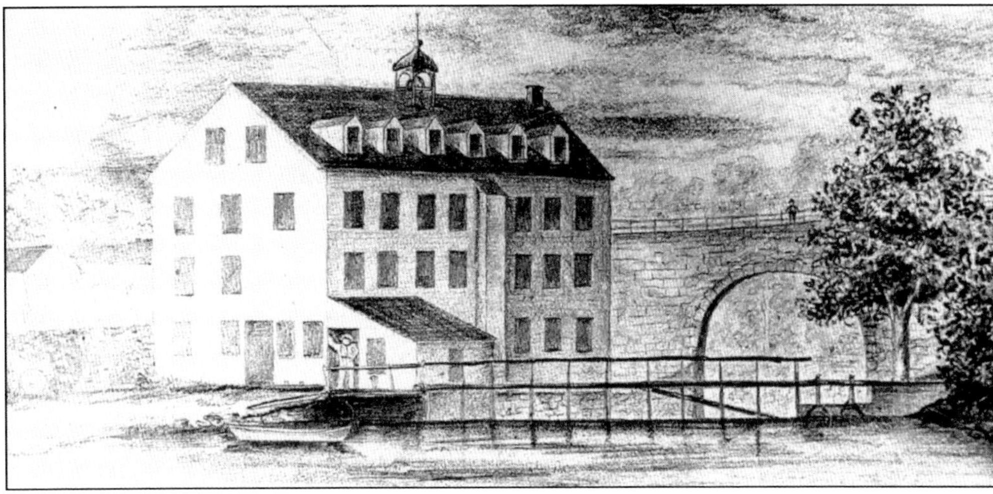

The White Mill was the second mill built at the falls; that is the site on Sanford Street now occupied by the Sanford Mill condominiums. The White Mill was built in 1811 to manufacture cotton thread and fabric and, eventually, woolen goods. This mill was sold to the Sanford Mill corporation in 1881, the building razed, and the present brick Sanford Mill built on the site.

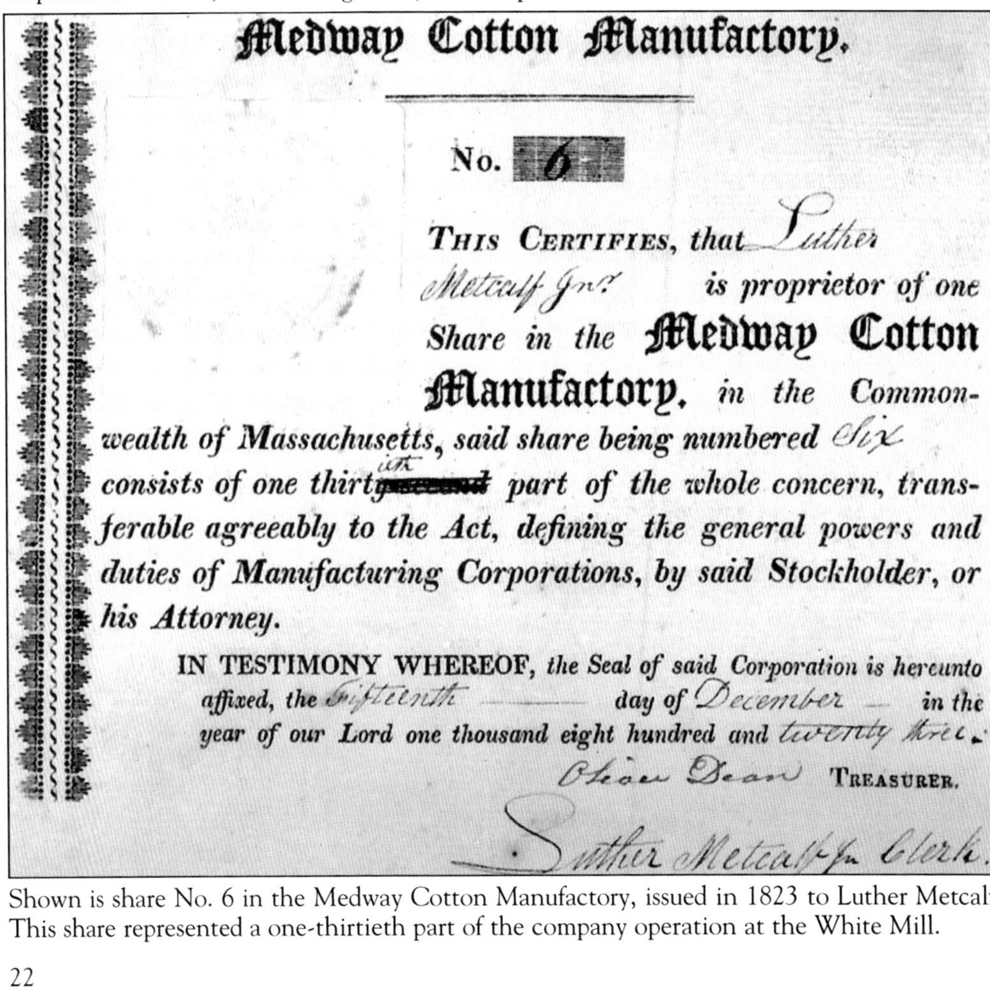

Medway Cotton Manufactory.

No. 6

This Certifies, that Luther Metcalf Jnr. *is proprietor of one Share in the* **Medway Cotton Manufactory,** *in the Commonwealth of Massachusetts, said share being numbered* Six *consists of one thirtieth part of the whole concern, transferable agreeably to the Act, defining the general powers and duties of Manufacturing Corporations, by said Stockholder, or his Attorney.*

IN TESTIMONY WHEREOF, *the Seal of said Corporation is hereunto affixed, the* Fifteenth *day of* December *in the year of our Lord one thousand eight hundred and* twenty three.

Oliver Dean TREASURER.

Luther Metcalf Jn Clerk.

Shown is share No. 6 in the Medway Cotton Manufactory, issued in 1823 to Luther Metcalf. This share represented a one-thirtieth part of the company operation at the White Mill.

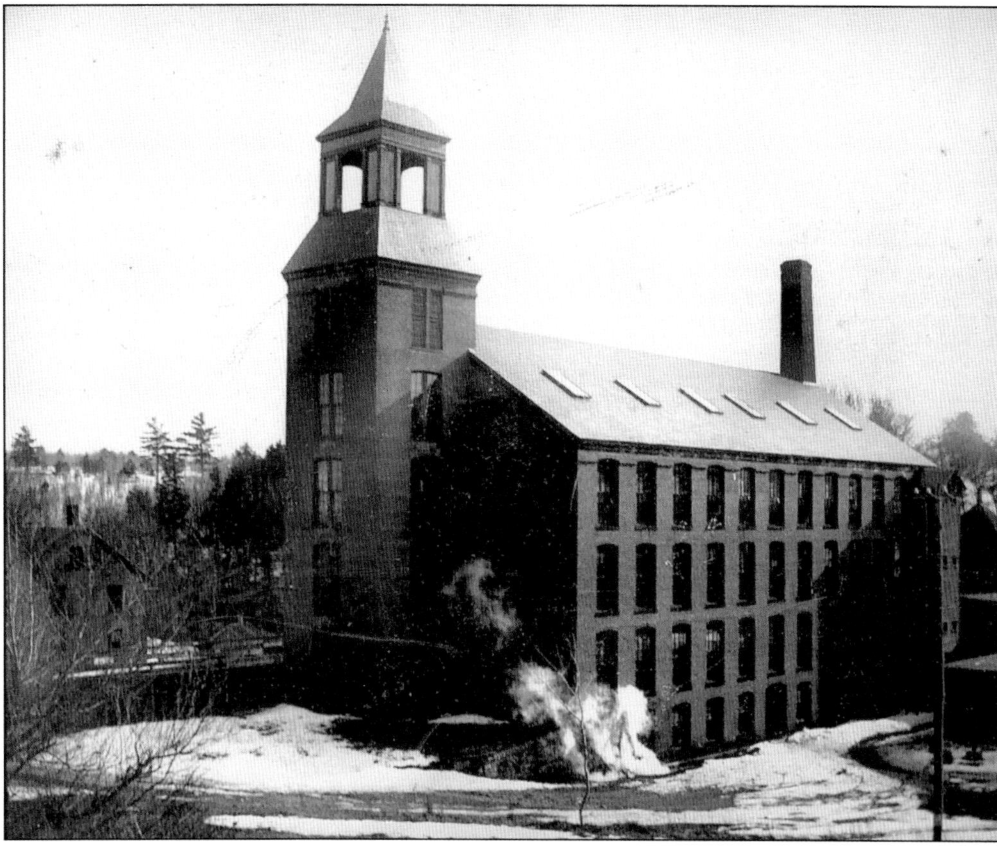

Pictured is Sanford Mill as built in 1885. Later changes included additions at the side and rear.

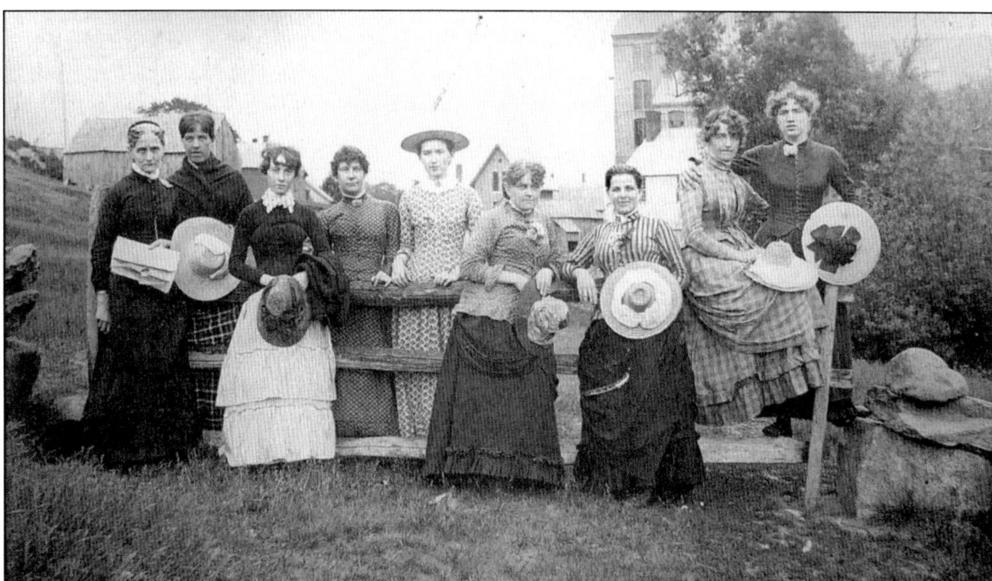

A group of mill workers is pictured in the field upriver of Sanford Mill in 1900. Hats were worn every day, not just for special occasions.

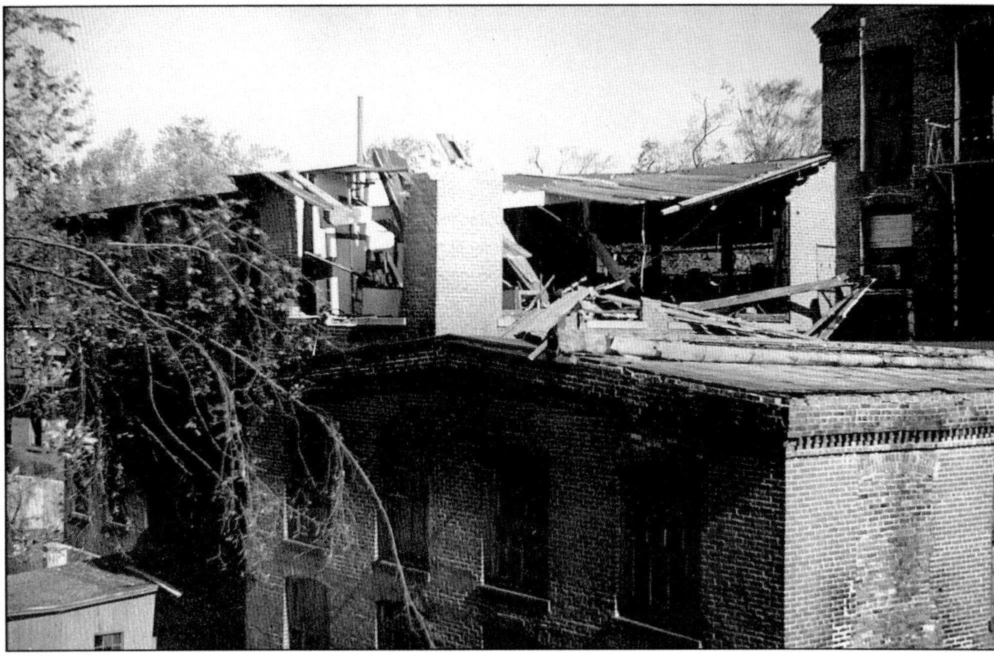

Sanford Mill is pictured after the hurricane of 1938.

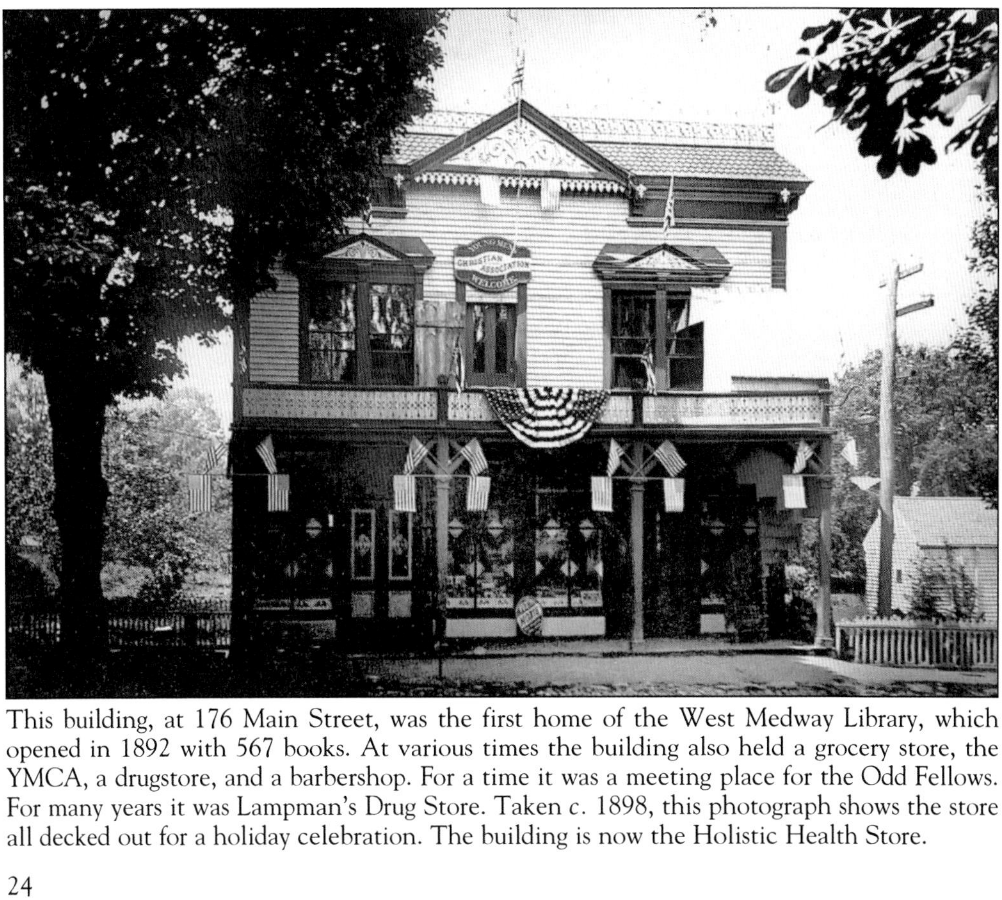

This building, at 176 Main Street, was the first home of the West Medway Library, which opened in 1892 with 567 books. At various times the building also held a grocery store, the YMCA, a drugstore, and a barbershop. For a time it was a meeting place for the Odd Fellows. For many years it was Lampman's Drug Store. Taken *c.* 1898, this photograph shows the store all decked out for a holiday celebration. The building is now the Holistic Health Store.

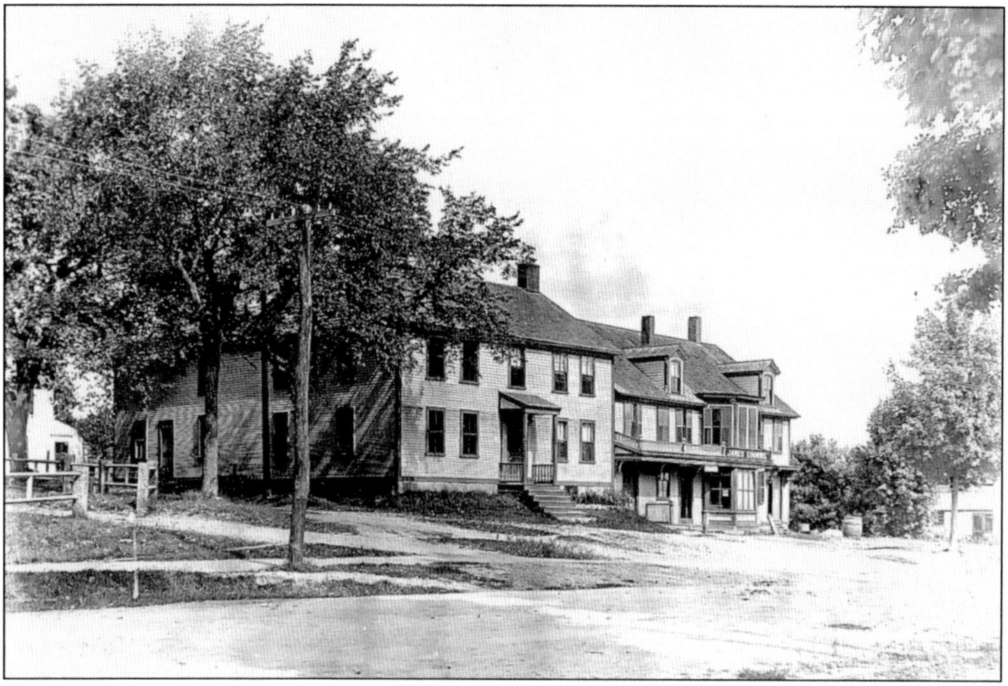

The ell of the tavern house, 194–198 Main Street, was used to house the workers who were building the Community Church in 1814. In 1816, the main part was built and became a popular tavern. James Coombs had a store here from 1859 to 1913, selling dry goods and groceries. After that, it was Anderson's Market. It is now apartments.

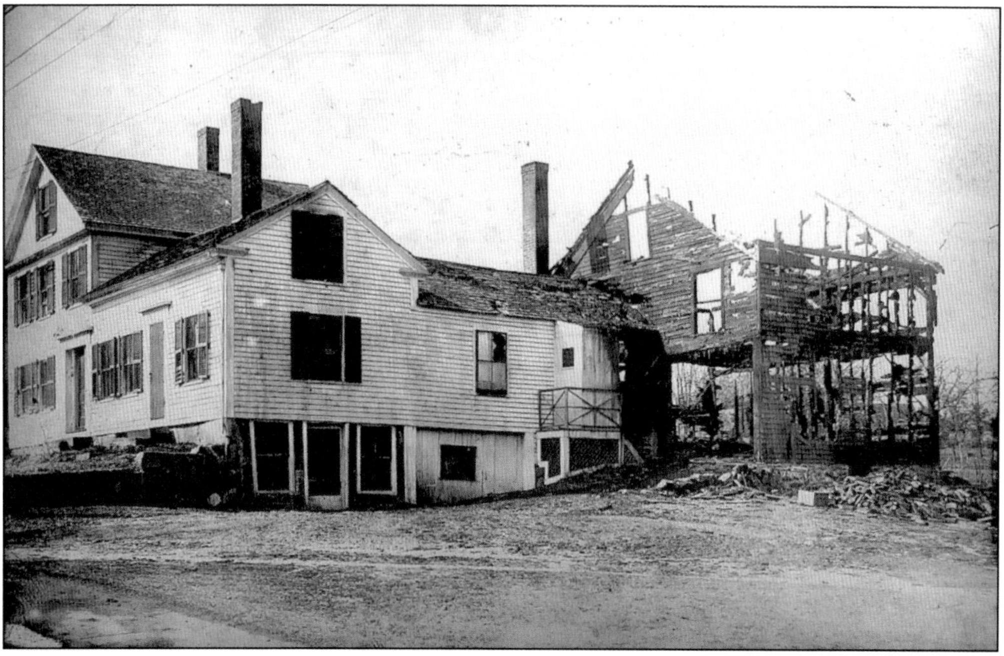

White's livery stable, where the fire department horses were stabled, was in the barn of this building. Previously, the horses were stabled behind Coombs' store, up the street, until that stable was destroyed by fire. Today, there is a bookstore in the basement. It is 168 Main Street.

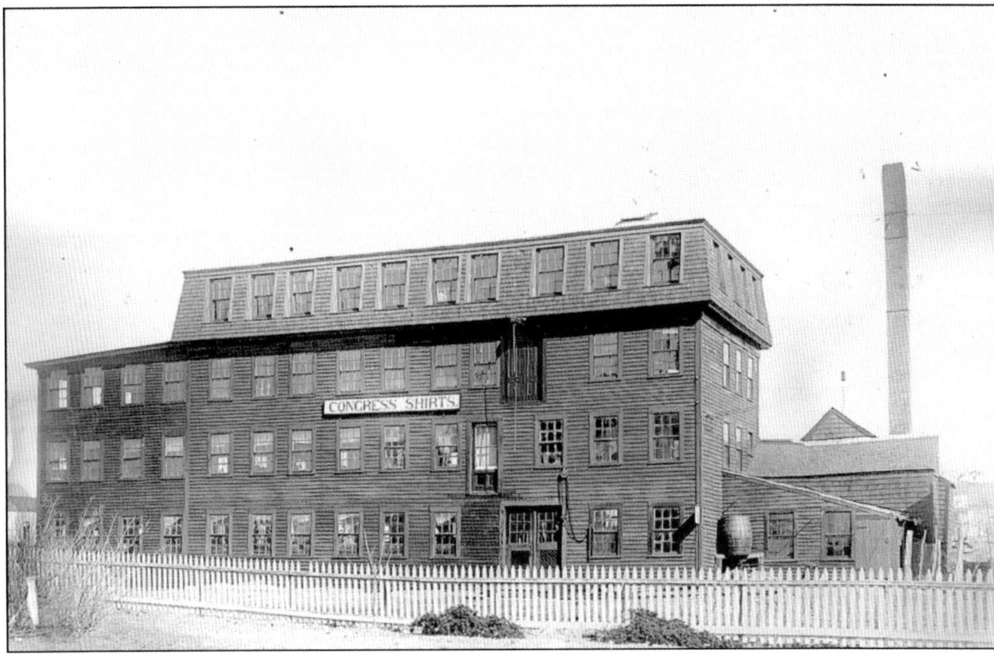

John Smith built a shoe factory between Temple and Winthrop Streets in 1832 and continued in business for several decades. Later on, the building became an elastic braid and suspenders factory and, eventually, the Congress Shirt Factory, pictured. It burned in 1910.

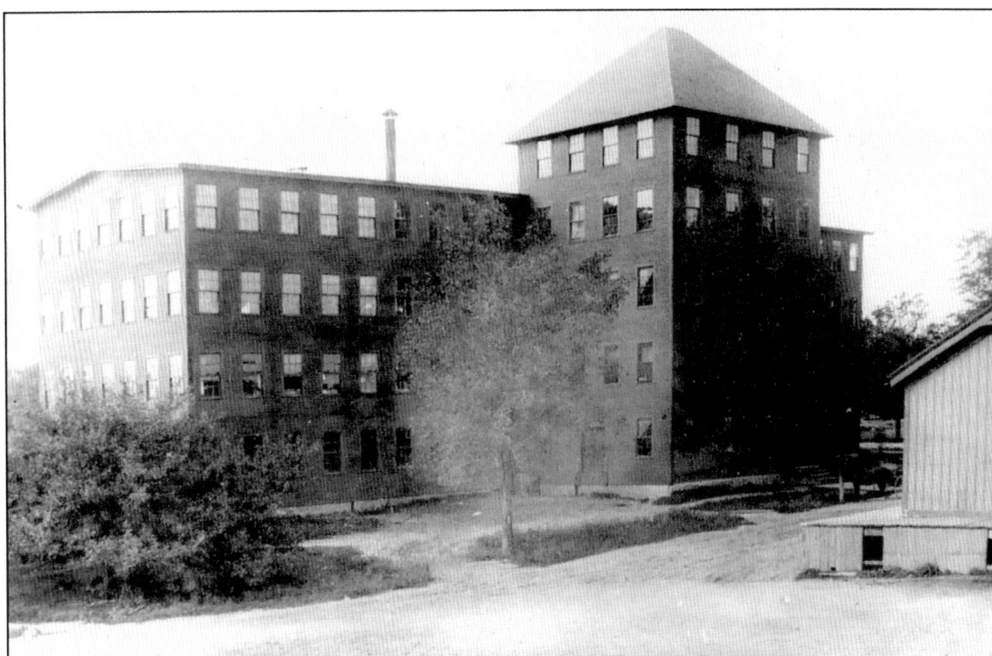

This large factory was a boot shop erected for the Seavey brothers *c.* 1890. The Seaveys produced boots and shoes, as well as cartons for shipping. A massive fire in 1965 destroyed this building and several others nearby, including the Medway Village depot, visible in the right foreground.

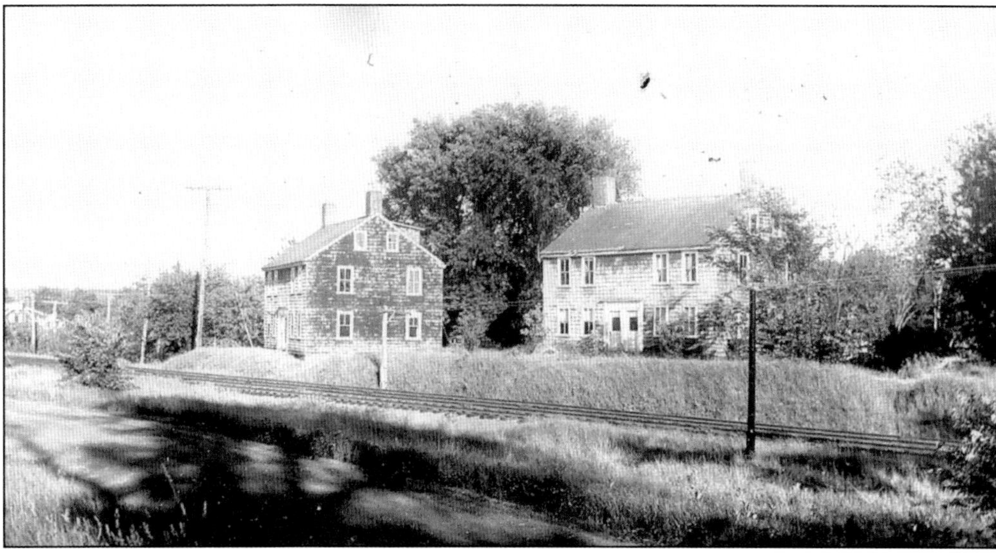

These two houses were built for workers at the mill on the Charles River in West Medway. The mill was originally Hunt's grist- and sawmill and later a cotton manufactory and a factory for making machinery. Then, in the 1850s, the property was purchased by T. and G. Campbell for the manufacture of paper. These houses were recently demolished.

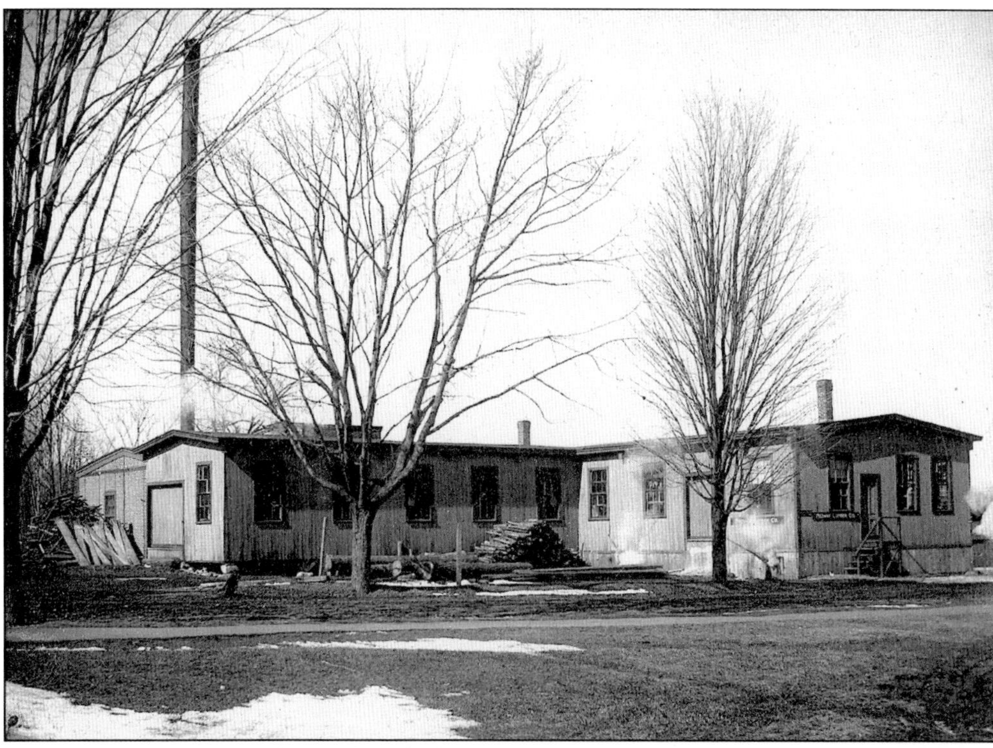

Clark's Box Shop was at the north end of Broad Street. It made boxes and cartons for shipping various products manufactured in the town. It was one of several box shops in town. This one burned in 1912.

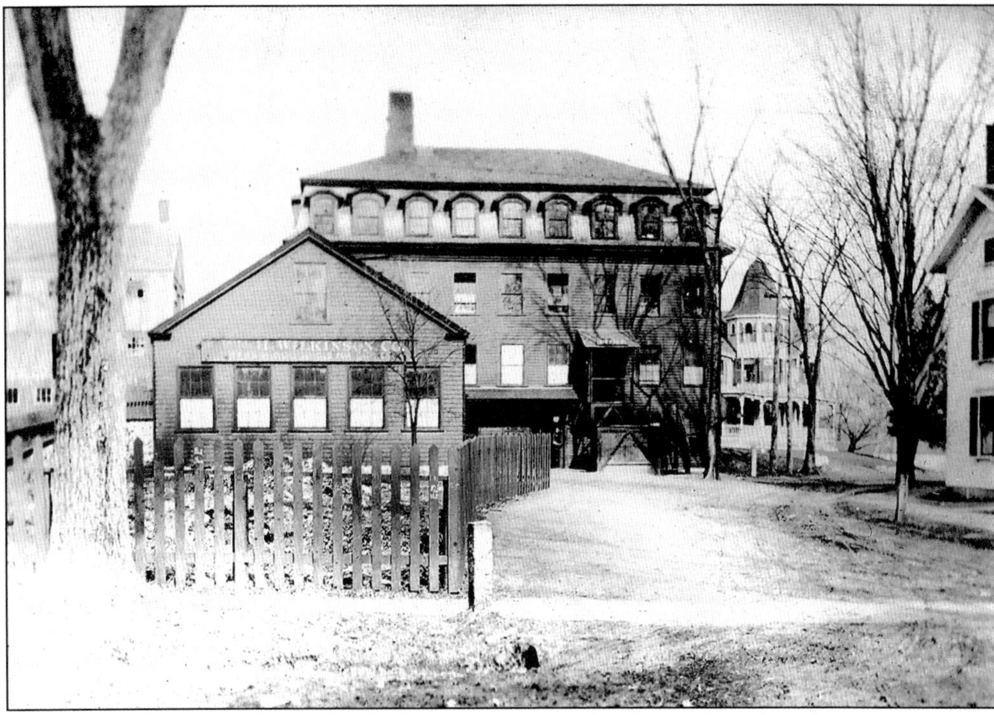

Daniels boot shop, later the Wilkinson brass machine shop, was located at the corner of Main and Mechanic Streets. After being vacant for many years, the building was torn down in 1964. At the right rear can be seen the large Queen Anne–style house at 5 Mechanic Street. A group of workers outside the building is pictured below.

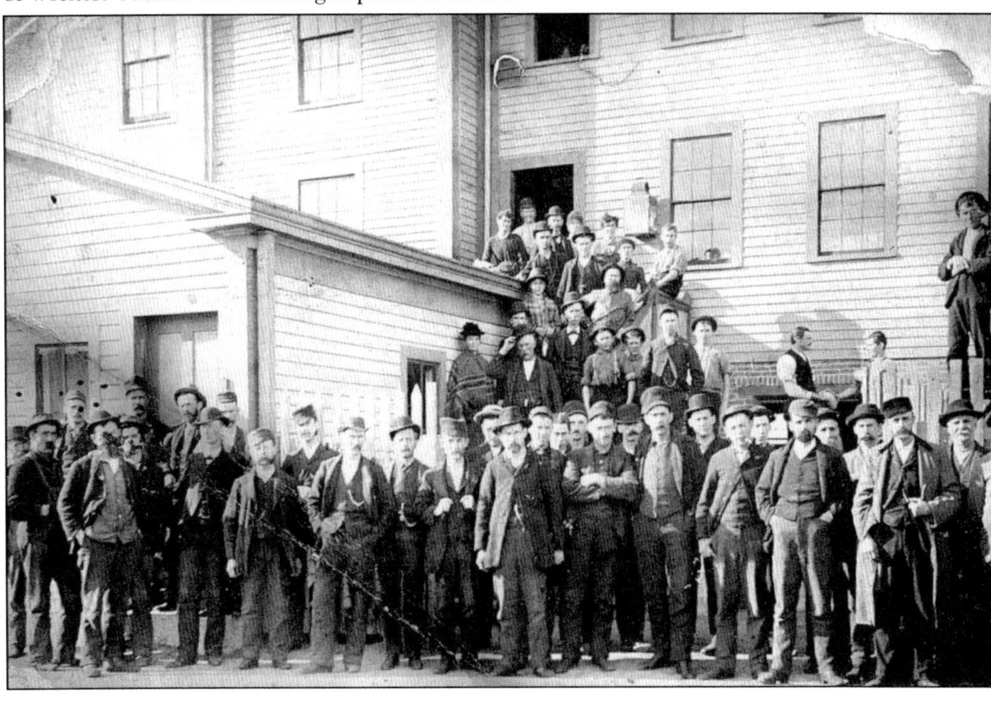

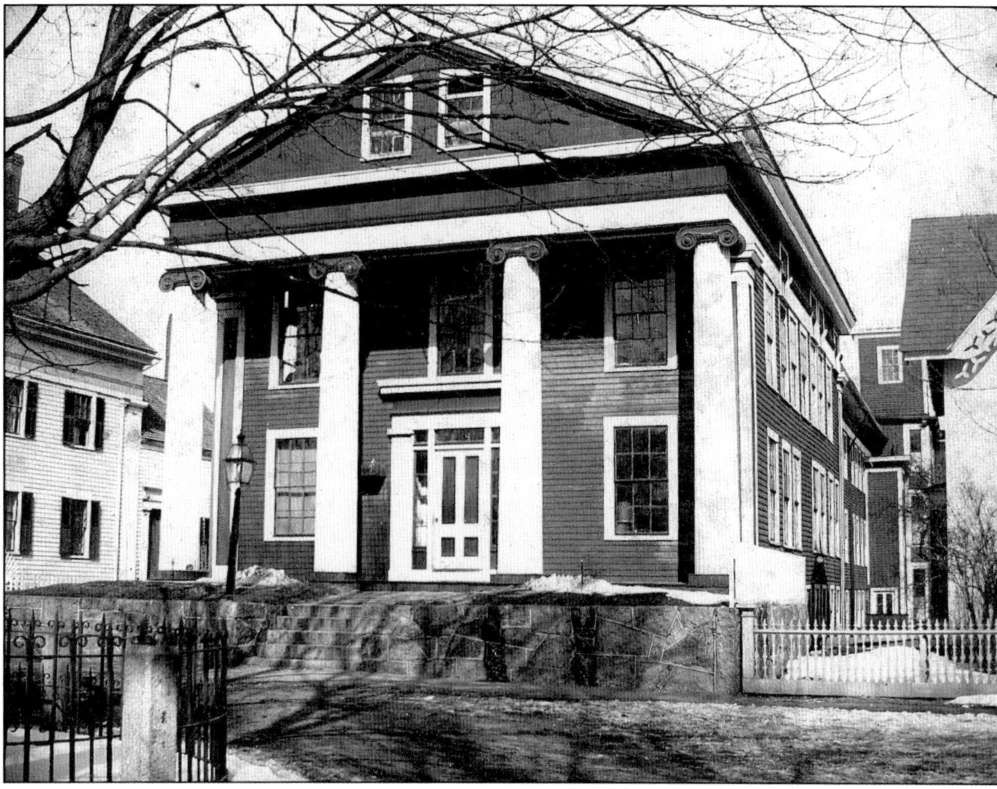

This beautiful building was built in the Greek style as a meeting hall by Amos Fisher. In 1847, Milton Fisher moved his straw shop into part of the building. It became exclusively a straw shop in 1857, and several additions were needed to accommodate the increasing business (below). Abram S. Harding became a partner of Deacon Fisher. The building, located on the lot near the Village Church, burned in a spectacular fire in 1935.

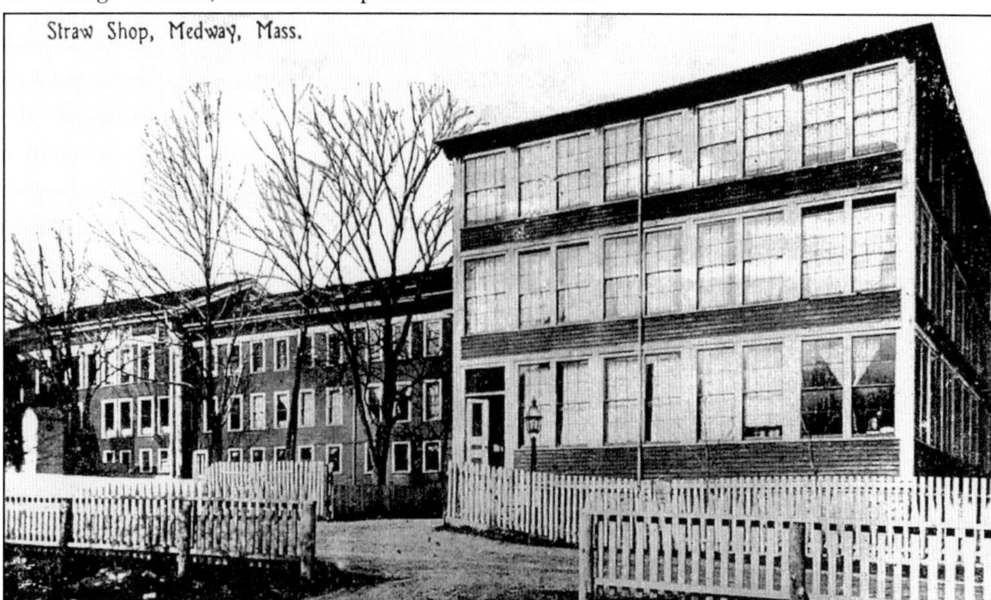

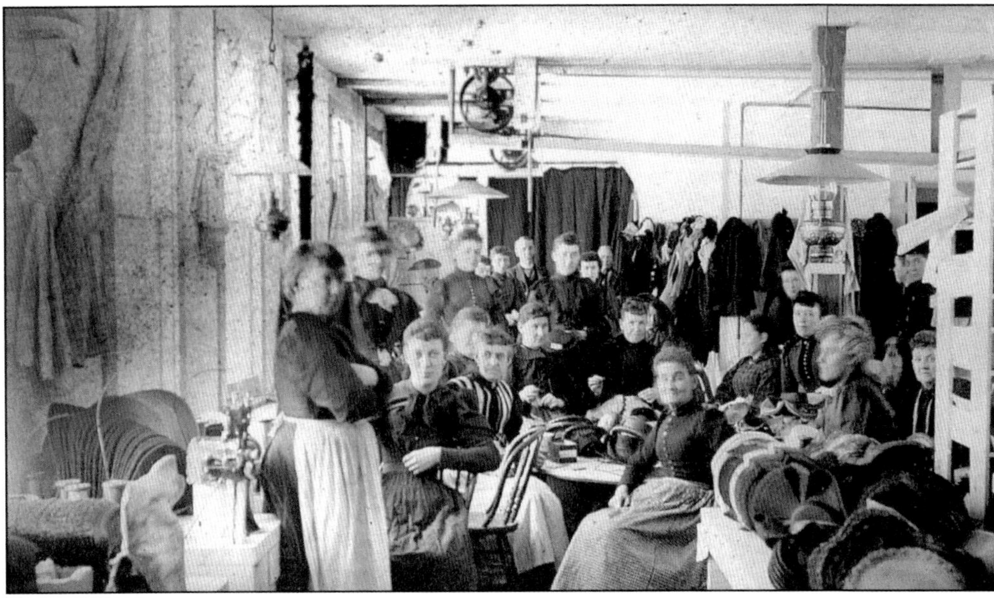

These are pictures of workers at the straw factory. The first is an interior view. The second shows the workers outside one of the additions to the building.. The straw and hat industries were major businesses in Medway. In 1854, some 100,000 bonnets were made in Medway.

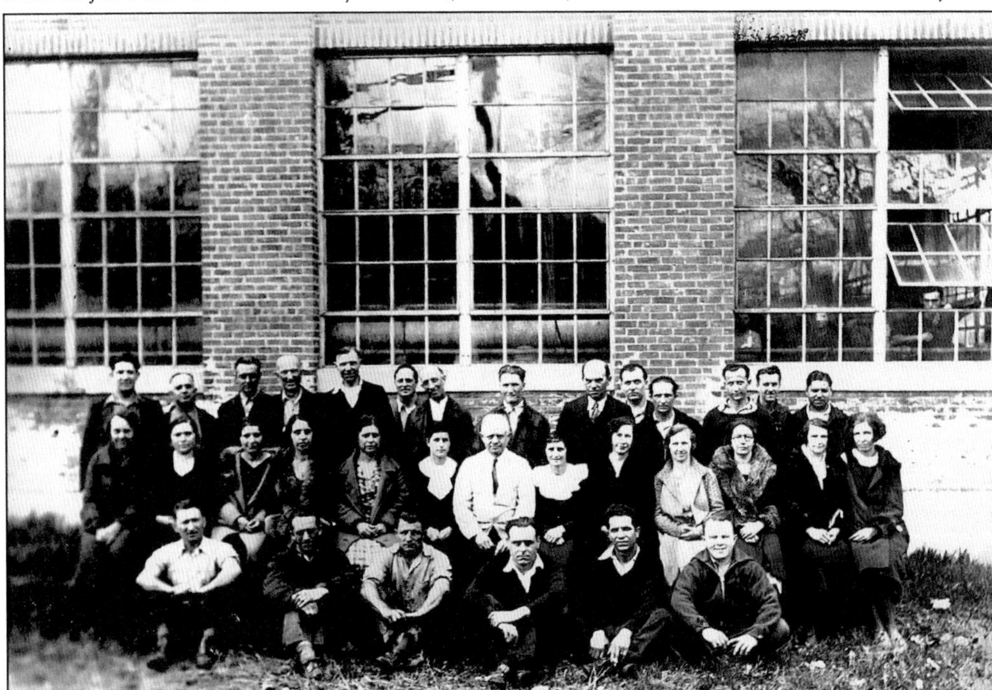

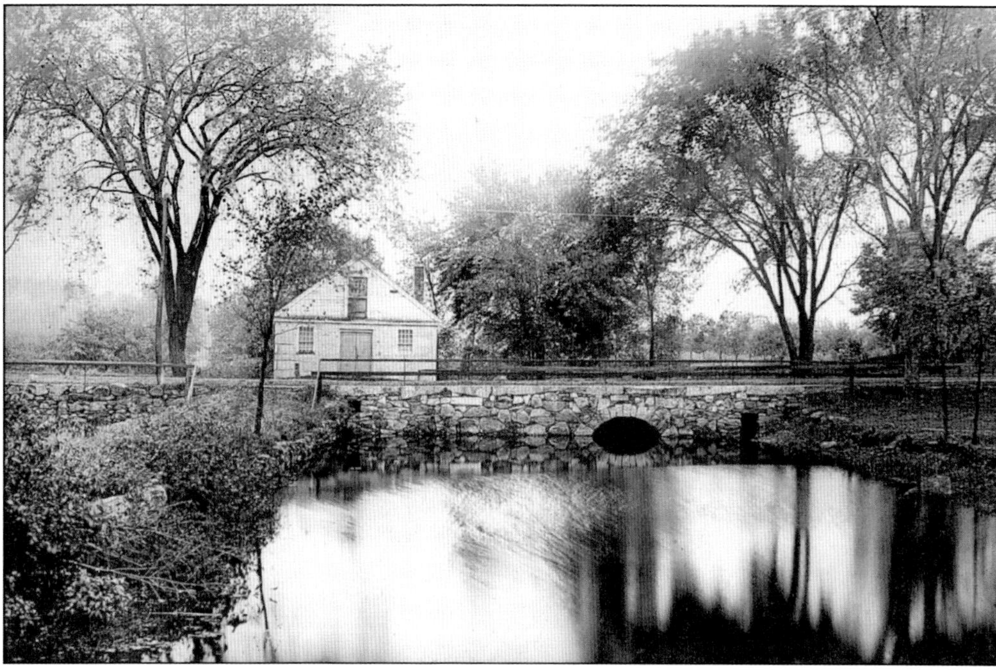

This little mill was built across the street from the present Choate Park by Cephus Thayer in 1838. Thayer dammed Chicken Brook for power, which made a pond across the street called Thayer's pond. It was a popular skating spot. The waterpower was used to make textile machinery and other textile products. The mill was enlarged in the early 1900s.

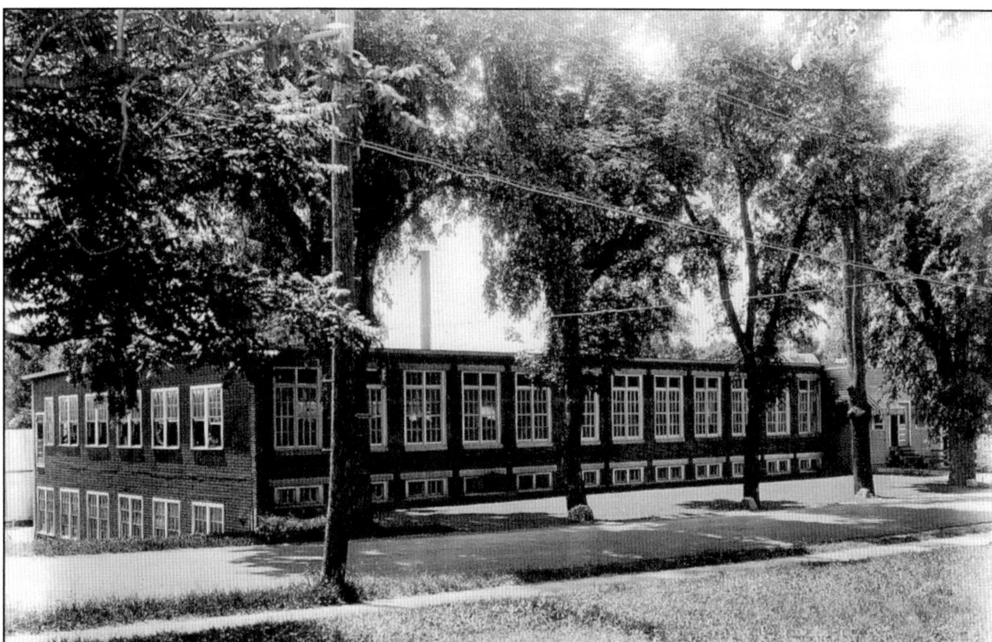

This 1950 view of the stone mill site shows a very different building. When this photograph was taken, the mill was occupied by the West Medway Woolen Company. Later, New England Awl and Needle moved in. Today, the space is shared by a variety of businesses.

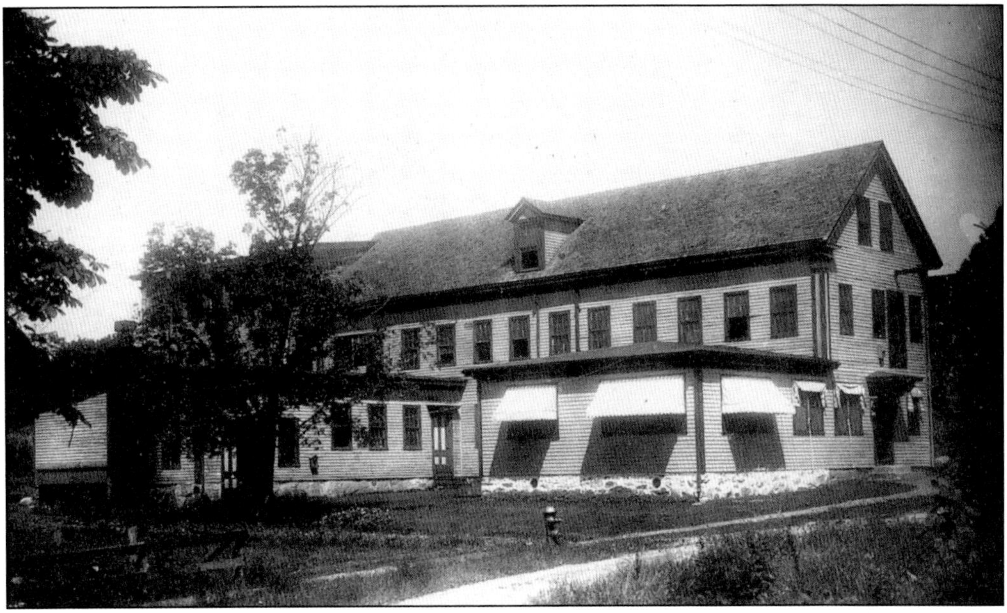

This postcard view shows the original building of the New England Awl and Needle Company, on Awl Street in West Medway. Founded in 1871, this business served boot makers and shoemakers throughout the country. The company later moved to the stone mill site on Main Street and finally merged with United Shoe Machinery Corporation.

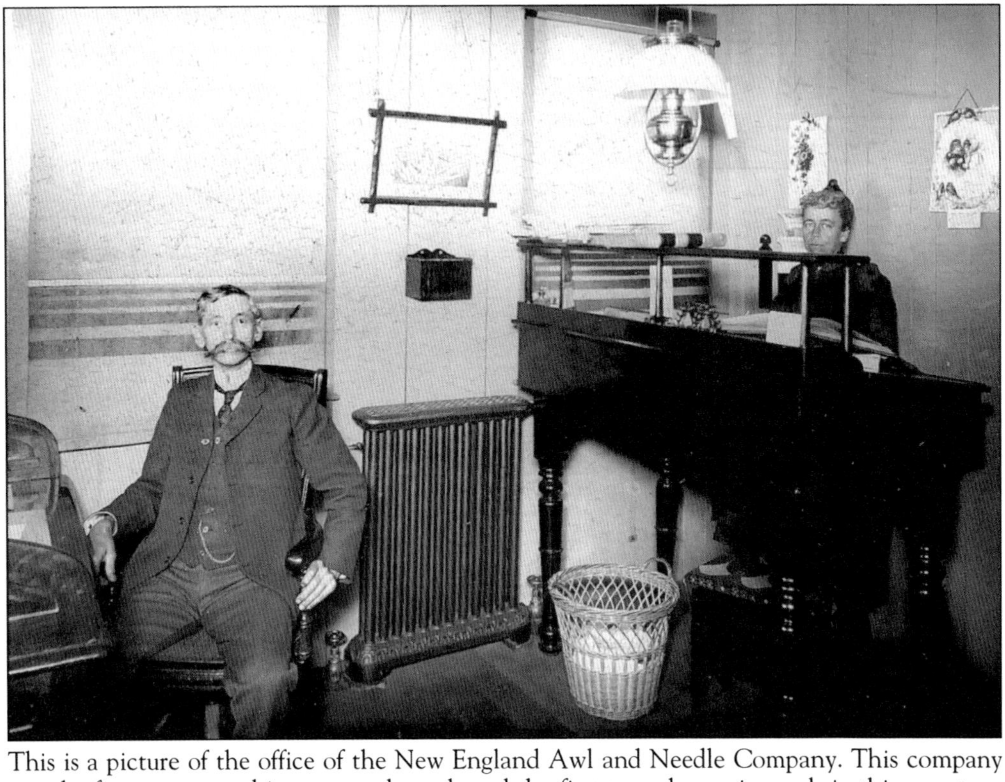

This is a picture of the office of the New England Awl and Needle Company. This company was the first to use machinery to make awls and the first to make sewing awls in this country.

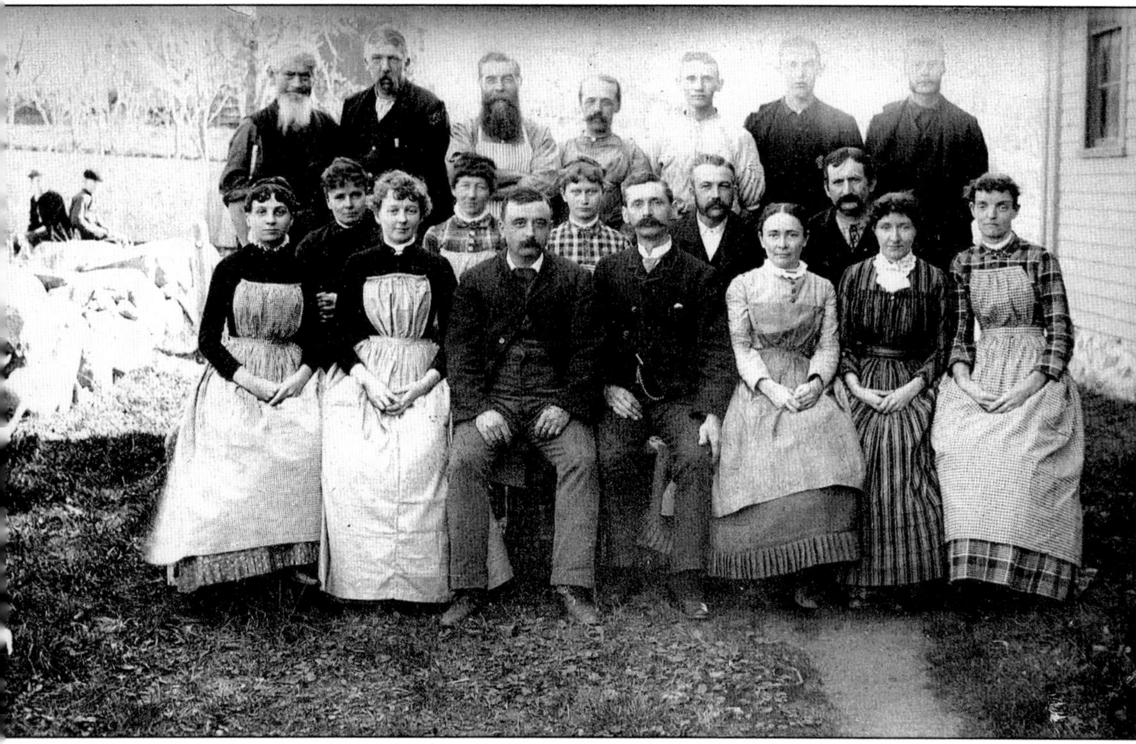

Workers at the original New England Awl shop gather for a photograph in 1885.

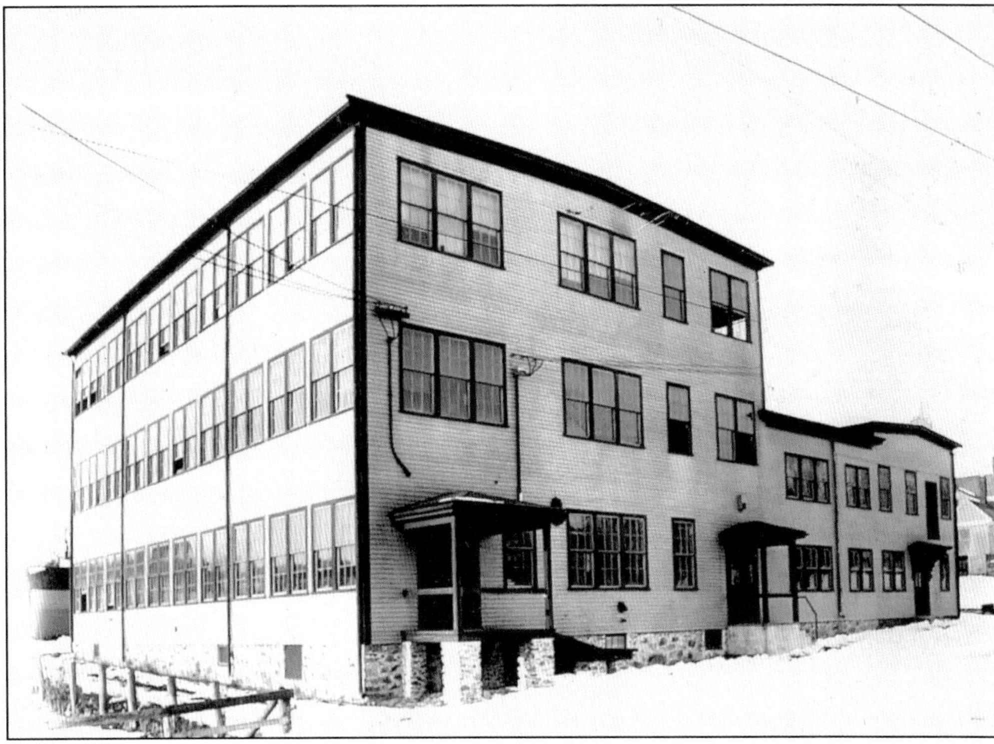

By 1920, the owners of the New England Awl and Needle Company had built a larger plant (above) and employed a much expanded work force (below).

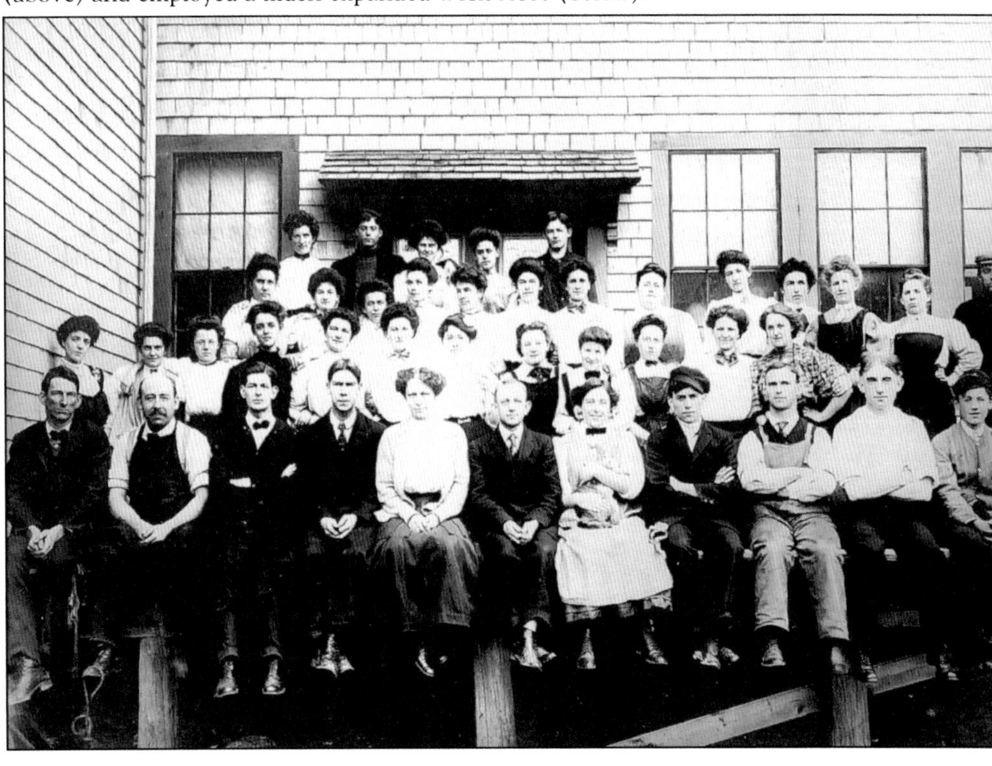

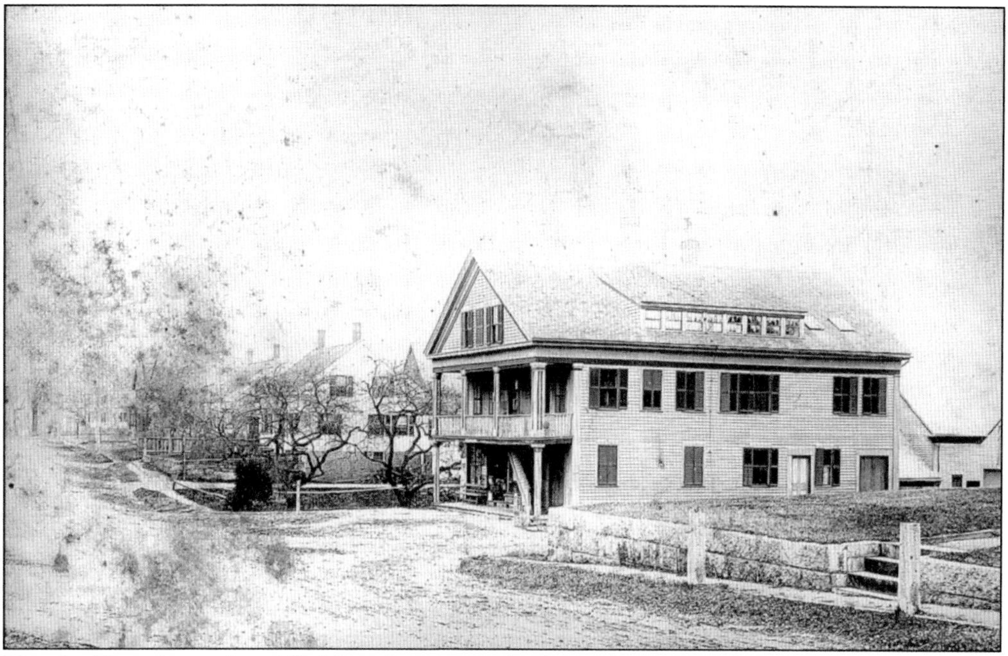

This building, located at 153 Main Street, was built as a boot manufacturing shop by Sumner Robbins *c.* 1850. Later, Robbins had a general store and fish market and stayed in this location for 40 years. There was a boot shop upstairs. It was known as the Plainville store. It was the home of Gordon Dress Shop during World War I. Ladies' jersey suits were manufactured on the second floor and sold on the first floor. From the 1930s, it was a real estate office owned by the Cerel family.

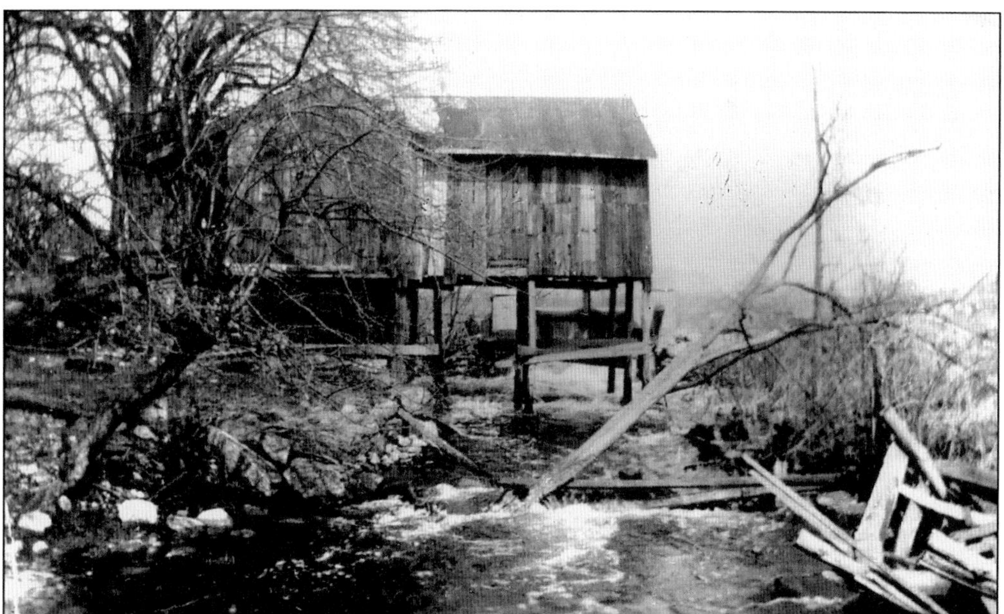

The remnants of an early shingle mill and sawmill on Chicken Brook off Winthrop Street are shown *c.* 1930, when the dam broke.

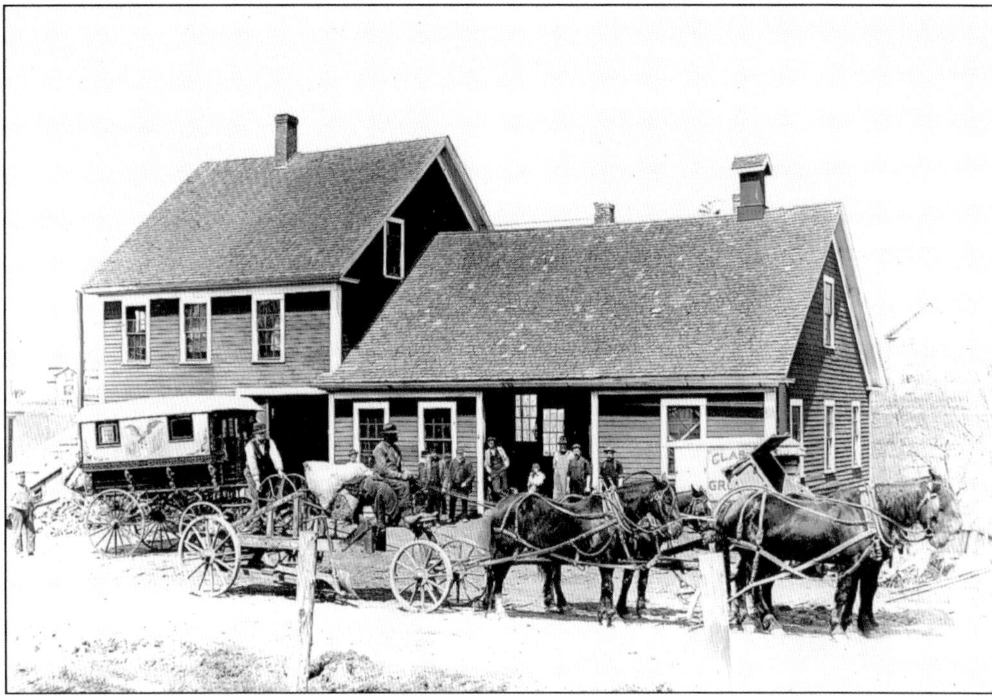

Blacksmiths were a necessity throughout the 18th and 19th centuries. Pictured in front of Hunt's Blacksmith Shop (above), at Wellington and Lincoln Streets, in 1901 are a road scraper (foreground) and a "barge" (left) used for carrying passengers and mail. The blacksmith shop (below) stands on Franklin Street *c.* 1925 and is now a residence.

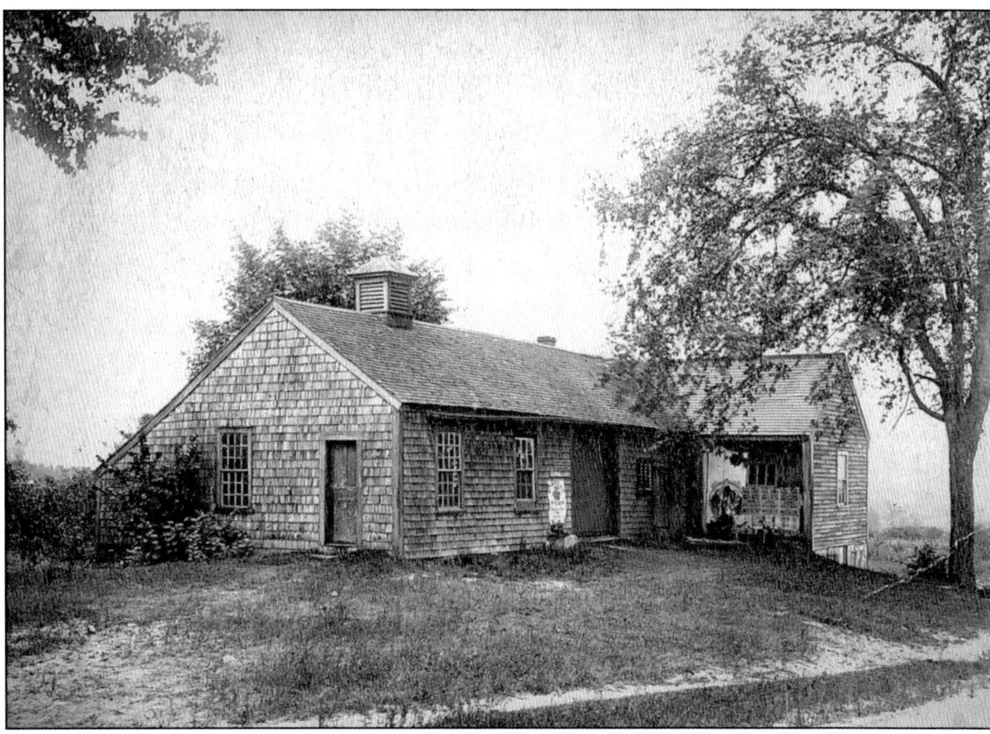

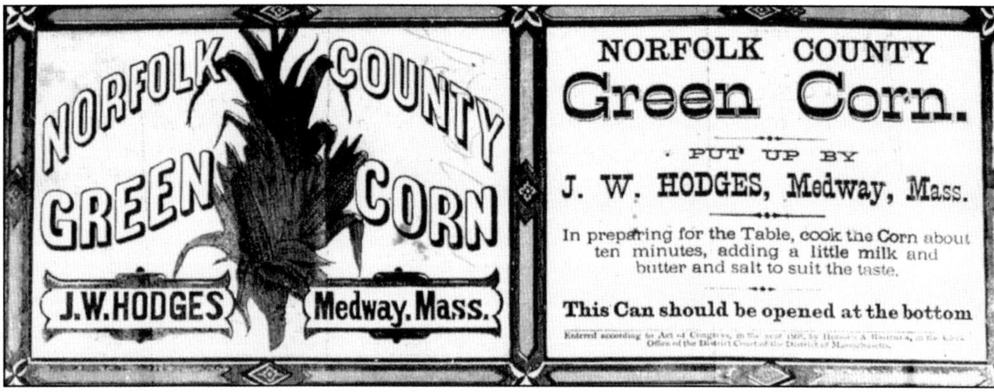

The J. W. Hodges Company operated two large canneries in Medway Village, supported by Mason and Hodges greenhouses producing tomatoes, cucumbers, and peppers. This 1868 label for canned corn indicates that the company also used produce grown outdoors through the summer.

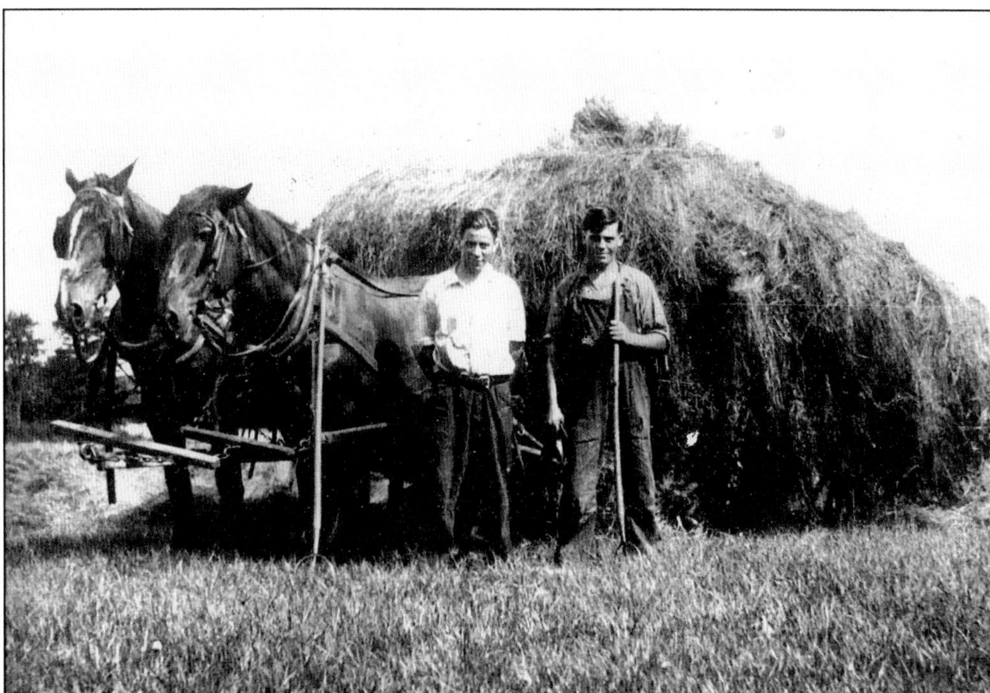

Brothers Philip (left) and Francis Cassidy take a break from bringing in the hay at the family farm *c.* 1928. This farm is now commercial property. (Courtesy Eileen Cassidy.)

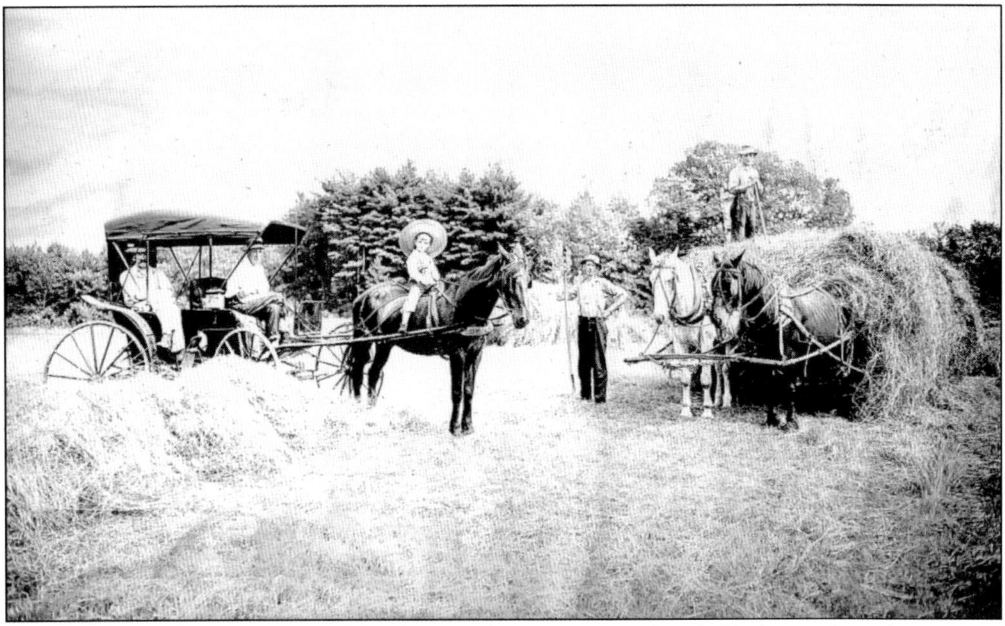

J. Gardner Sanderson and a helper harvest hay c. 1900. This field, located to the west of Winthrop Street above Choate Pond, is still a part of Robert Briggs's Shady Oaks Farm. The men in the carriage (left) are representatives of a fertilizer firm.

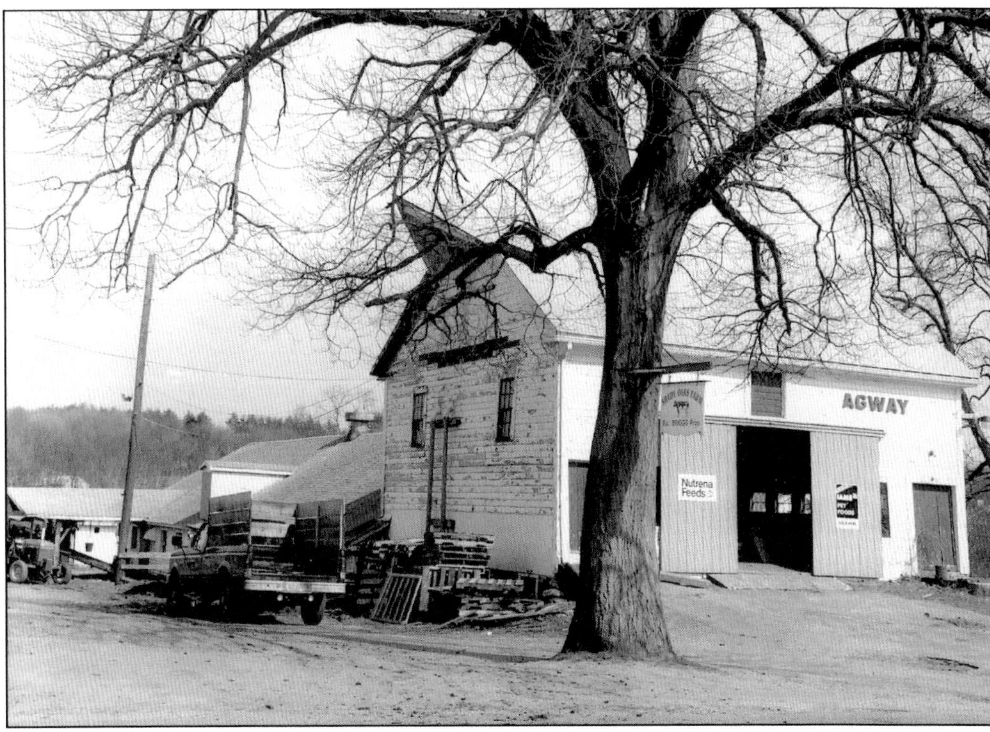

Shady Oaks Farm, at 38 Winthrop Street, was until recently an active dairy farm with home delivery. Today, milk, cream, eggs, and ice cream are available on site, as well as hay and all kinds of animal and pet feeds.

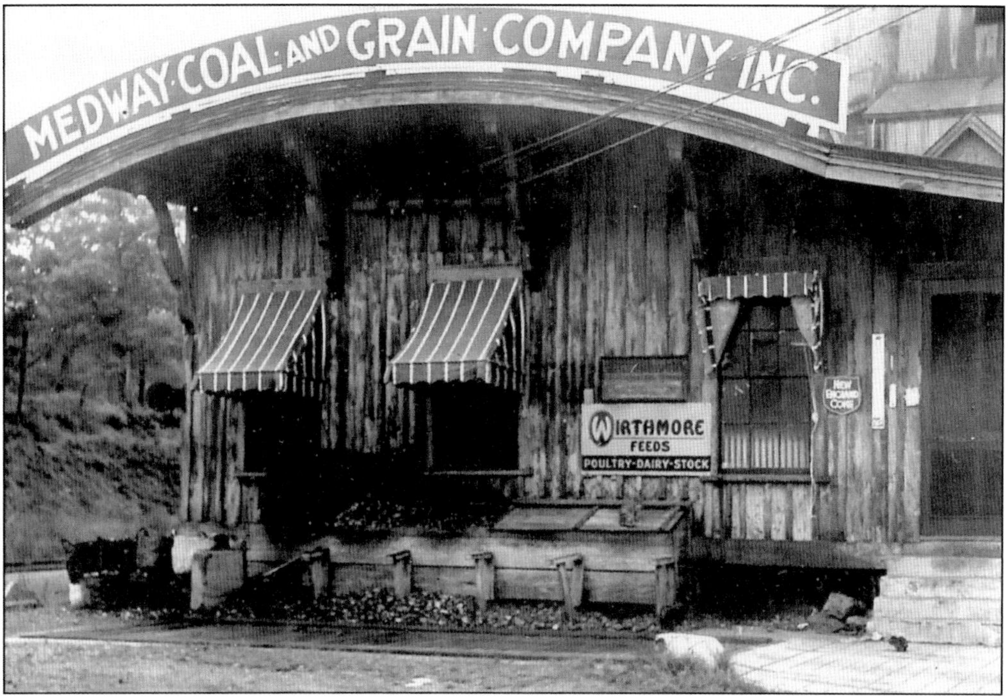

Medway Coal and Grain, formerly the W. L. Palmer Feed and Grain store, was on Broad Street. It was near the railroad tracks, which simplified the grain delivery. The building was once a railroad station. This photograph was taken in 1946.

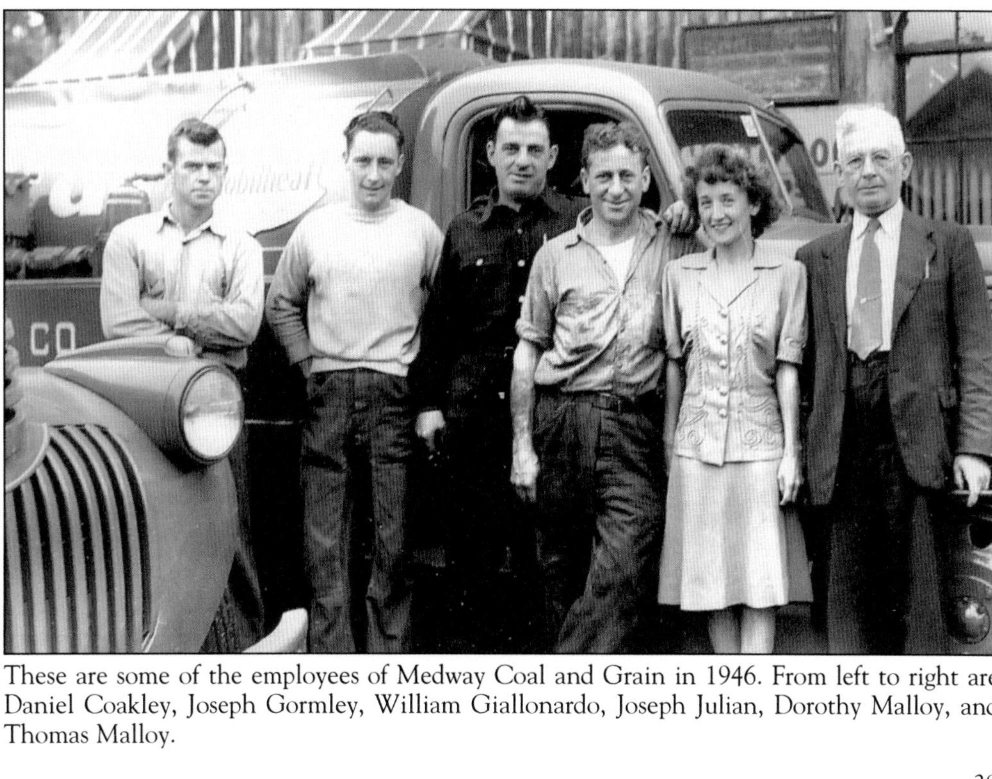

These are some of the employees of Medway Coal and Grain in 1946. From left to right are Daniel Coakley, Joseph Gormley, William Giallonardo, Joseph Julian, Dorothy Malloy, and Thomas Malloy.

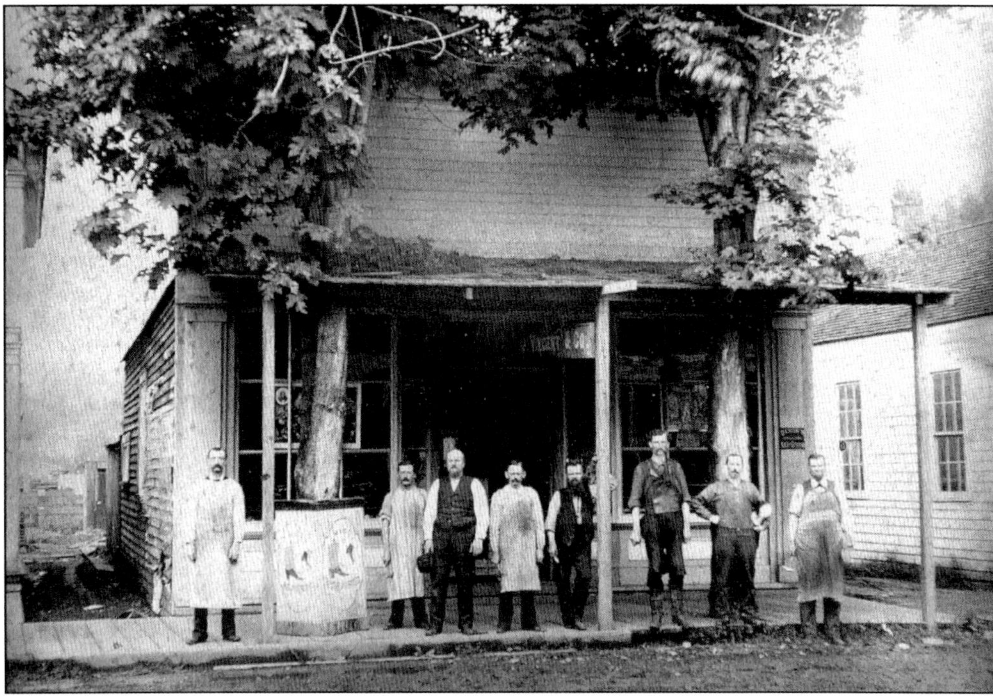

Gilmore's Market was on Village Street where the Medway Savings Bank later stood. Note the trees growing through the roof of the porch.

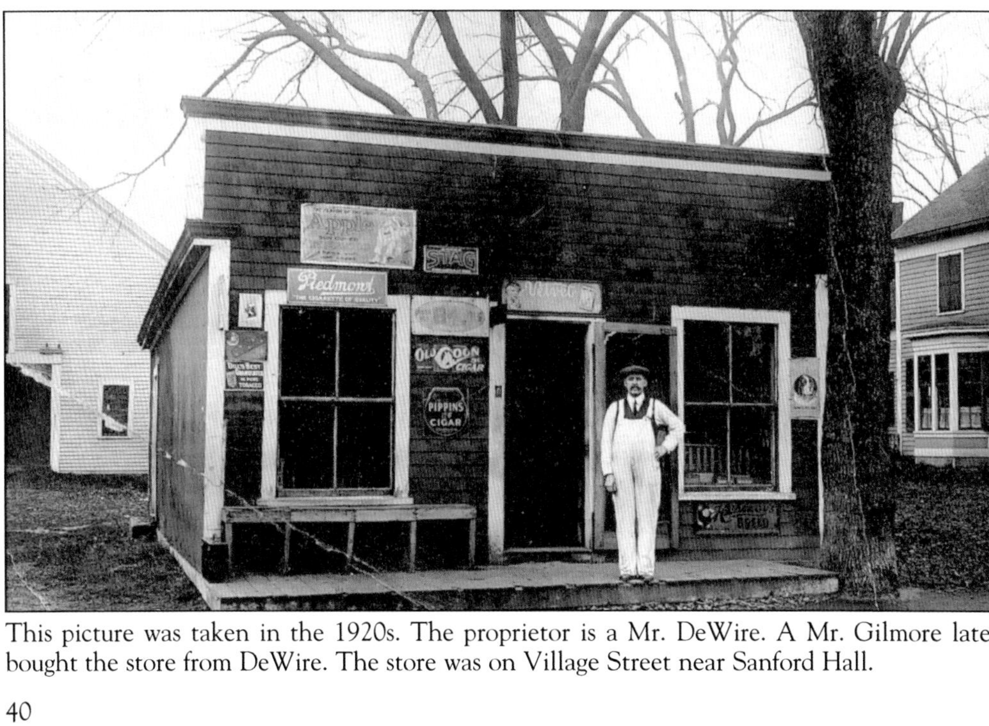

This picture was taken in the 1920s. The proprietor is a Mr. DeWire. A Mr. Gilmore later bought the store from DeWire. The store was on Village Street near Sanford Hall.

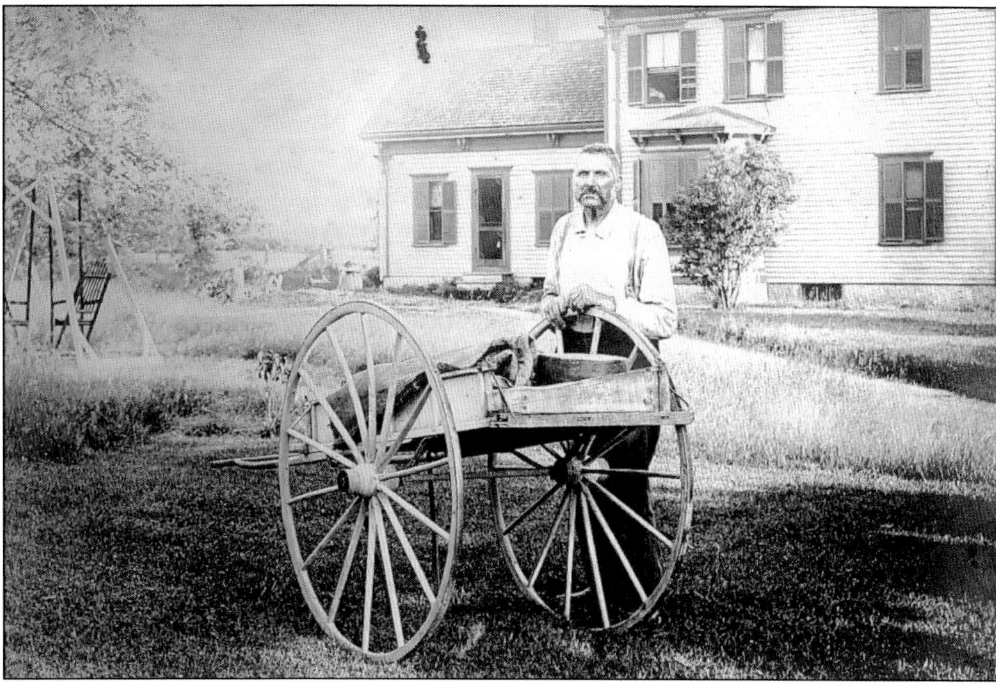

Bill Gay was a familiar figure around town in the late 19th and early 20th centuries. Always on foot, he delivered produce door to door, summer and winter. He is pictured on a warm summer day using his jacket for extra protection from the heat for goods in the handcart.

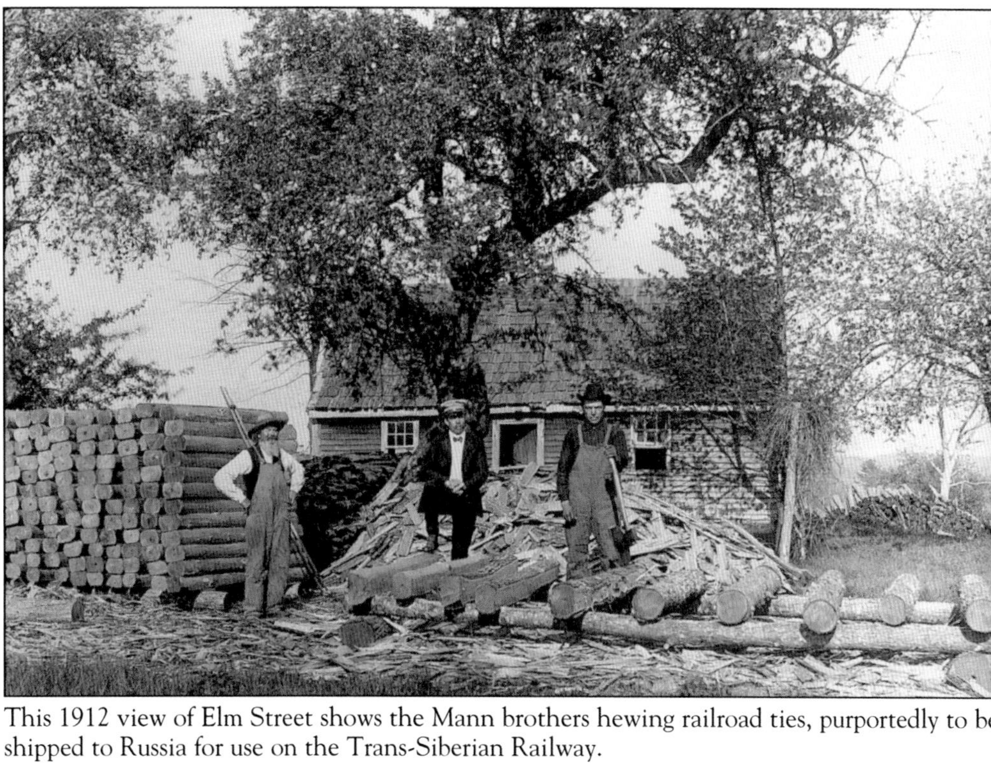

This 1912 view of Elm Street shows the Mann brothers hewing railroad ties, purportedly to be shipped to Russia for use on the Trans-Siberian Railway.

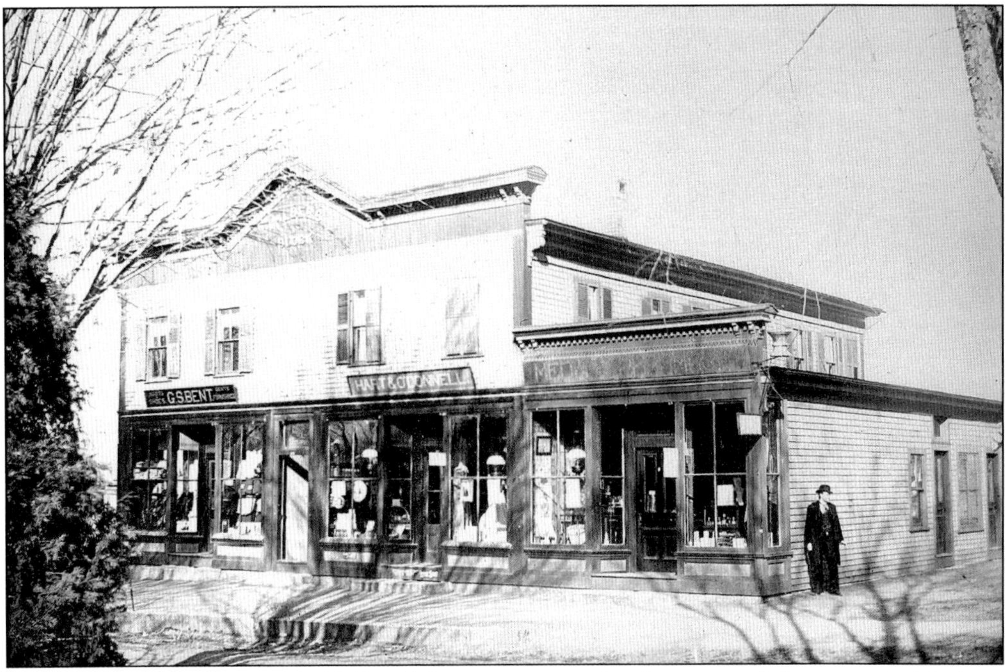

This block of buildings, at 8–10 Broad Street, contained a few more of the stores in Medway Village. Two of them are the G. S. Bent Store and the O'Donnell Store.

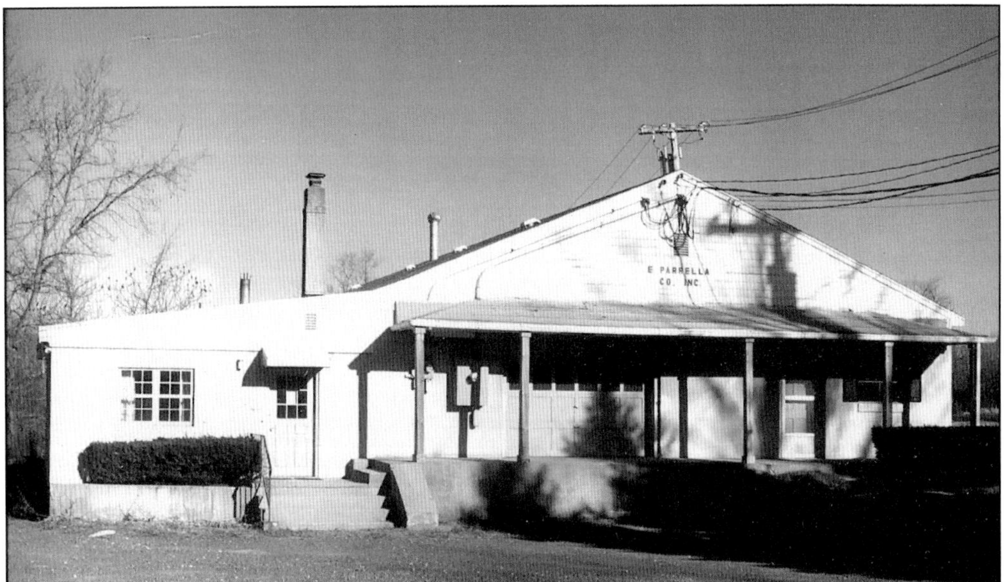

This building was constructed at 84 West Street by the Emilio Parrella company in 1969 to manufacture innovative composition bowling balls. Since that time, the company has developed many other products including track balls for military surveillance systems. Operated today by Parrella's sons, Paramount and the E. Parrella parent company have facilities at 42 Milford Street and 36 Alder Street, as well as at the original location. (Courtesy Paramount Industries.)

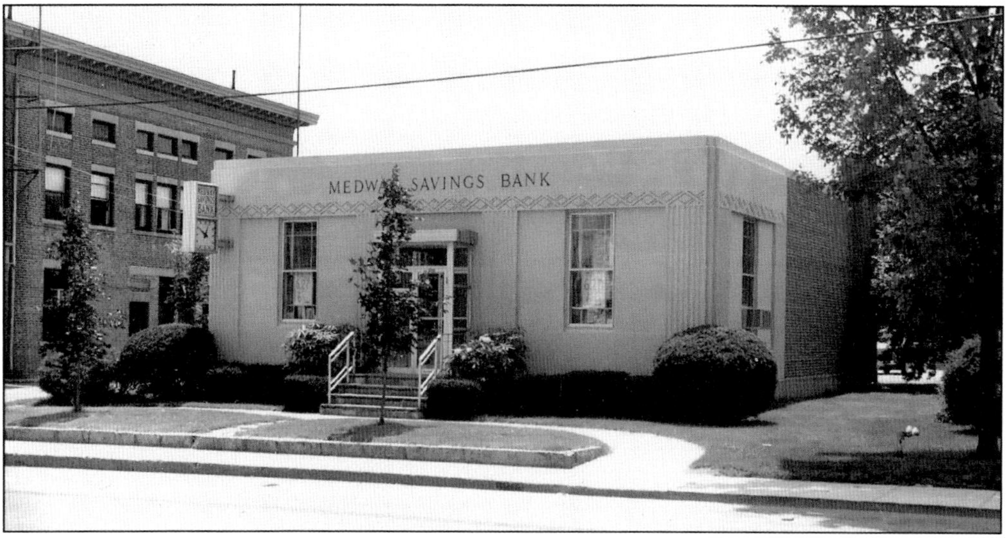

The town's earliest banking institution, the Medway Savings Bank, was incorporated in 1871 and had offices on the street level of the original Sanford Hall until it burned in 1911. Undaunted, the bank kept its offices in the new Sanford Hall when it was rebuilt in 1912. Later, the building pictured here, on Village Street, was home to Medway Savings through much of the 20th century. The bank was offering 6.27 percent compounded interest when this undated photograph was taken. Today, after relocating on Main Street, the renamed Strata Bank has its headquarters in Franklin and branches in several neighboring towns. (Courtesy Strata Bank.)

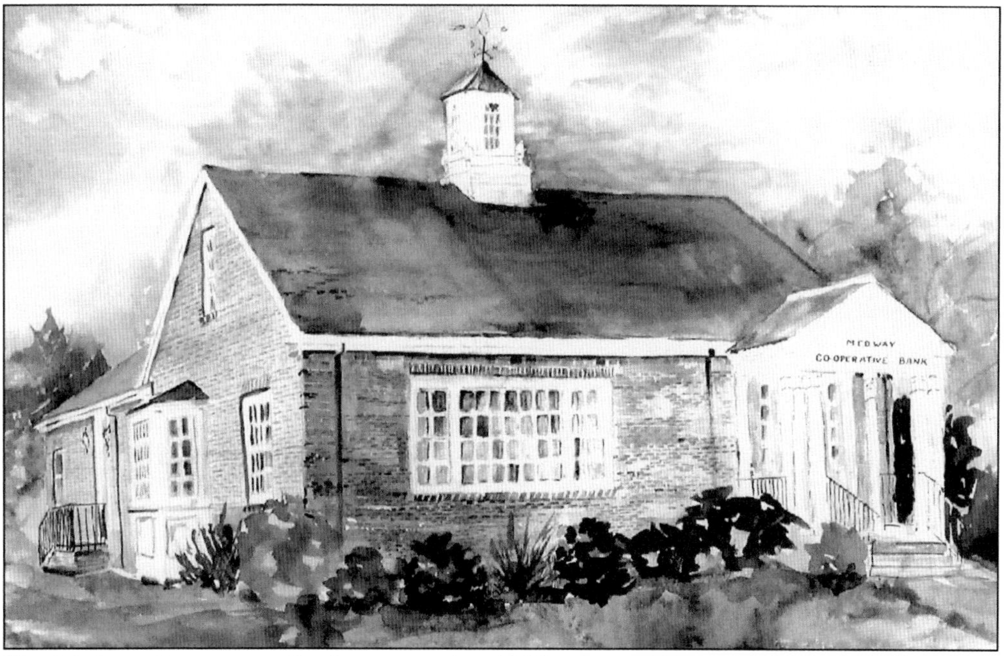

The Medway Cooperative Bank organized in 1915, using space in the Medway Village train depot. In 1932, the bank established an office in the new Medway Hotel, at Broad and Village Streets. From 1950 to 1982, the bank was located in this building, on Village Street. Since that time, the bank has expanded, requiring even larger quarters. In 1997, it opened a new building at the corner of Holliston and Main Streets. (Courtesy Medway Cooperative Bank.)

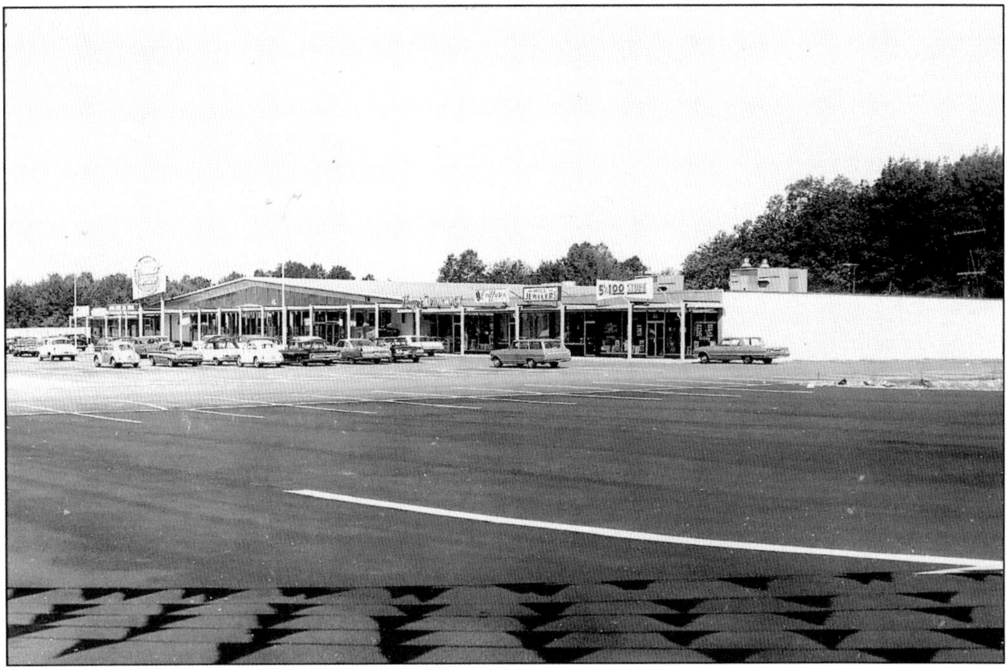

Fernandes, Medway's first supermarket, is shown here as it opened in 1965. Mammoth Mart discount store stood out of view at the left. These original Medway shopping center businesses have been replaced by others at the same location, now called Medway Plaza.

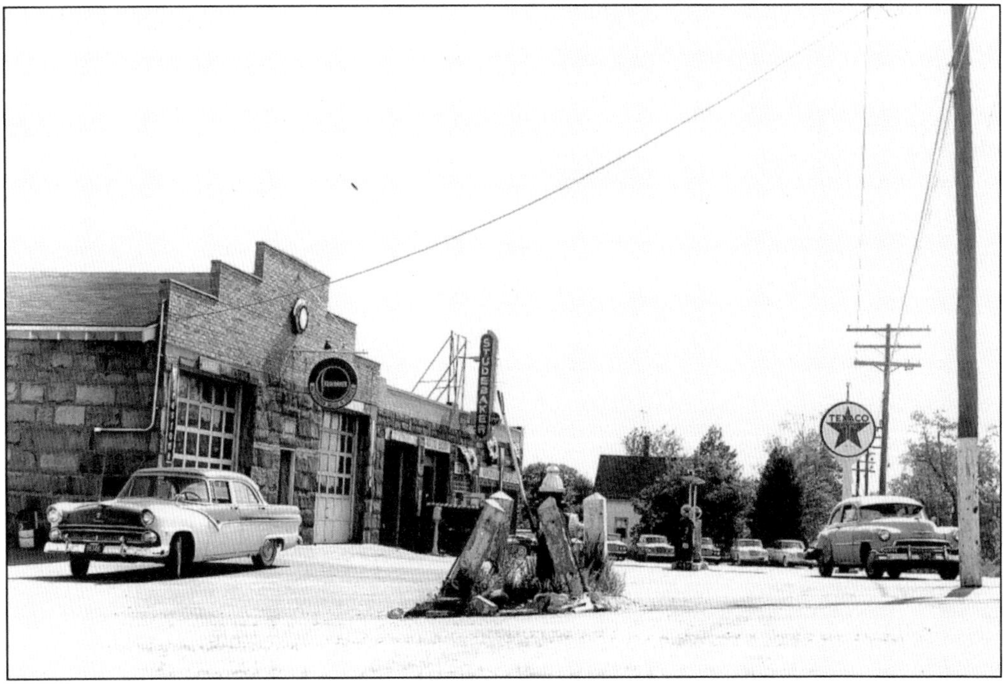

Goodwin's Garage and Auto Sales, on Main Street, was the place to go to look over the new Studebakers, one of the first passenger cars produced after World War II. The automobiles' Raymond Loewy designs were a big departure from prewar styles and became very popular.

Three

CIVIC MATTERS

Many of the buildings pictured in this chapter survive today, although serving different functions. In a time when transportation was more difficult, the street level usually held neighborhood stores, with a meeting room on the upper floor. Today, these buildings are more often given over to either complete commercial or office space.

Fire protection was also local; whatever firefighting was possible was done by small volunteer companies often located near the site of the fire. Before town water or telephones were available, when heating was provided by wood or coal stoves, fire took its toll.

Buildings, however, were salvaged; when the roof burned on the Odd Fellows Hall, the top floor was removed. After a new roof was added, the same building served for another 70 years. The Gladstone-New Medway Hotel-Quinobequin House rose from the ashes multiple times before finally succumbing to a fire in the 1990s.

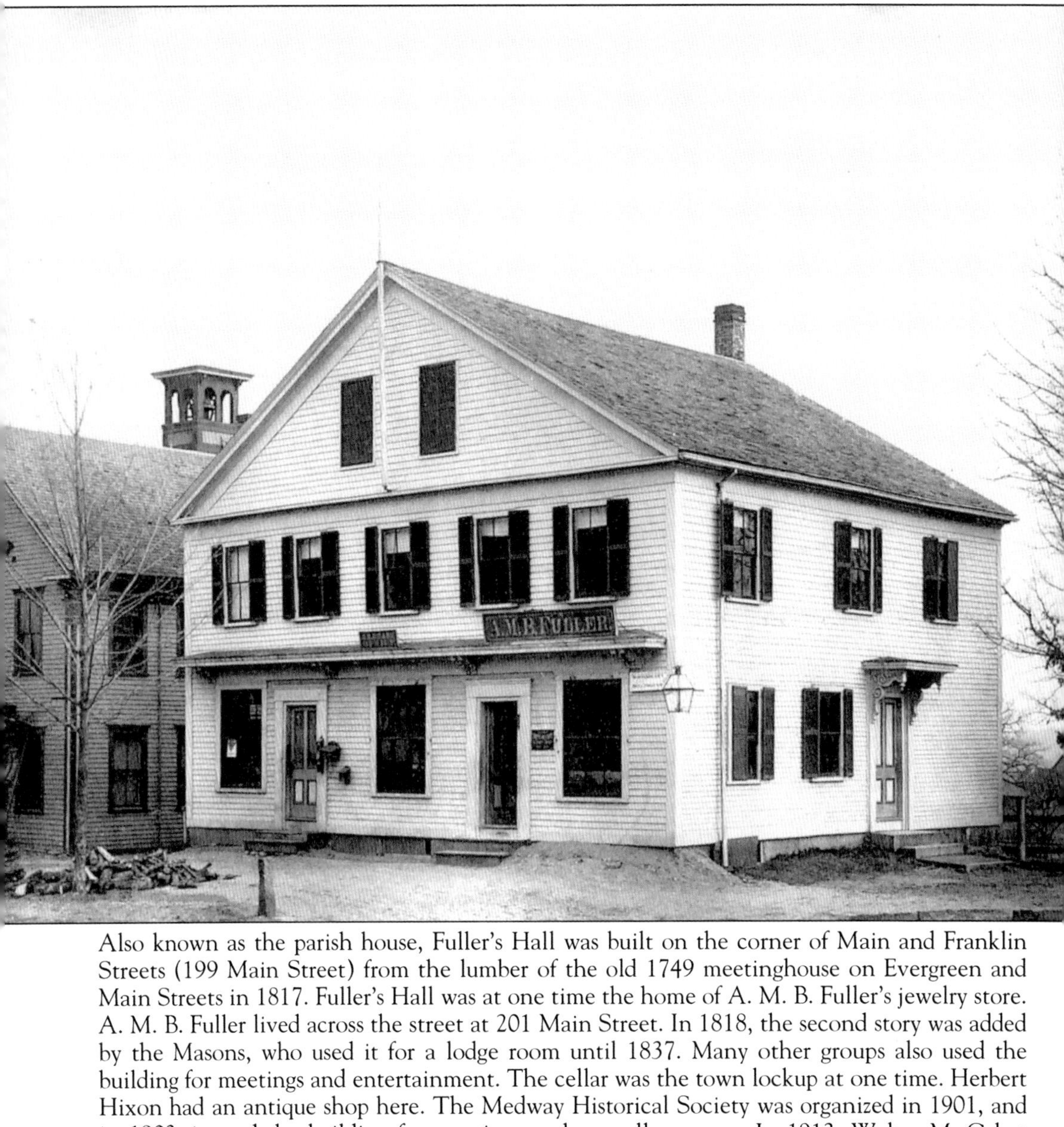

Also known as the parish house, Fuller's Hall was built on the corner of Main and Franklin Streets (199 Main Street) from the lumber of the old 1749 meetinghouse on Evergreen and Main Streets in 1817. Fuller's Hall was at one time the home of A. M. B. Fuller's jewelry store. A. M. B. Fuller lived across the street at 201 Main Street. In 1818, the second story was added by the Masons, who used it for a lodge room until 1837. Many other groups also used the building for meetings and entertainment. The cellar was the town lockup at one time. Herbert Hixon had an antique shop here. The Medway Historical Society was organized in 1901, and in 1903, it used the building for meetings and a small museum. In 1913, Walter M. Cabot bought the building and restored it to its Colonial condition. It was bequeathed to the Community Church as a parish house in 1954 by Katherine Cabot, and the historical society moved out. During the 1950s and 1960s, the Medway Community Nursery School held classes here for at least 10 years and the backyard was a playground for the group.

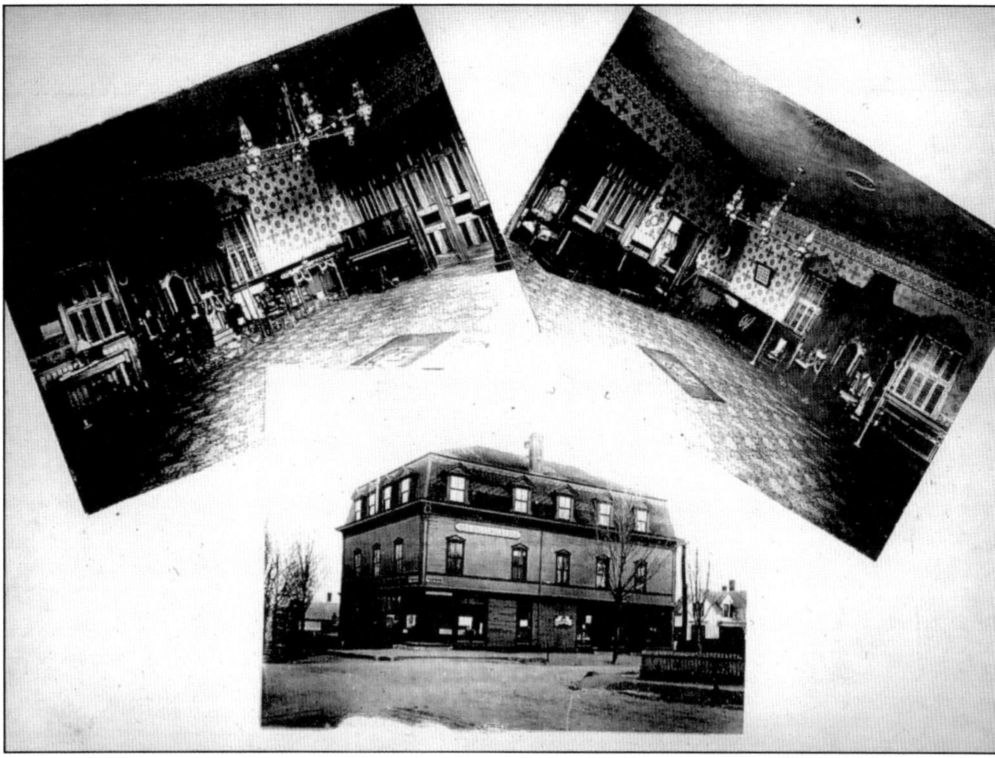

Odd Fellows Hall was built at the corner of Main and Lincoln Streets in 1896. The Odd Fellows met upstairs, and the first floor housed the post office as well as a barbershop and a grocery store at times. As the interior photographs show, the meeting rooms were very luxurious. In 1911, the roof burned. Then, in the 1980s, the entire building burned. It has been replaced, and it is still the Odd Fellows Hall.

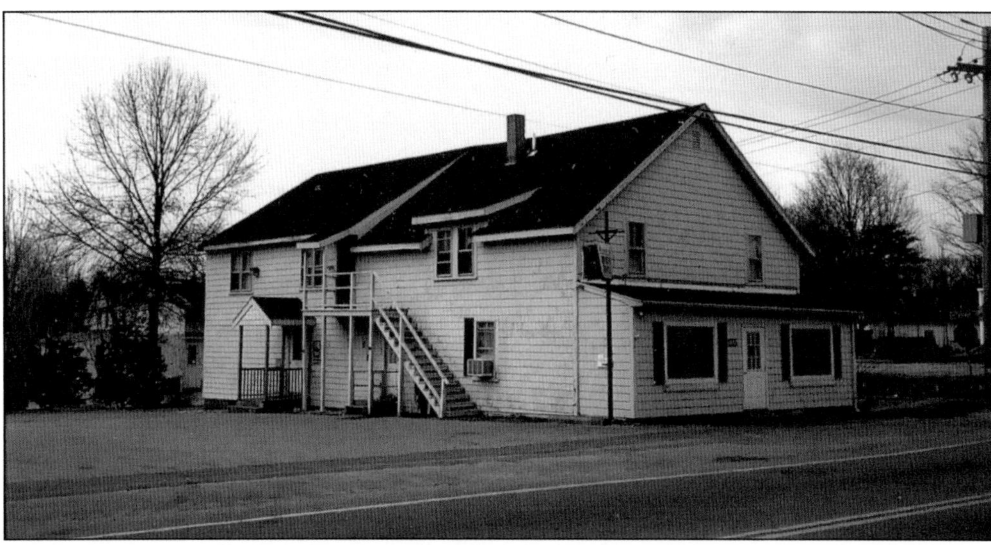

This building was called Mechanics Hall. When first built in 1819, it was used for Universalist church services. Later, it was a meeting hall for lectures, concerts and other entertainments. A new building was constructed in 1840. It is now a furniture store, at 135 Main Street.

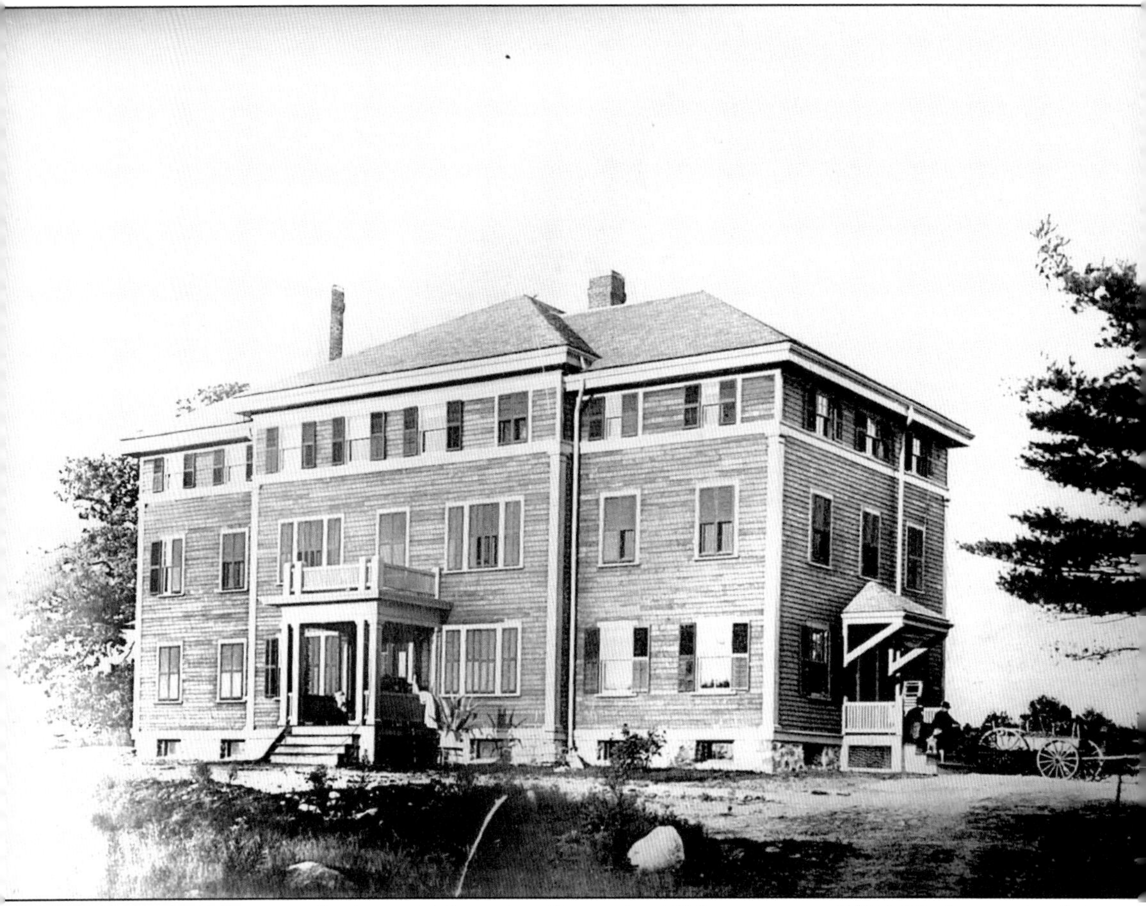

The almshouse was built at 66 Lovering Street in 1898 at a cost of $7,000. It remained in operation until 1927. The maximum number of residents during that period was 24. It was sold in 1927 for a summer resort. Later, it was used as a farm, and eventually, it became apartments. In 1974, it was struck by lightning and the roof and top floor burned. This is a 1901 photograph. The building is still standing.

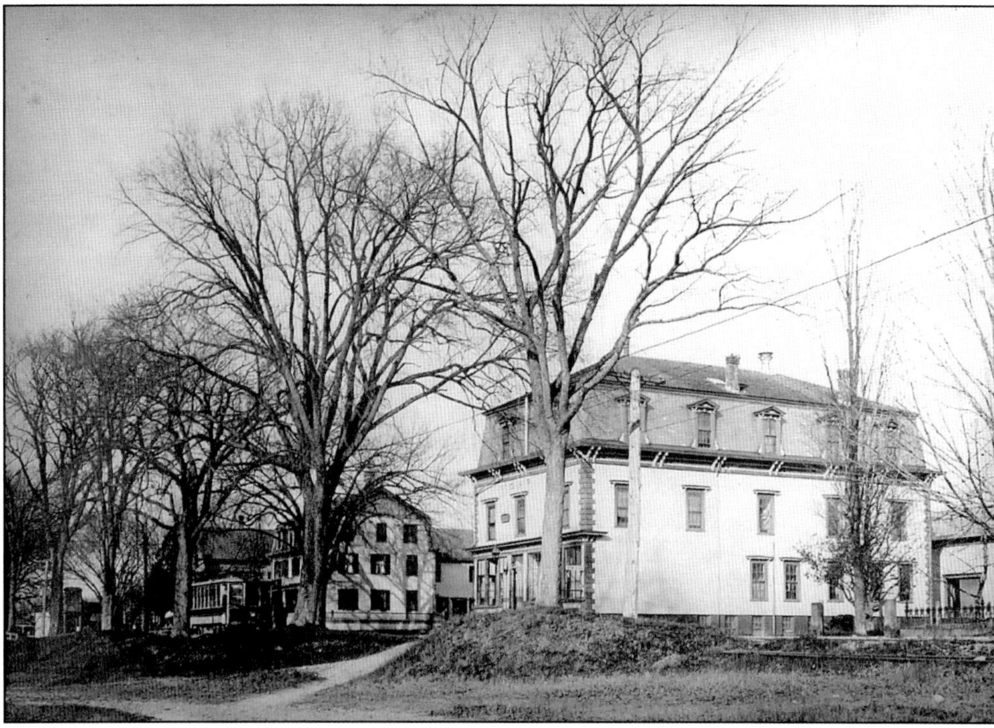

The Grand Army Block on Village Street was built as a meetinghouse for the Grand Army of the Republic and the Masons. For some time, it housed the town offices. It burned to the ground in 1918. Luckily, the town records were saved.

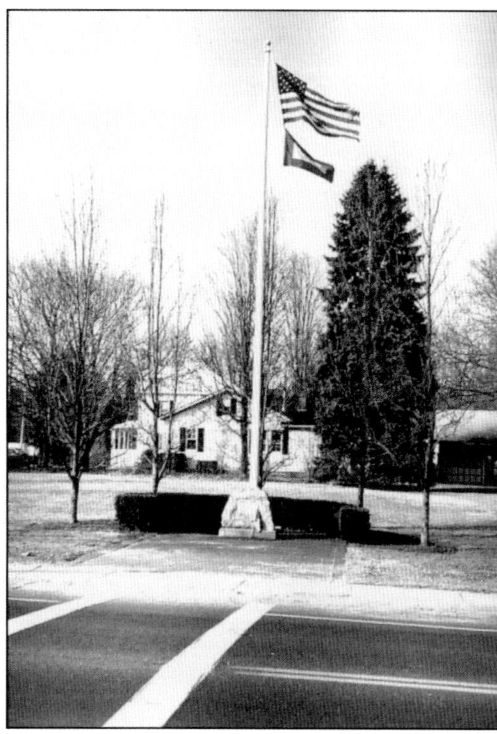

A granite marker commemorating Medway's Civil War soldiers stands on the site today, opposite the police station. It was put in place in 1961.

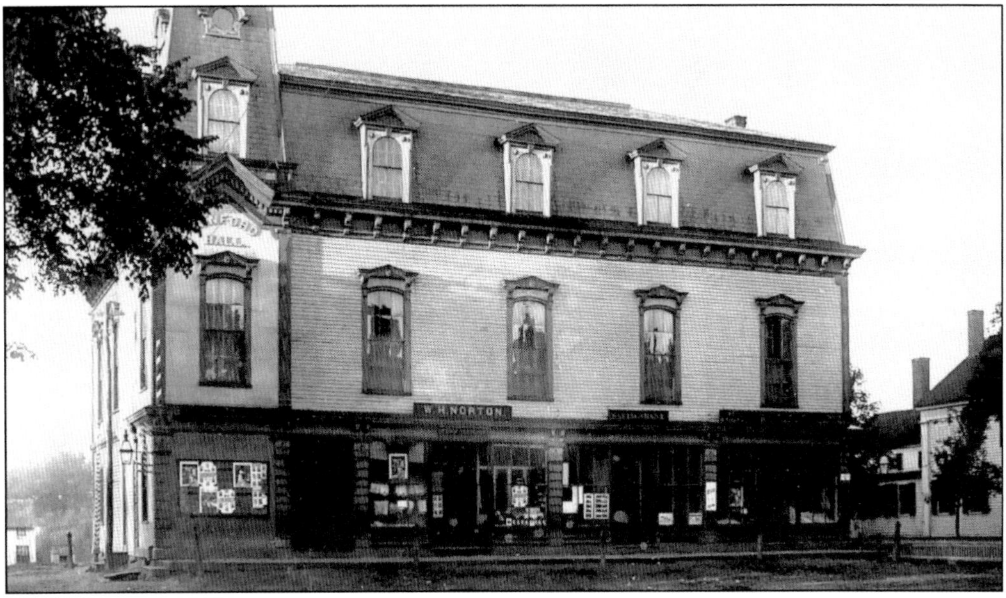

In 1871, Medway Village residents sought to construct their own large public meeting hall, but the idea was refused at a town meeting. Sanford Hall (above) was constructed nonetheless and offered to the town to no avail. The first money was raised by the women of the town. The building was named for Milton and Edward Sanford and their "venerated mother," Edena. The first town meeting was held there in 1873. On the first floor, there were at various times stores, a bank, the post office, the Dean Library, and a barbershop. The second floor was used for meetings and social events. Henry Ward Beecher lectured here in 1881. Minstrel shows and dances were popular events. On June 24, 1911, Sanford Hall burned to the ground. Everything was lost, including the Dean Library books. A new brick structure (below) was built to replace it at a cost of $20,000. It is now the town hall. Until 1990, the building also housed the police station. (Below, courtesy Louise Smith.)

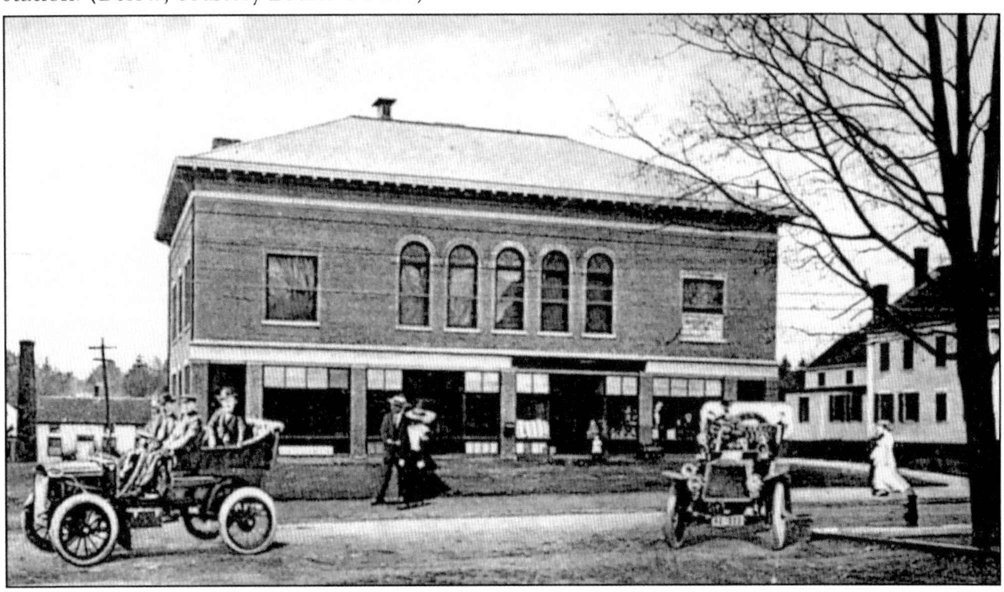

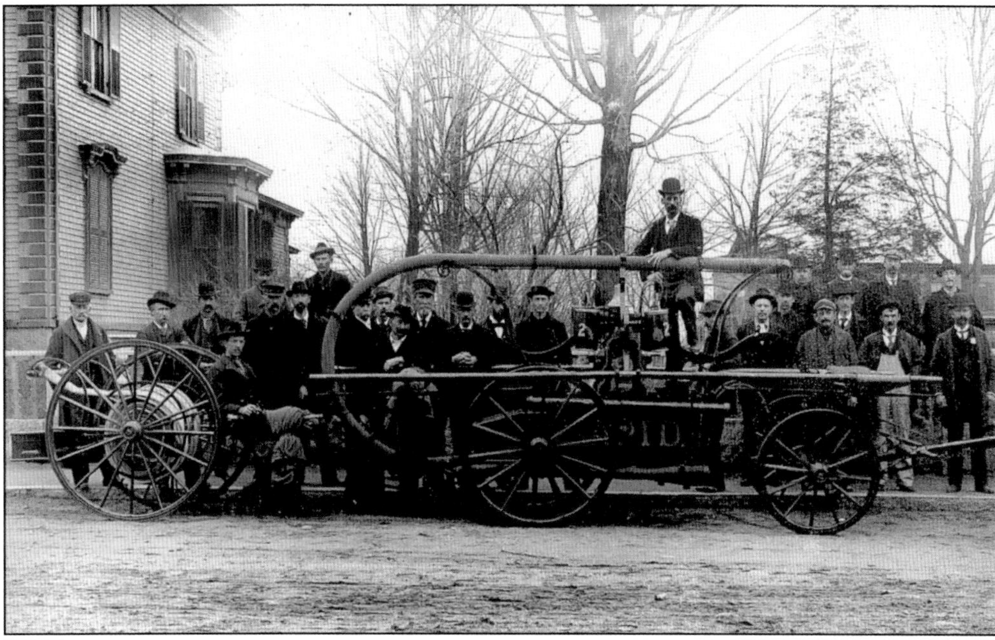

In the early 1850s, Medway purchased its first fire engines. The Rapid engine, assigned to Hose No. 2 Company in Medway Village, is pictured here with hose reel in front of the Clark Partridge house, at Broad and Village Streets, *c.* 1897.

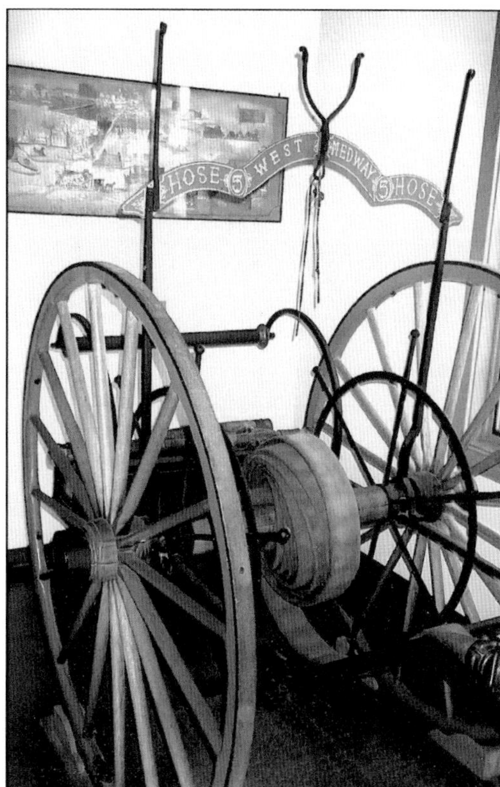

A hose reel from Hose No. 5 Company, West Medway, is pictured on display at the Milford Street fire station. When declared surplus, the reel was bought by the Hixon brothers and moved to California. In 1987, at the request of the heirs of the estate, Philip Boczanowski was able to return it to Medway, where it was restored. Hubs and spokes are replaced; the outer wooden and iron rims are original.

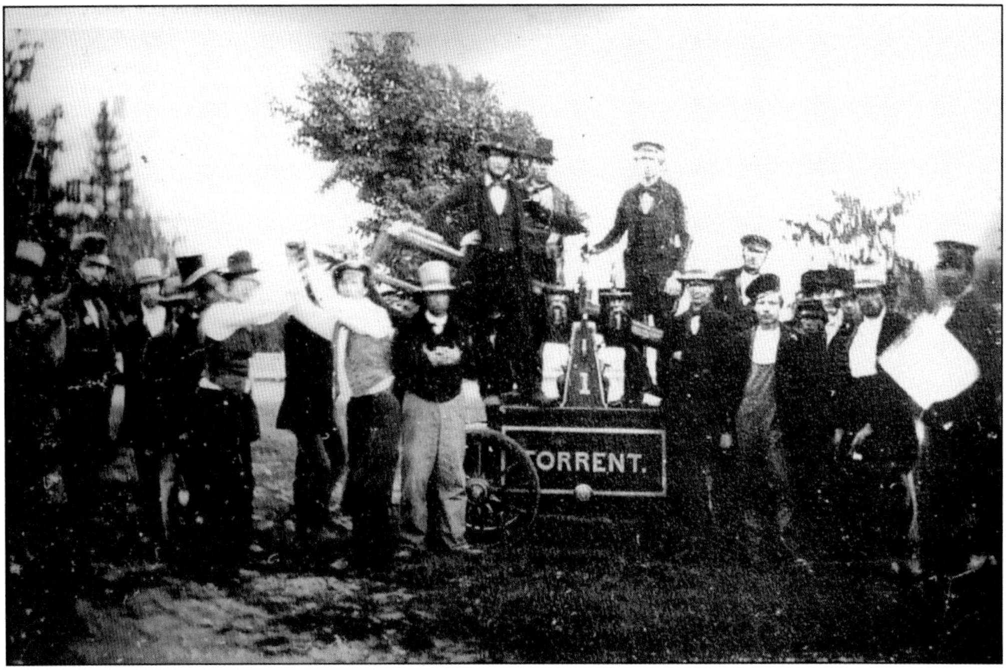

The 1851 Torrent engine of Hose No. 1 West Medway is pictured here with volunteers in 1865. These first hand engines cost between $400 and $500 each. At the time, Medway had several small volunteer companies located in different parts of town—thus, the Hose No. 5 sign on the restored hose reel.

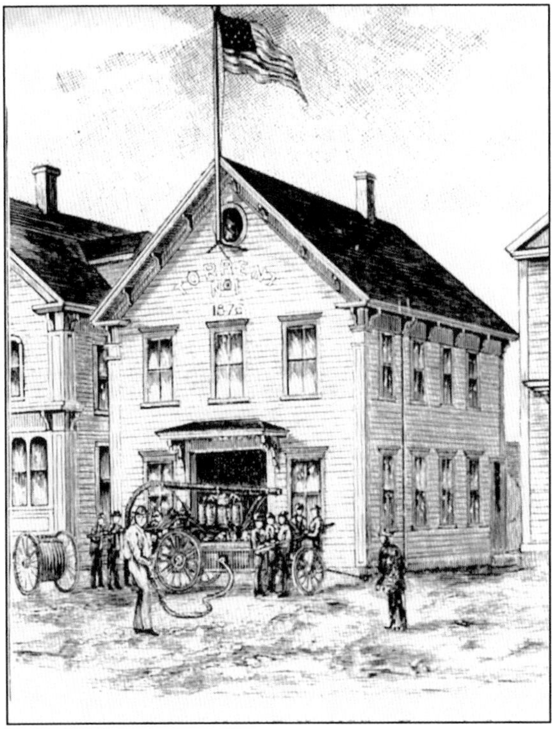

The Torrent Firehouse was built at 197 Main Street in 1876; the hose drying tower was added later. This is one of the few remaining unaltered examples of later-19th-century firehouse architecture left in Massachusetts. At one time, the building had one door in front with windows on each side. In 1900, this was changed to two doors with a window in the middle. The upstairs meeting room has a very beautiful parquet floor. This building remained in active duty until 1991. In 1885, the first permanent fire department was organized, consisting of six companies. The first engine house of Torrent No. 1 was between 201 and 203 Main Street.

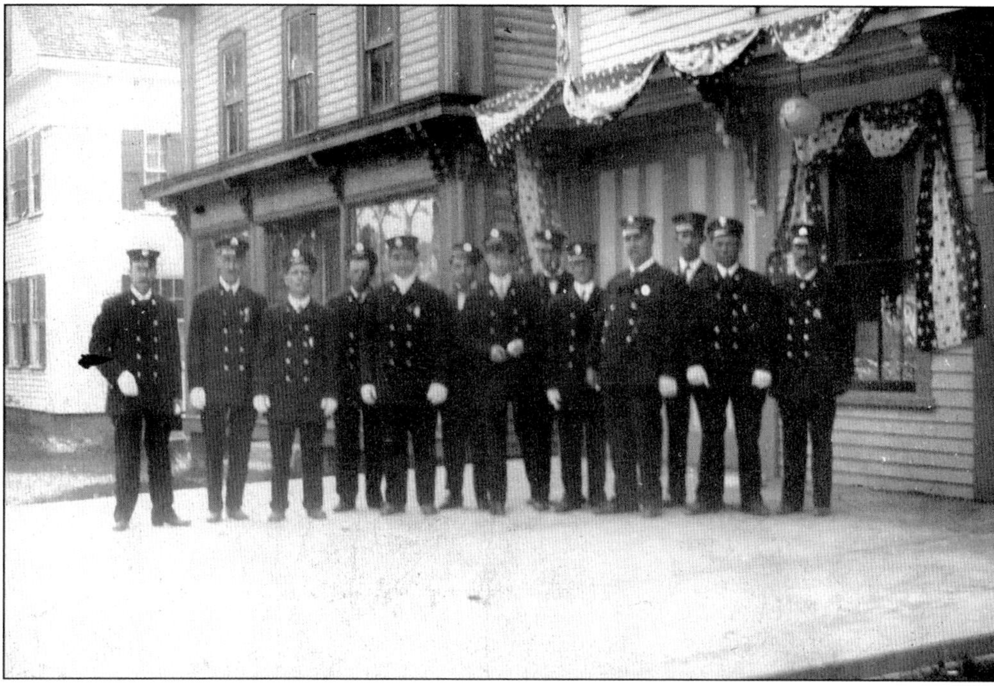

Some of the members of the Hose No. 1 Company line up in front of the Torrent Fire Station, which is decorated for an occasion.

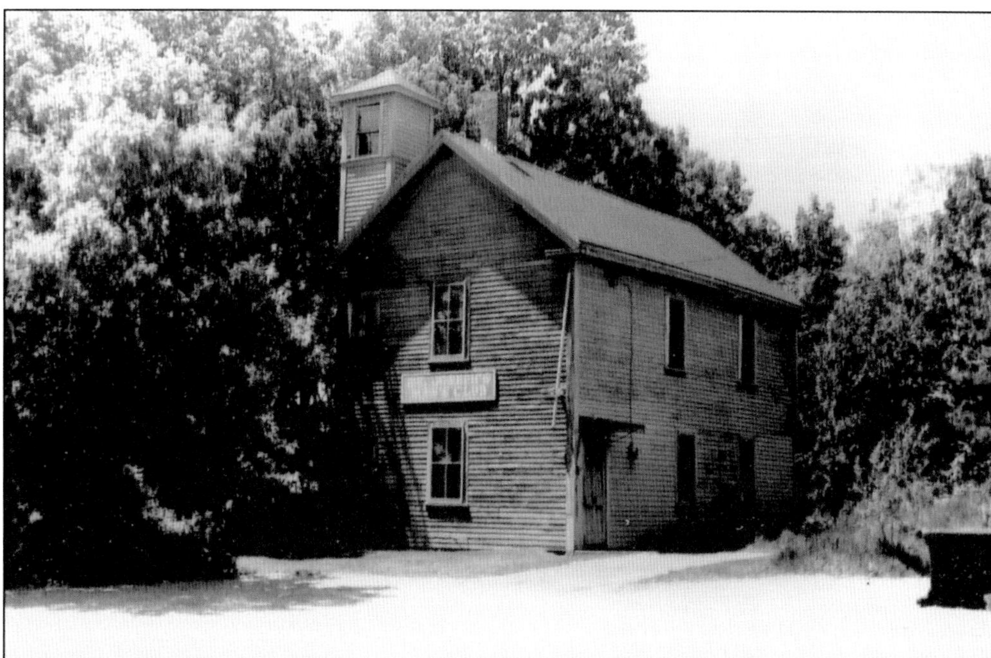

This building, now standing at the rear of the town hall parking lot, was the old fire station at Medway Village. It was moved back so that the present fire station could be built on the front of the site. When this photograph was taken in 1974, the building was home to St. Joseph's Men's Club.

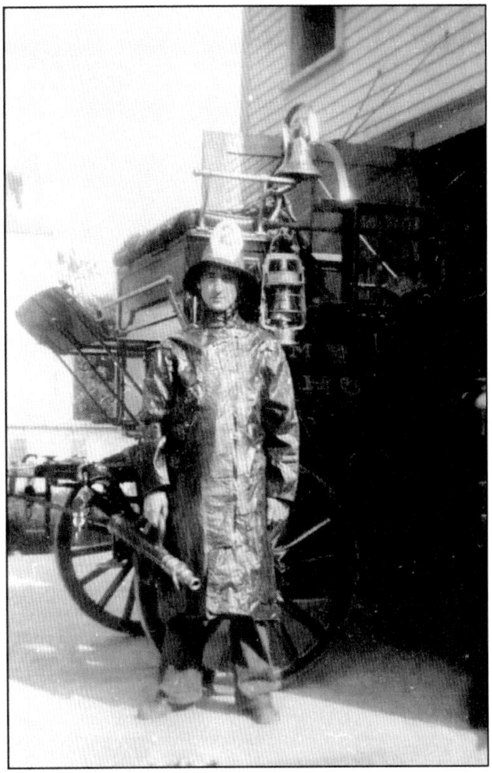

A young Daniel Malloy is shown in front of the old firehouse at Medway Village in 1913. This building, on the site of the present village fire station, now stands at the rear of the parking lot. (Courtesy Stephen Malloy.)

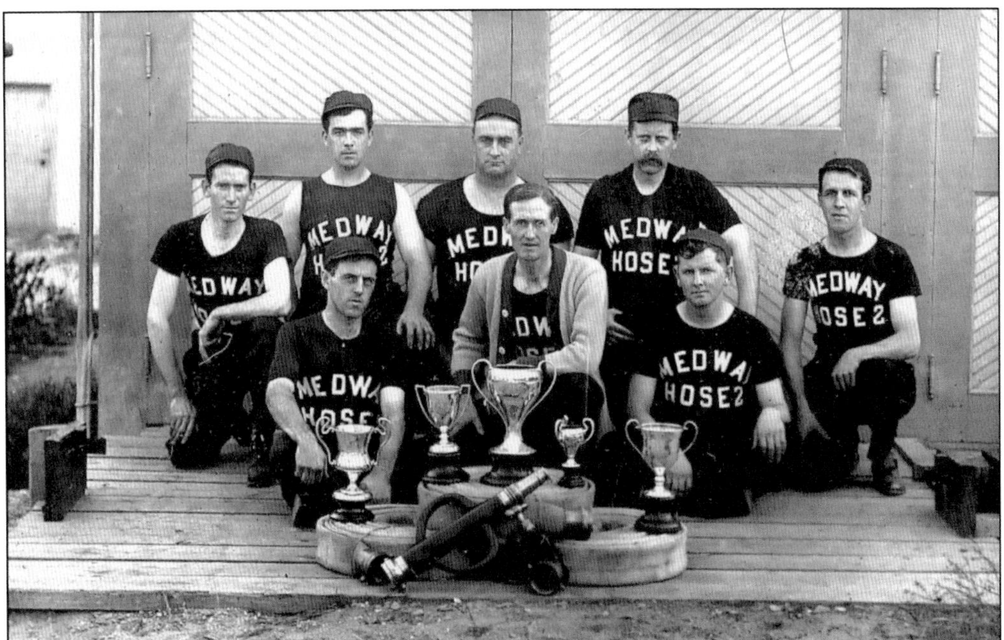

Shown in front of the Medway Village station in 1912 are firemen of Hose No. 2, with trophies won in muster competitions. Among those pictured are Clyde Hunt, Joe Irving, and Peter Caouette. (Courtesy Louise Smith.)

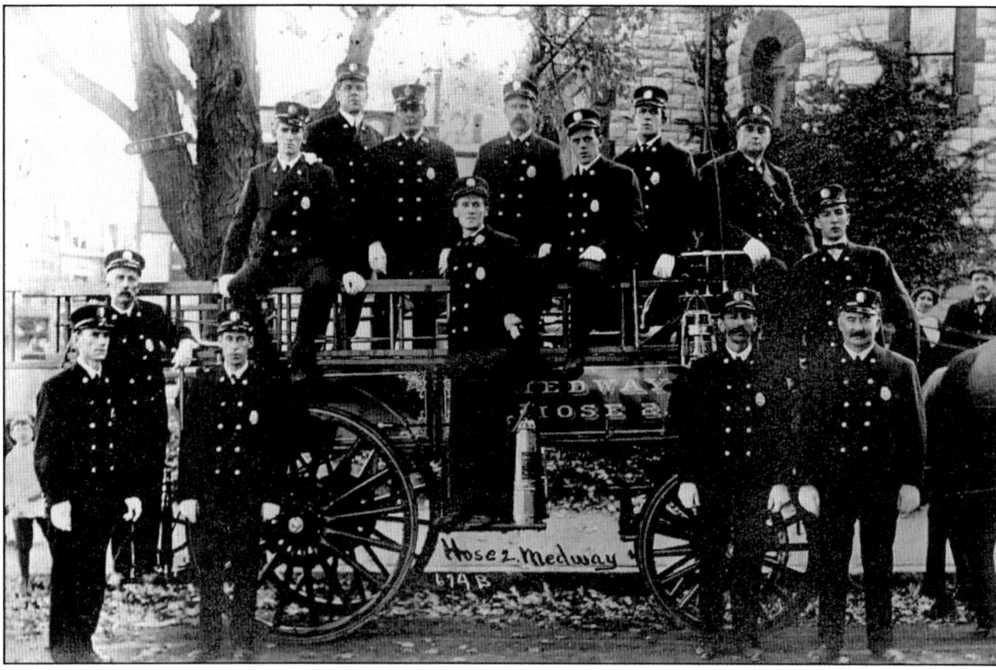

Firemen of Village Station Hose No. 2 are pictured with their new ladder truck in front of the Milford Library. This photograph was taken at a firemen's muster in 1912.

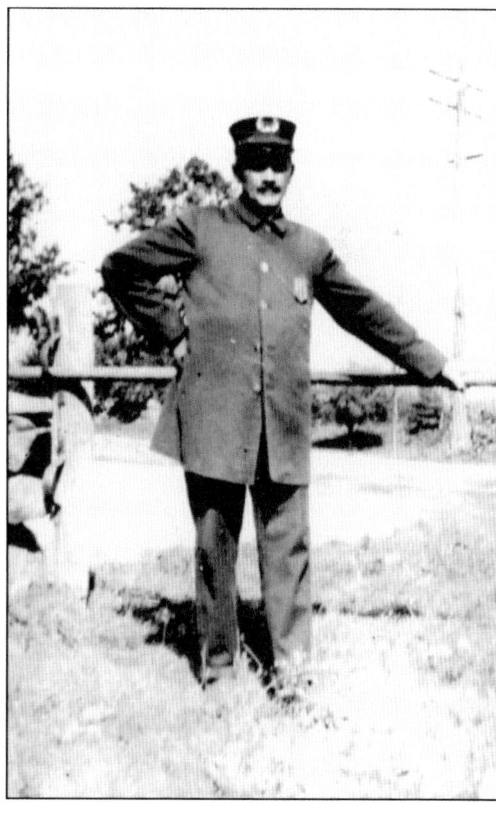

Pictured in 1918, Michael J. Connolly is perhaps Medway's longest serving police officer. Appointed in 1901, Connolly served on the force until 1930. (Courtesy Medway Police Department.)

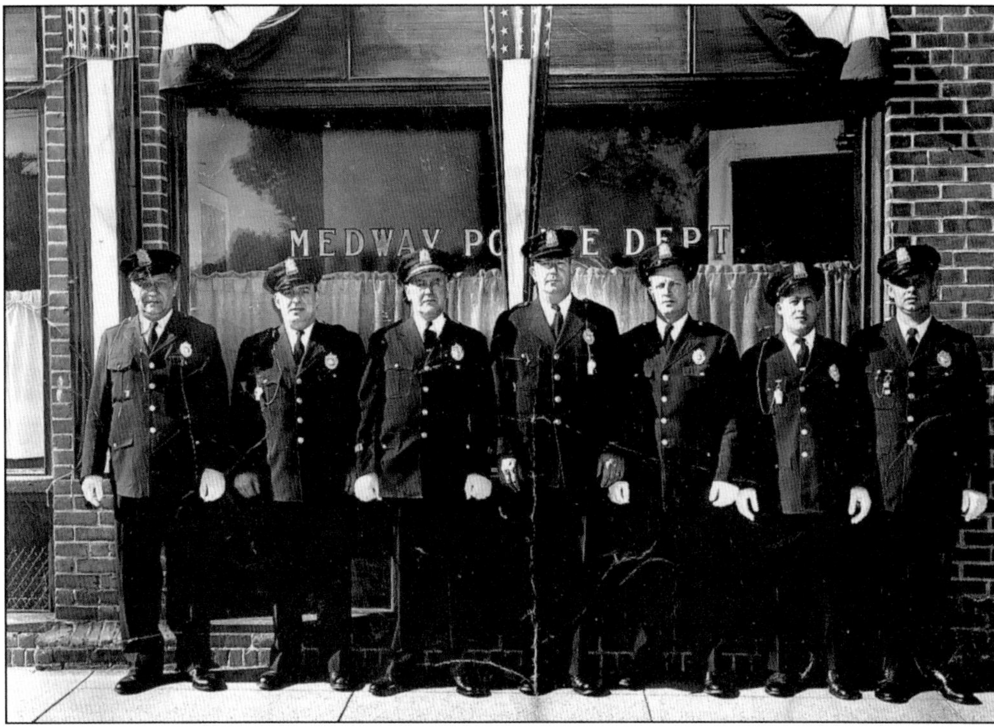

Medway police officers are shown in front of the station at town hall in 1955. From left to right are Michael Beksha, William Giallonardo, Chief Leo Cassidy, Joseph Hennessey, Richard Coakley, Harris Kochansky, and Joe Regan. (Courtesy Medway Police Department.)

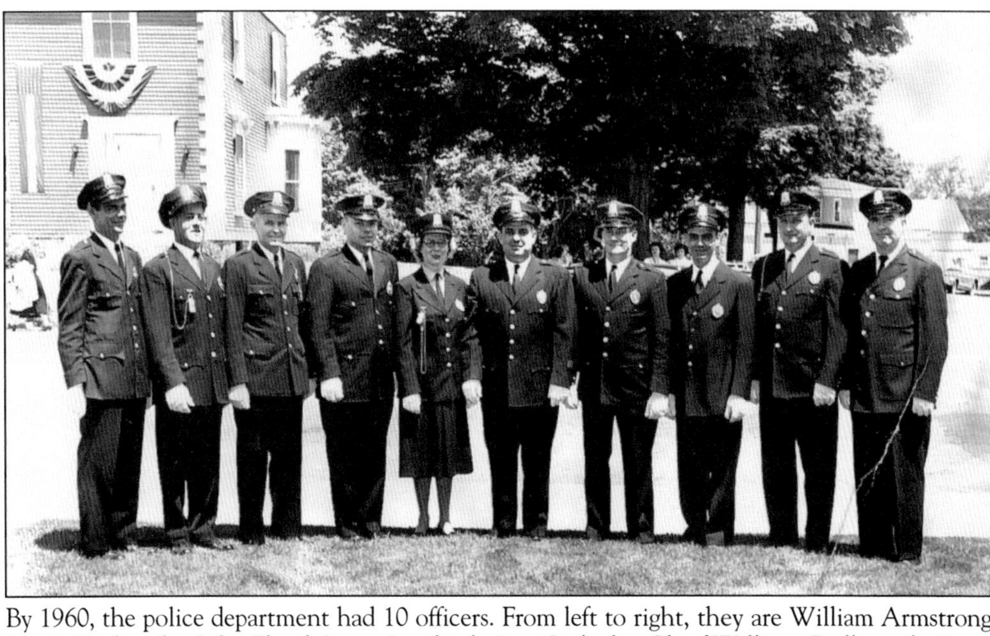

By 1960, the police department had 10 officers. From left to right, they are William Armstrong, Harris Kochansky, John Flood, James Lambirth, Inez Szelepka, Chief William Giallonardo, Leroy Eisner, Elias Rojee, Larry Burns, and Robert O'Brien. (Courtesy Medway Police Department.)

Joseph Julian served the fire department for 47 years, 27 of these as chief, before retiring in 1975.

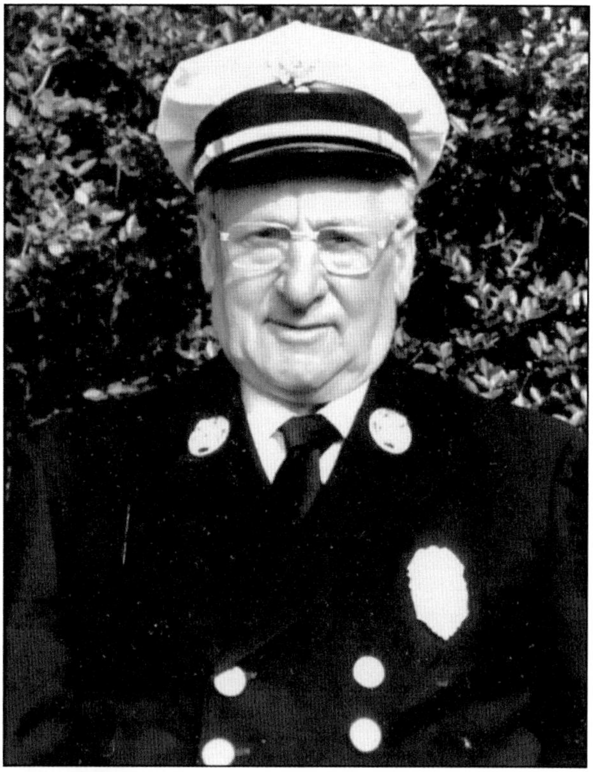

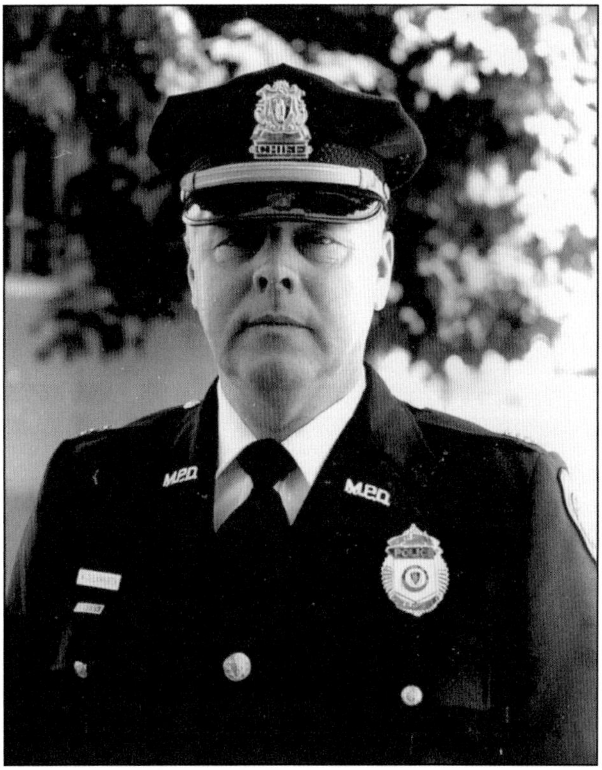

David Lambirth was appointed chief of police in 1980. Retiring in 2003, he was succeeded by present chief, Robert Saleski. (Courtesy Medway Police Department.)

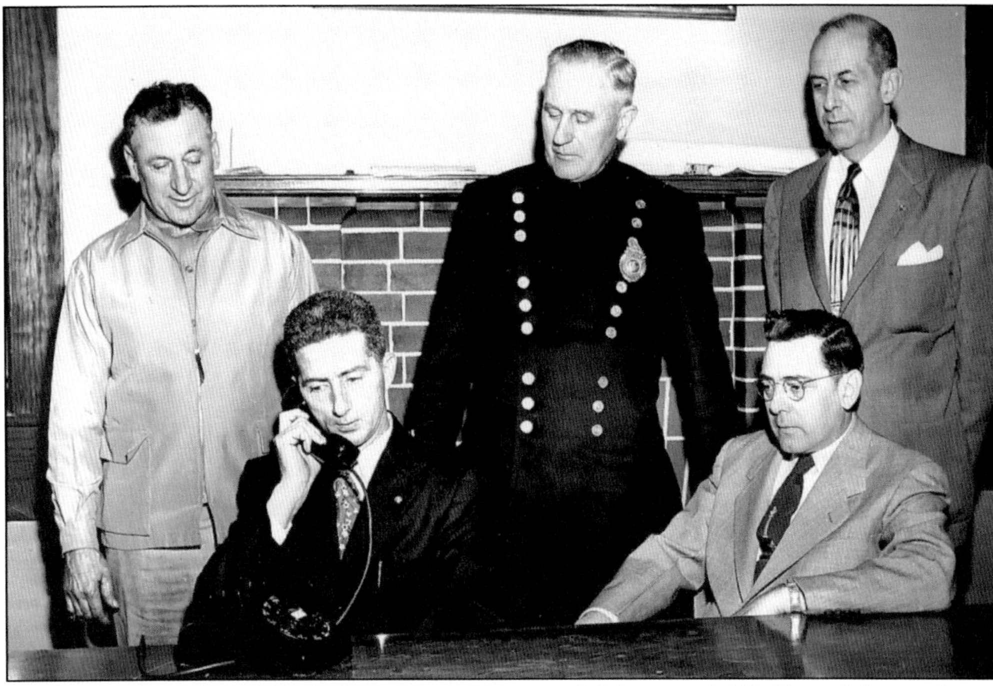

It was a big day when dial telephone service came to Medway in 1953. From left to right are the following: (first row) Ed Higgins and Bob O'Donnell, selectmen; (second row) Joe Julian, fire chief; Leo Cassidy, police chief; and a telephone company representative.

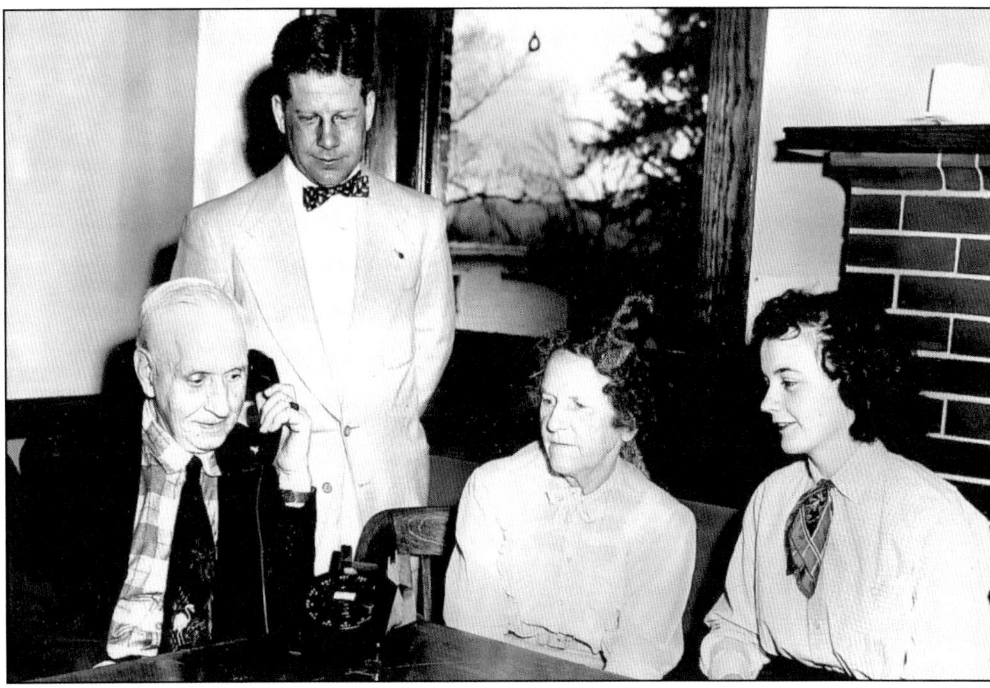

Pictured at town hall trying out the new dial system in 1953 are, from left to right, George Sanford, Isabelle McGourty (town clerk), and Eunice Hanlon. With them is a telephone company representative.

Four

Houses of Worship, Schools, and Libraries

The churches have always been an important part of Medway's life. In the early days, there was a lot of dissension among the churches. Occasionally, the dissension involved politics and personal matters rather than theology. Some prominent members were even excommunicated from the Second Church of Christ and formed the Third Congregational Church. The separation to form the Village Church was, however, amicable and deemed necessary.

For many years, there was a number of small schools around town. For the most part, they were very primitive and often did not even have water. They were not well heated and were very stuffy and overcrowded. As a result, there was a lot of sickness among the students. In spite of this, the townspeople voted down improvements including wells year after year. For some time, the high school students moved from village to village until it was finally decided to have a central high school

For many years, Medway had two libraries: Dean Library in Sanford Hall and the library at West Medway, which was first located upstairs in Smith's Block and later in the Thayer Building. The libraries were combined in 1980, when the High Street School was converted to a central library.

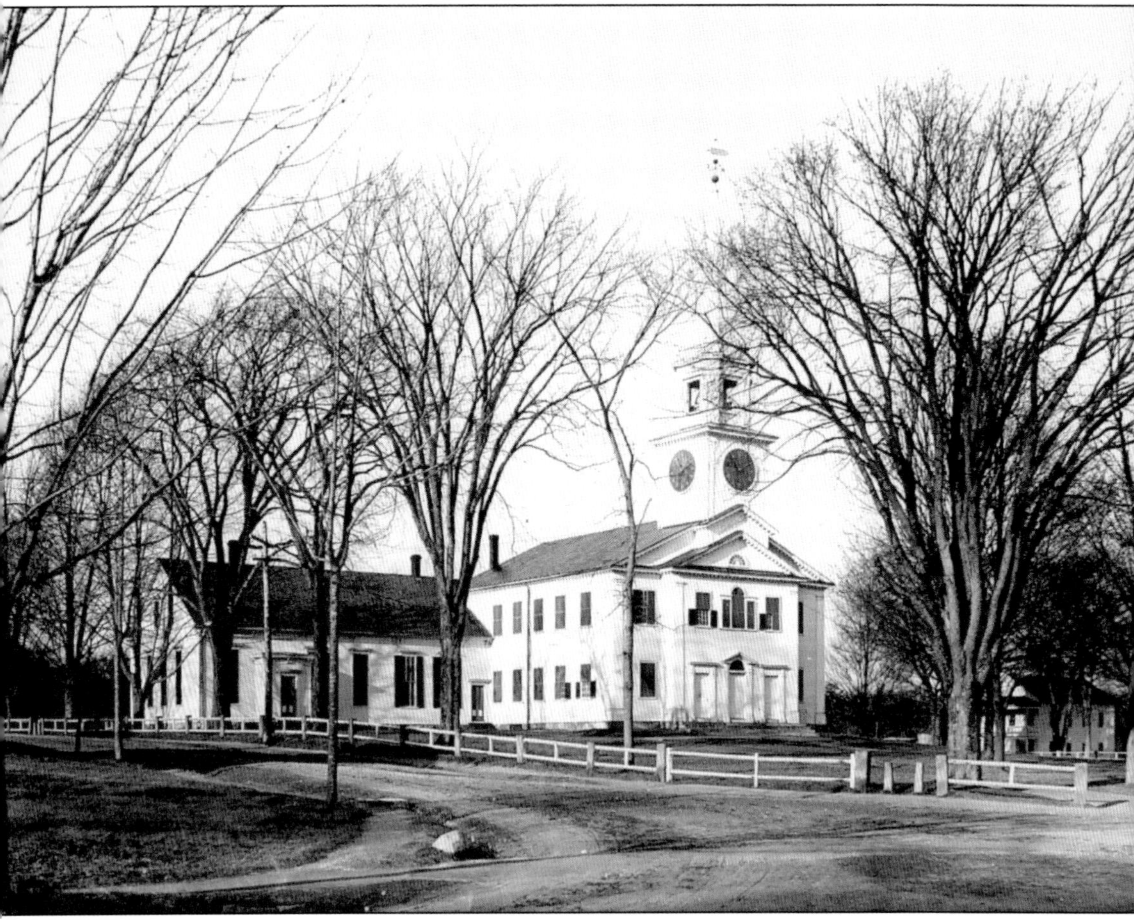

The Second Church of Christ in West Medway was constructed on Rabbit Hill by builder Malachi Bullard in 1814. It replaced the original 1749 meetinghouse, located on the corner of Evergreen and Main. At that time, there were no homes near the Rabbit Hill site. The ell of the church was added in 1875. In 1886, the Third Congregational Church was organized by excommunicated and disaffected members of the Second Church. In 1891, the Second Congregational and Third Congregational Churches united.

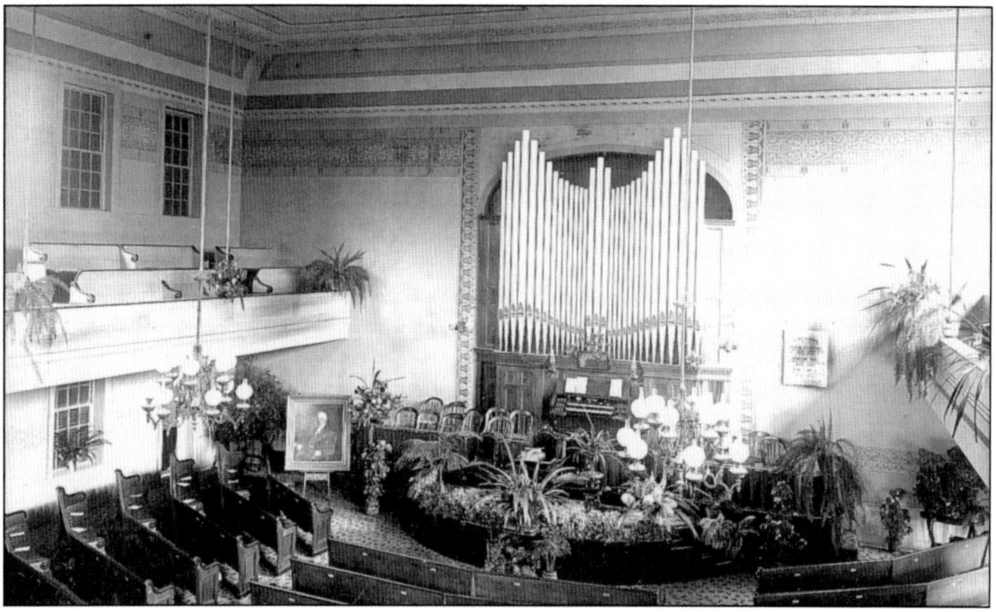

This 1900 photograph shows the interior decorated to celebrate the 150th anniversary of the church. By this time, the church had changed its name to the Second Congregational Church. A portrait of Dr. Jacob Ide, pastor from 1814 to 1880, is on display. In 1846, the church was modernized. The square pews were removed, the aisles carpeted, and the windows opposite the entrance closed in. In 1873, more remodeling was done. The first pipe organ was installed in 1900. In 1910, the auditorium was restored to the Colonial style. Other changes were made in 1986.

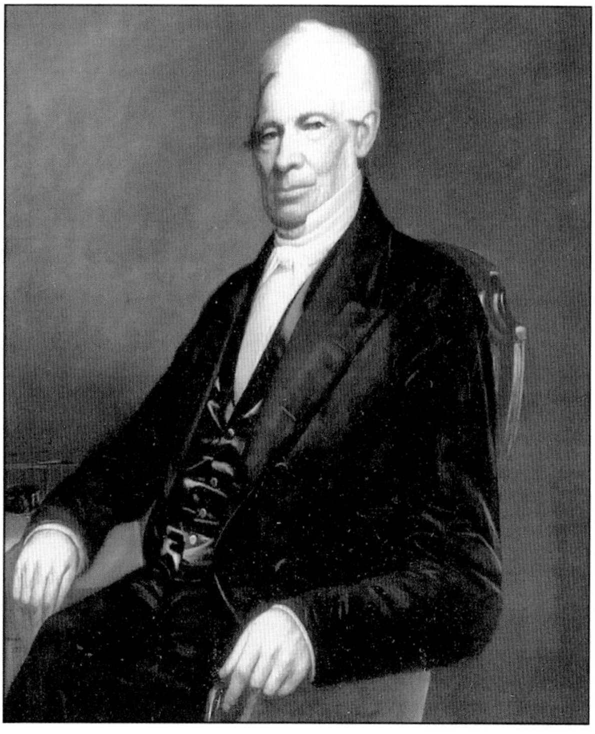

Dr. Jacob Ide, seen here in a portrait by Anson Daniels, was the first pastor of the church on Rabbit Hill. His 65 years with the church spanned the development of the West Medway area that is now Rabbit Hill Historic District. This portrait hangs in the entry hall at the church.

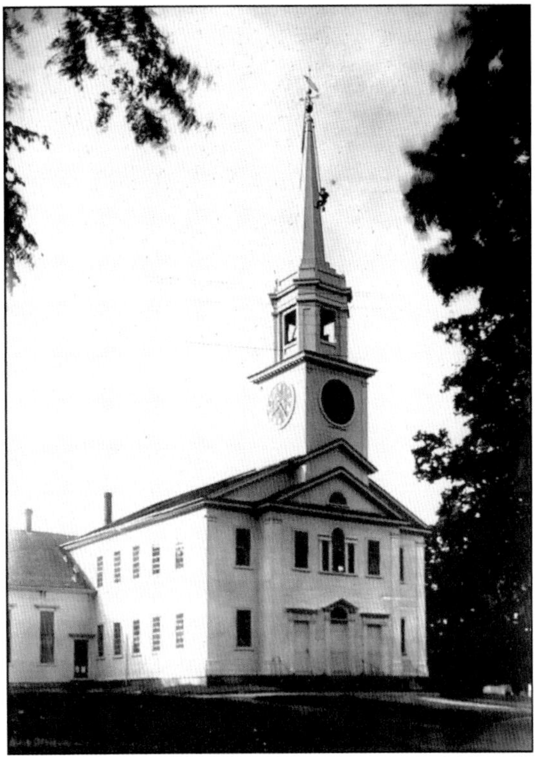

This Second Congregational Church steeple has had a dramatic history. When the church was built, it had a dome instead of a spire. The spire was erected in 1846. According to a September 30, 1882, report by the parish committee, "the steeple was rebuilt after the great blow of July 28, 1882 at which time the steeple was whirled in the air like a top and sent through the roof point first into auditorium room below and striking a large timber in the floor bounded back and lay on top of the pews in front of the pulpit doing a very little damage." In the hurricane of 1938, the rebuilt steeple was destroyed. Then, in 1945, it was struck by lightning and severely damaged. This photograph was taken in 1896 while the steeple was being painted.

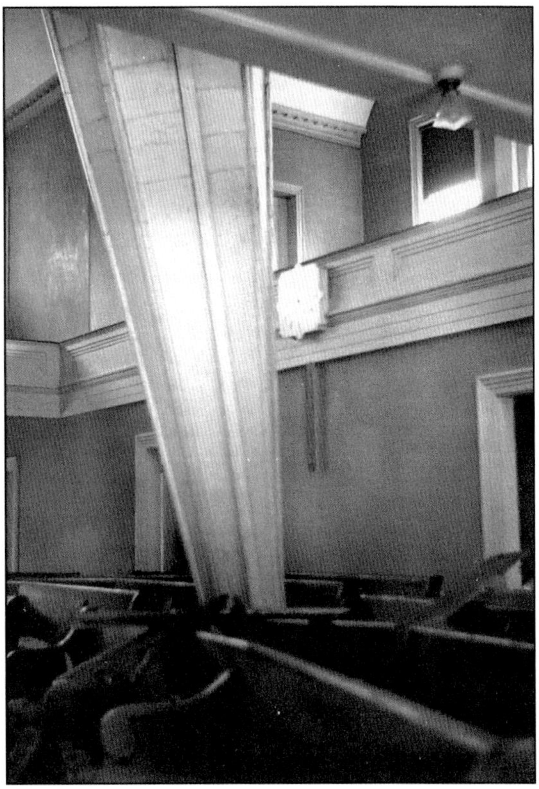

The hurricane of 1938 also brought the steeple into the sanctuary.

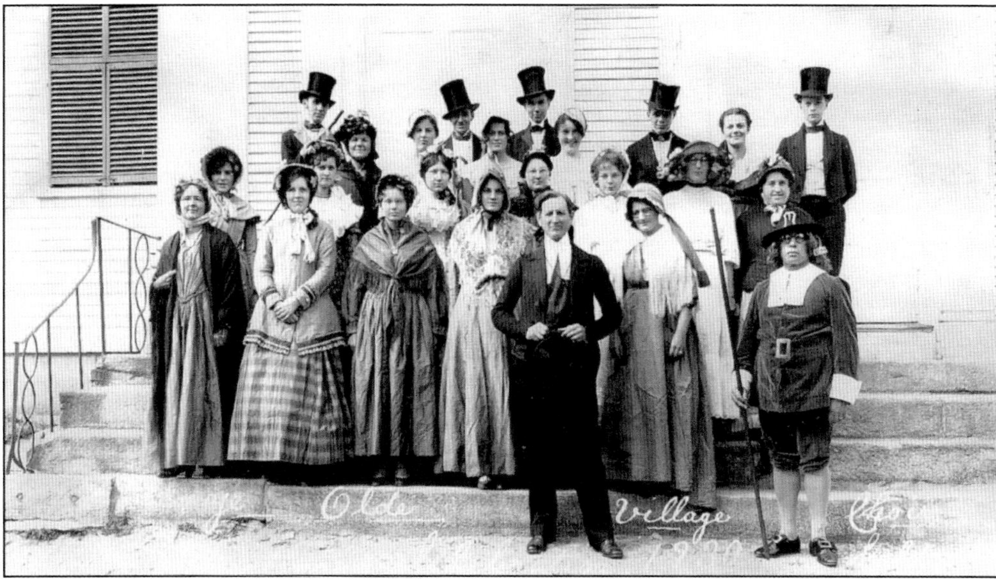

This 1930 photograph celebrates the 300th anniversary of the Massachusetts Bay Colony and the 180th anniversary of the founding of the old West Parish Church. The people standing in front of the Second Congregational Church are members of the Old Medway Choir. From left to right are the following: (first row) Mr. Howard and Edgar Woodman; (second row) Margaret Labaree, Myrtis Hill, Virginia Saunders, Sylvia Hodgson, and Esther Clough; (third row) Maude Fairbairn, Meta Hunter, Marion Clark, Lilla Fales, Nina Turner, Doris Turner, and Mary Stella. The fourth row included Kelsey Haynes, Nadine Anderson, Walter Force, M. Ollendorff, Harlan Moore, Peggy Page, Newton Cole, M. Ollendorff, and Harold Mill.

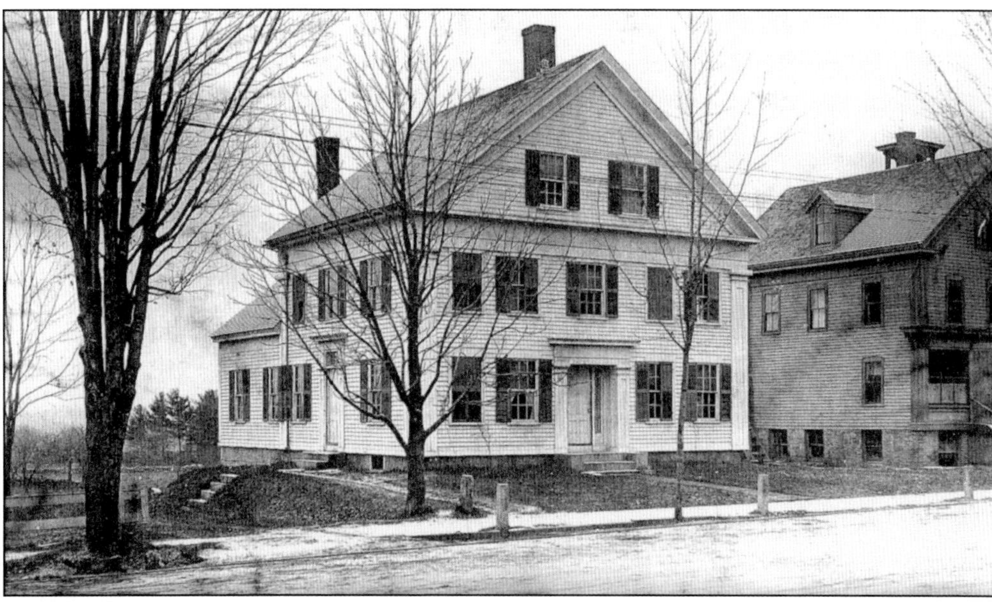

The parsonage of the Community Church was built at 193 Main Street in 1850. It was used as a parsonage until recently. It now holds the church offices and library. The house that was originally on this site was moved to Slocumb Place. This photograph was taken in 1900. Thayer's Block (right) later became a town library.

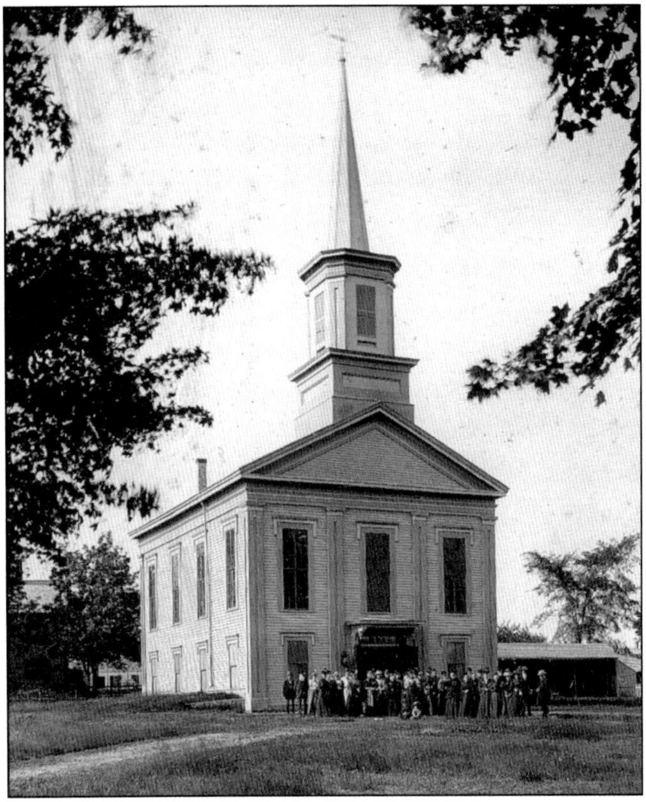

A Baptist society was formed in Medway in 1819. It included a few Baptists, some Universalists, and several others. A meetinghouse was built on the corner of Winthrop and Main Streets in 1823. For the first seven years, the Universalists held control and they met in this Baptist church (left). In 1832, the Baptists gained strength, and in 1852, a new meetinghouse was built on the same site. The church was destroyed in the 1938 hurricane, and the members joined with the Second Church of Christ to form the Community Church. Shown below is an interior view of the church.

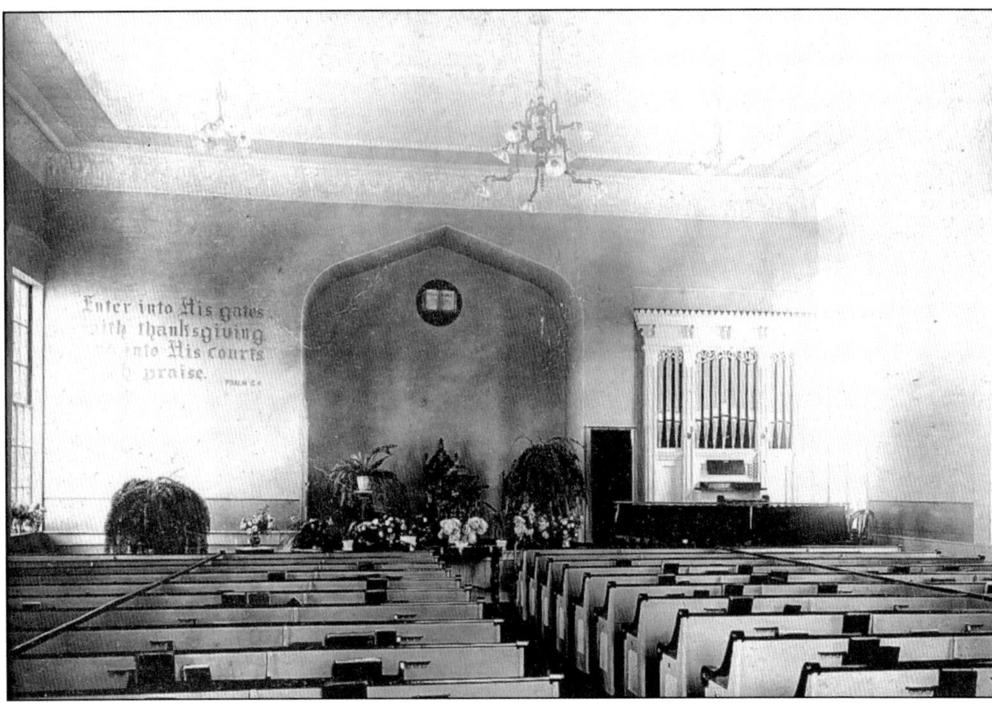

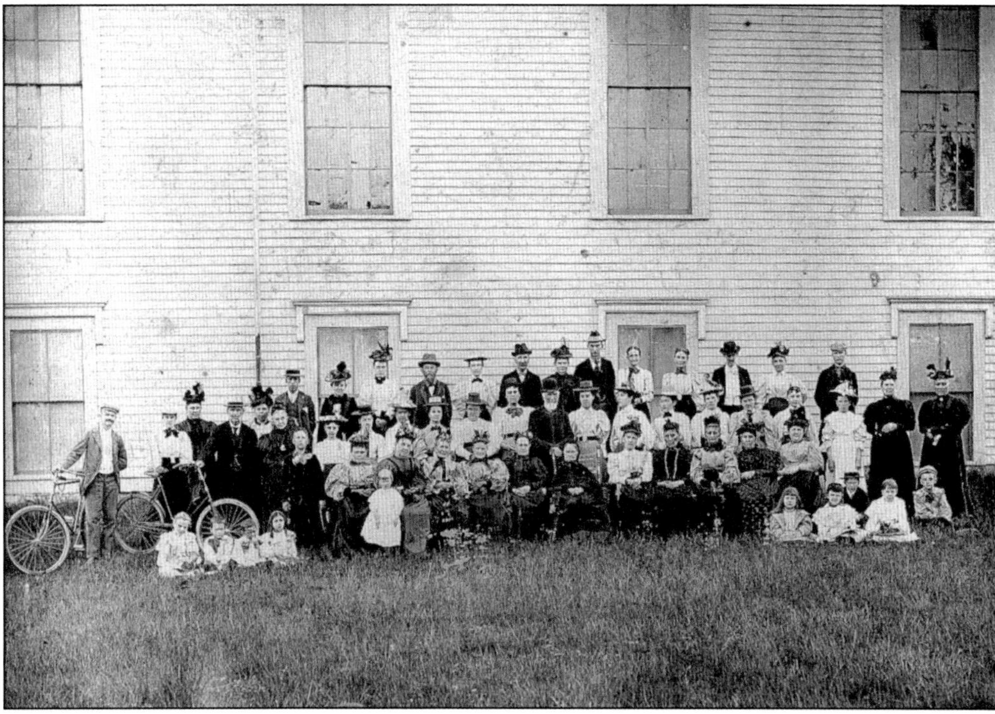

The rather somber people in this group are members of the Baptist church, gathered outside of the church on a Sunday *c.* 1900.

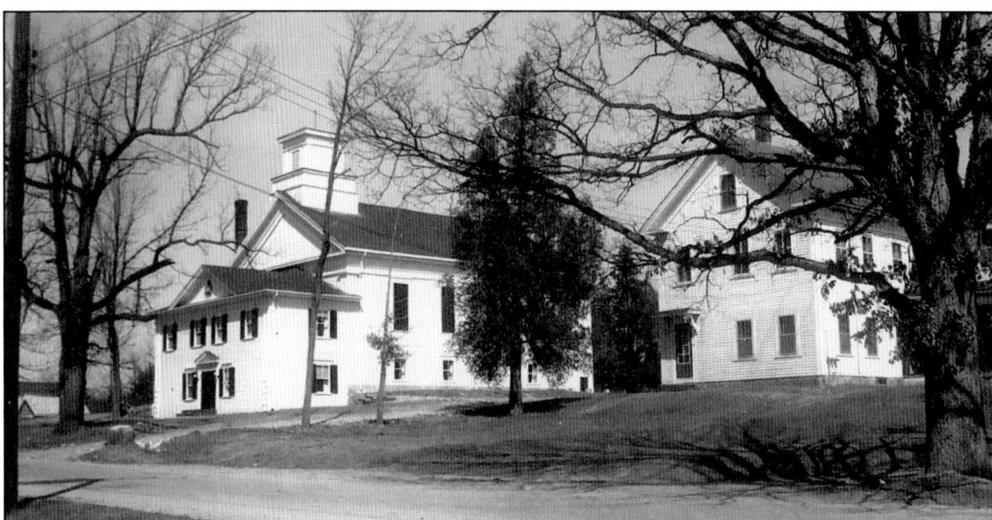

The Methodist church was organized in 1857. The Methodists met at first on Slocumb Place, with the eccentric Dr. William Jackson presiding. This building was constructed on Cottage Street and was eventually finished in 1860. In 1880, the church reached its peak membership of 186. Gradually, membership declined, and in 1930, the building was sold to the Charles River Lodge and dedicated to Masonic use. It continues as a Masonic temple, at 37 Cottage Street.

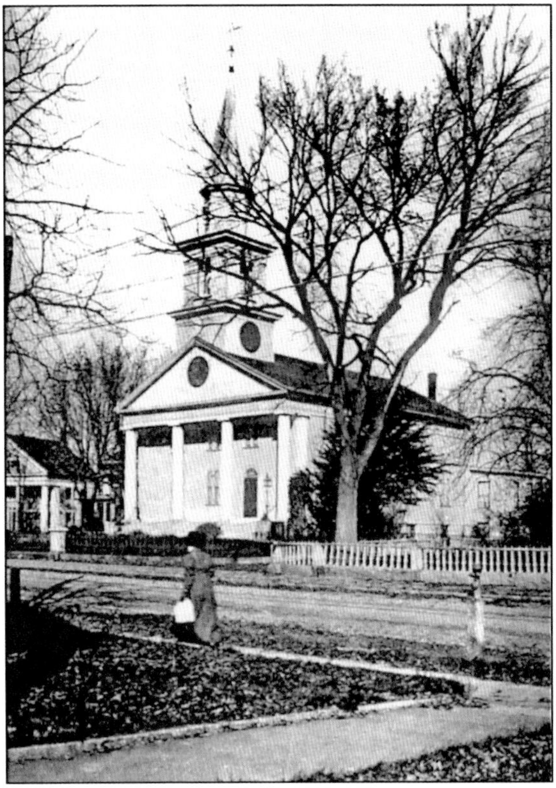

Attending services in West Medway was a hardship for the residents of Medway Village. A total of 31 members of the Second Congregational Church were dismissed, and they built and dedicated the Village Evangelical Congregational Church in 1838. Their first pastor was David Sanford, grandson of a former pastor of the mother church. Side galleries were added in 1840. In 1849, the church was presented with a tower clock. In 1861, Milton Sanford gave the church an organ. Town meetings were held in the church until Sanford Hall was built in 1872. In 1873, the church was remodeled.

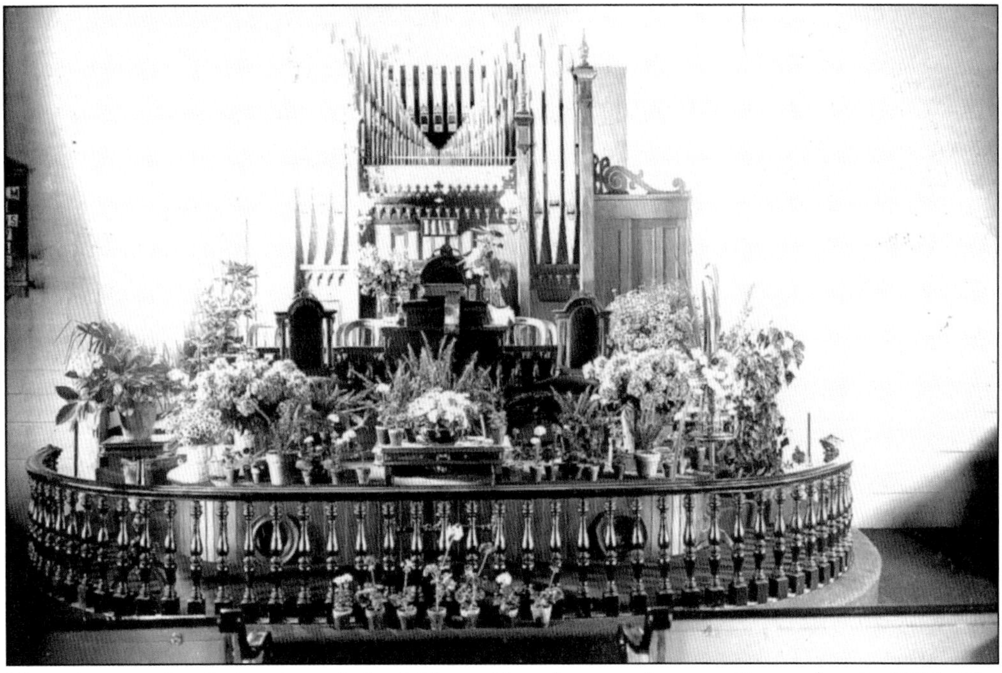

This photograph of the altar of the Village Church was taken on September 7, 1888. The church was decorated for the 50th anniversary celebration of the church. Rev. Rufus Harlow was the pastor at the time.

This is a photograph of St. Joseph's Church in 1885. In the middle of the 19th century, many Irish came to Medway to work in the mills and on the railroad. The first Mass in Medway was held in 1849 on John Street in a private home. A Catholic society was organized in Medway in 1862. The society purchased the Village Street schoolhouse in 1864 and then moved it to use the site for the present church. St. Joseph's Church was built in 1876, and the first service in it was held in 1877 in the basement. The steeple was added in 1890, with a bell pitched to match the one in the Village Church. The steeple was removed in 1993.

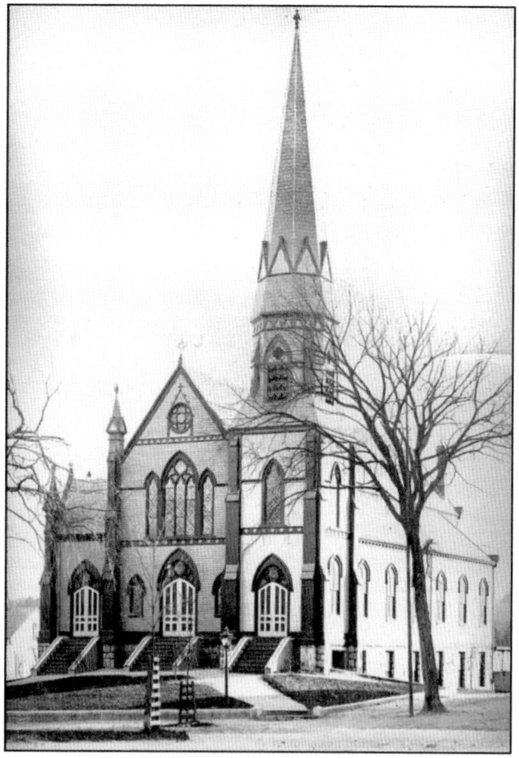

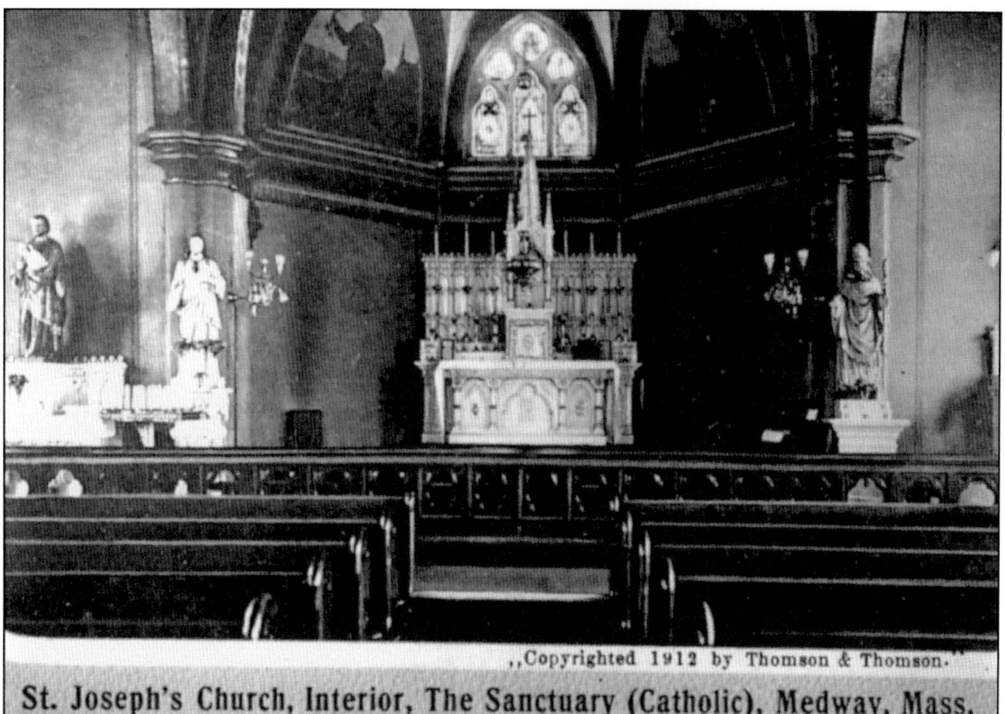

This photograph of St. Joseph's sanctuary was taken in 1912. The interior of the church has been renovated several times since then.

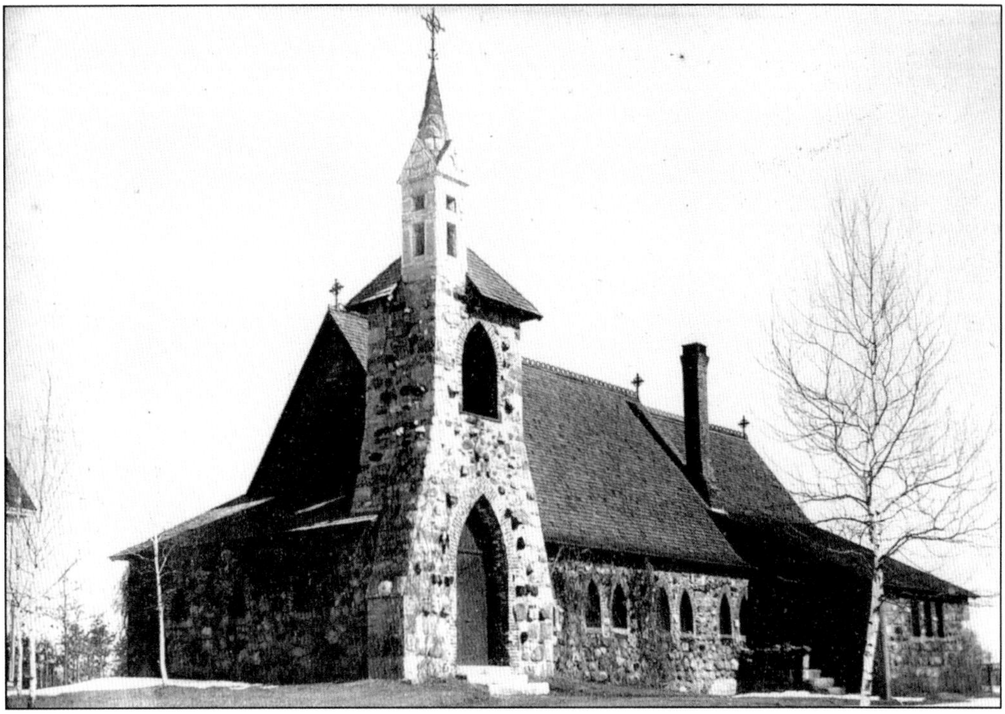

Christ Episcopal Church, on School Street, was designed by Stephen C. Earle, a prominent architect in the last third of the 19th century. Earle was one of the most skillful architects of his time. Dozens of his buildings are listed on the National Register of Historic Places. The church was constructed in 1874 by Elmer Videtto, a local stonemason who used local stones. Croswell Hall was added in 1899.

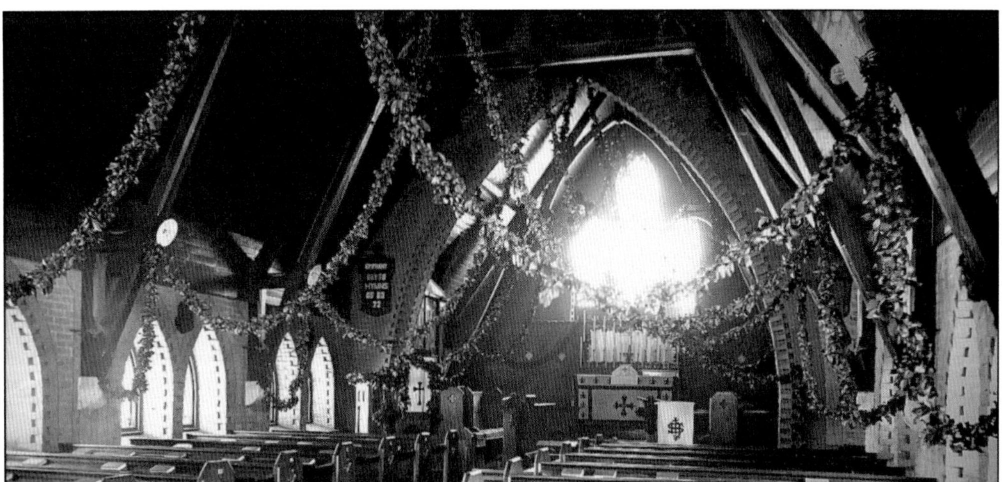

Prof. Curtis Dahl of Wheaton College has this to say about Stephen Earle and the Episcopal church. "In many respects nothing he would ever do would equal the quiet charm and perfection of this little sweeping-roof sanctuary with its deep chancel, low nave, superb interior brick work and small brilliantly-stained arched windows." Dahl devoted much time to the study of Stephen Earle and organized an exhibition having to do with his work. In this view, the church is decorated for a special occasion.

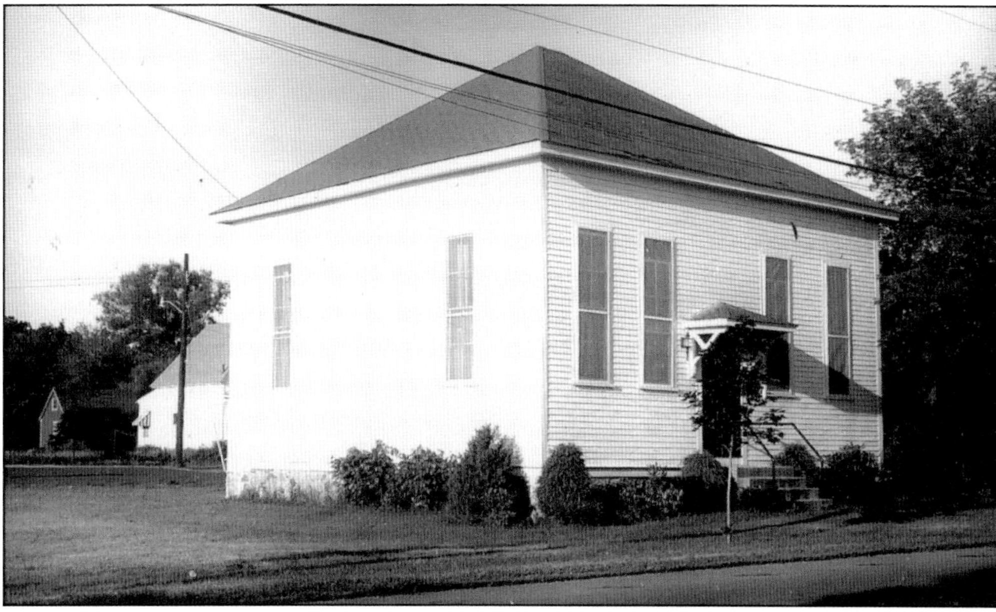

Congregation Agudath Achim was built on lower Village Street in 1919 and continued actively until 2003. Village Street in Millis near the Medway line was a Jewish summer resort for many years. Starting in 1881 with the arrival in Medway of Abraham Charak, Medway had a sizeable population of Jewish residents who had fled from Russian persecution. Many settled in the northern part of town in the vicinity of Hill and Winthrop Streets. A synagogue was built on Hill Street in 1899 and was later moved to the corner of Mechanic and Main Streets. Another synagogue was located at the corner of Partridge and Winthrop Streets, where Schoolhouse No. 5 had been. That area is now a playground.

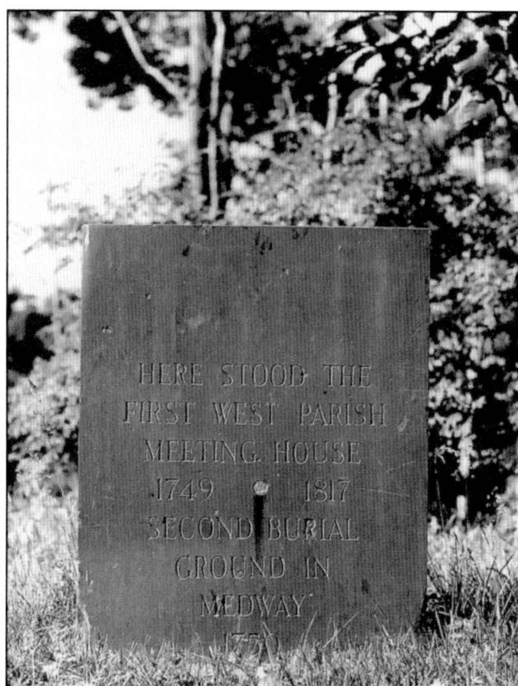

"Here stood the First West Parish meeting house 1749–1817. Second burial ground in Medway 1750." This stone marker stands at the west end of Evergreen Street, as it curves north to join Main Street. Medway's earliest cemetery lies on the rise beyond it. The town's first settler, Henry Garnsey, is buried here.

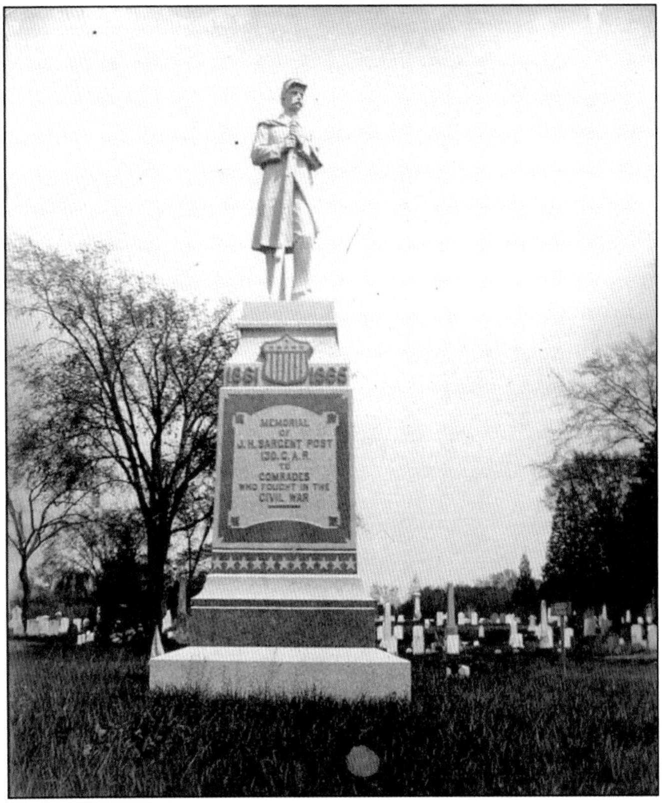

The Evergreen Street burying place was laid out in 1750, shortly after the Meeting House was constructed. It is still an active cemetery. The Soldiers Monument, Medway's only statue, was erected and dedicated by the Grand Army of the Republic (GAR) in 1896. In 1904, a monument was dedicated to the memory of Dr. Jacob Ide, longtime pastor of the Community Church. Most of the early settlers of the New Grant (see map on page 2) are buried in the older part of the cemetery.

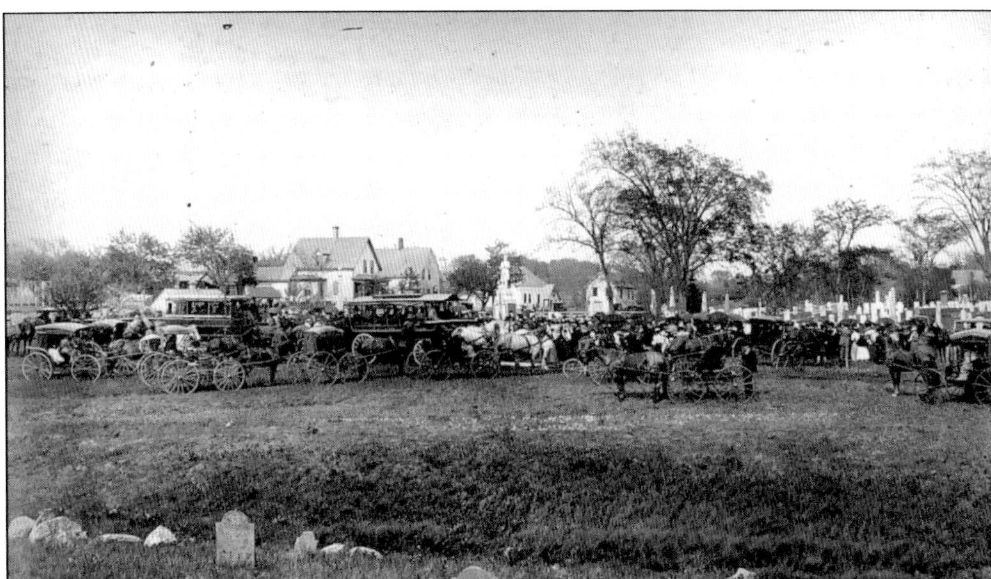

Taken from the old burial ground at Evergreen on Memorial Day 1898, this view looks toward the newer burial area that expands the cemetery to Cottage Street. Visible in the center distance is the newly erected monument to soldiers of the Civil War.

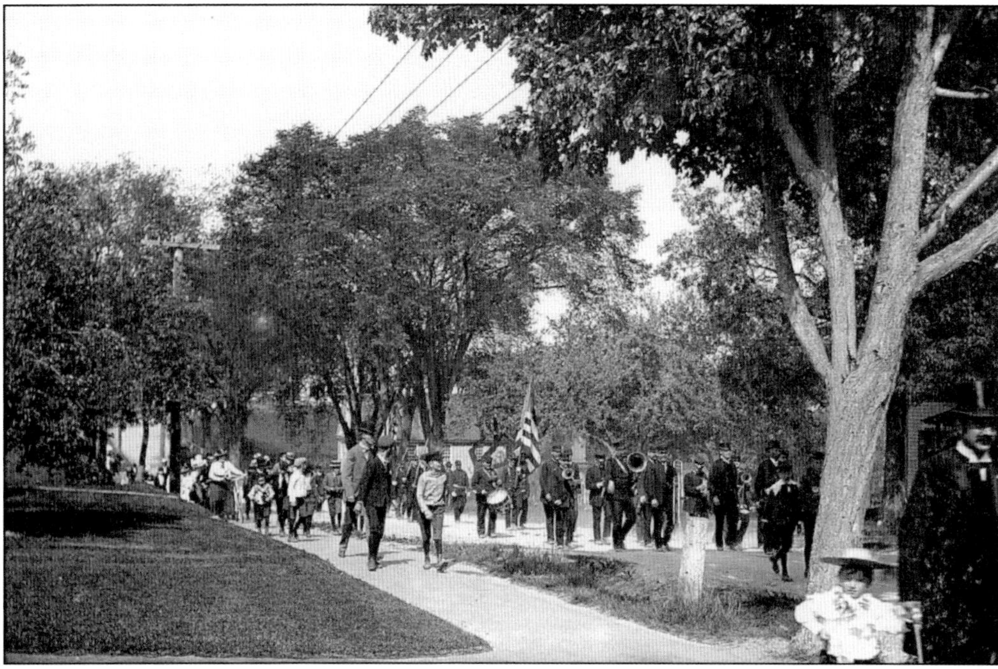

The Memorial Day parade is a longstanding tradition in Medway. The James Sargent Post of the Grand Army of the Republic started the town-wide Decoration Day observance in the 1880s. Today, it is carried forward by the local chapters of the Veterans of Foreign Wars and American Legion. Shown is the 1909 parade on Main Street, with the Fales Band.

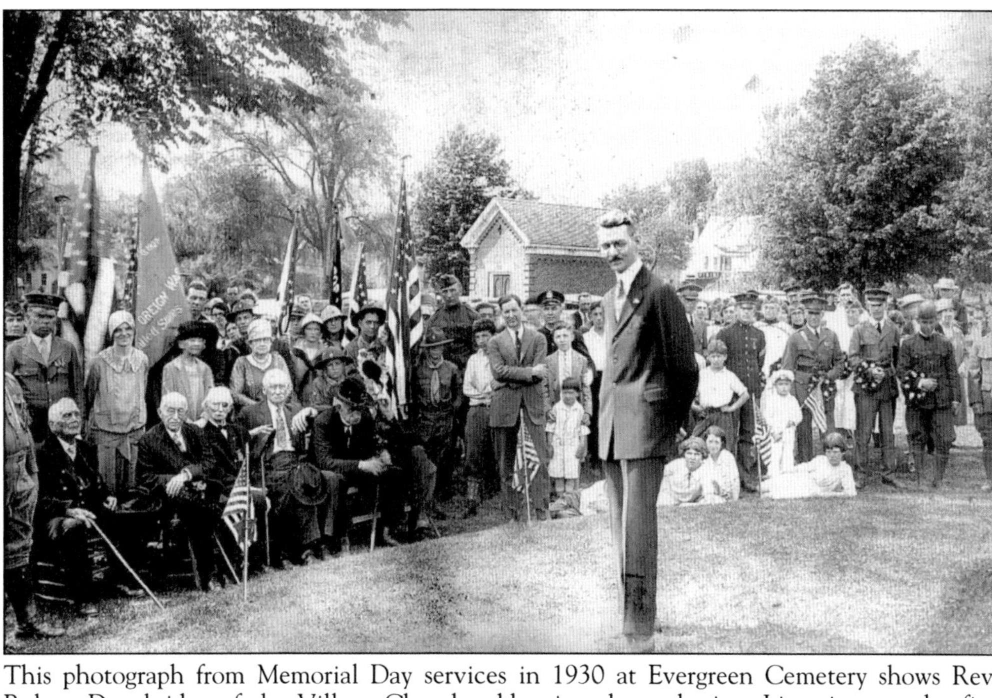

This photograph from Memorial Day services in 1930 at Evergreen Cemetery shows Rev. Robert Drawbridge of the Village Church addressing the gathering. Listening are the five surviving veterans of the Civil War (seated, left).

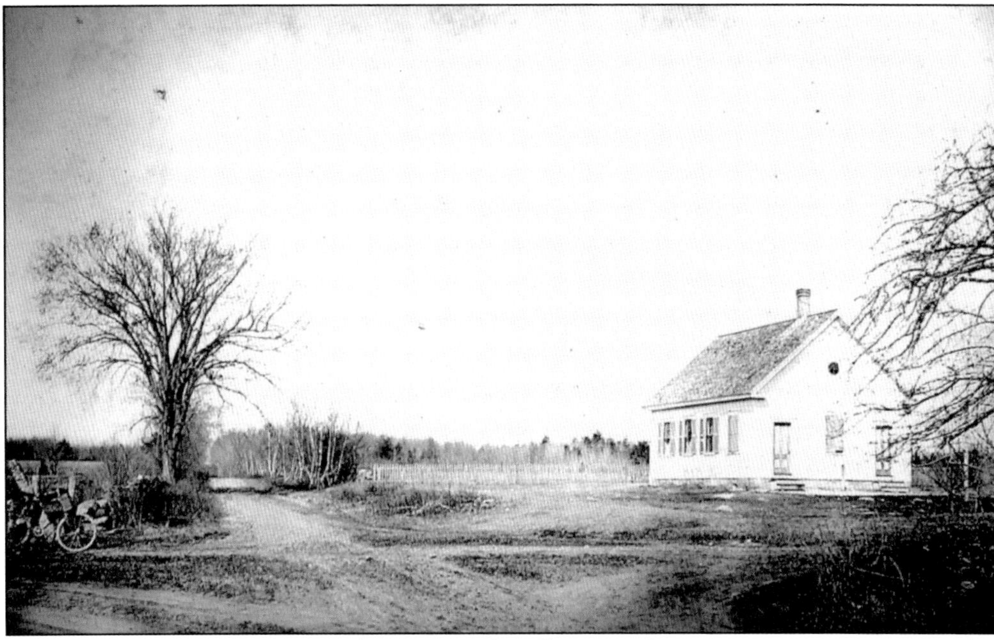

The Drybridge schoolhouse, at the corner of Holliston and Lovering Streets, is pictured in 1905. This building was typical of small one-room schools located throughout Medway.

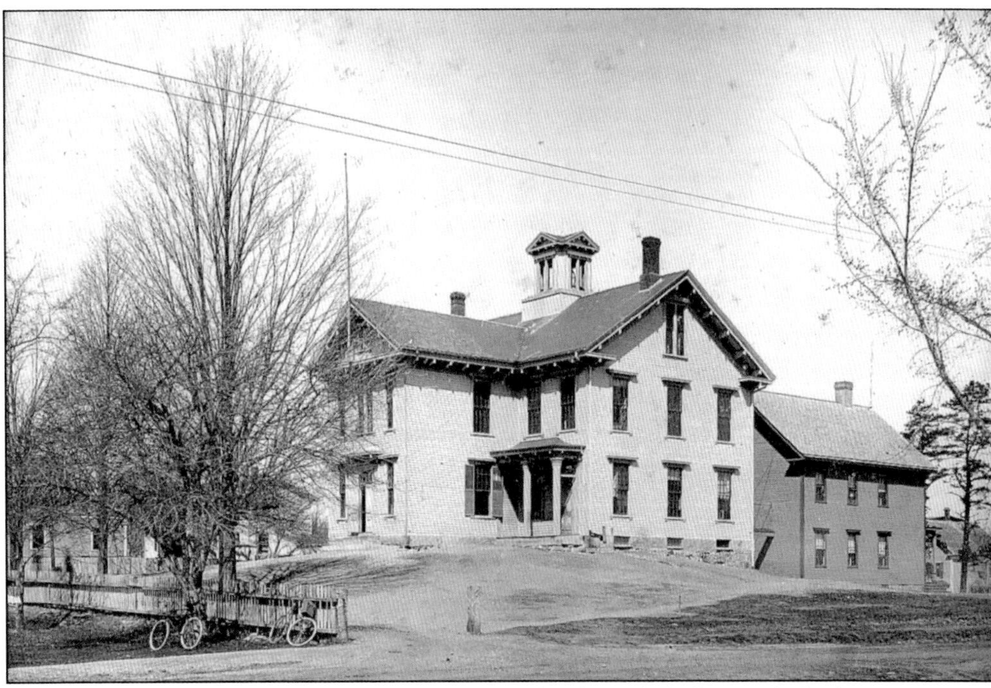

A 1900 photograph shows the Medway High School (with bell tower), built in 1851, and adjacent Lillian Hodgson Elementary School, at the corner of School and North Streets. These buildings stood until the new high school on Holliston Street opened in 1962. They were then razed, and the North Street playground was developed at the site. The bell from the high school is mounted in front of the Holliston Street School.

The Plainville schoolhouse was built on Cutler Street in 1873. Now the home of American Legion Post 367, the building looks much the same today.

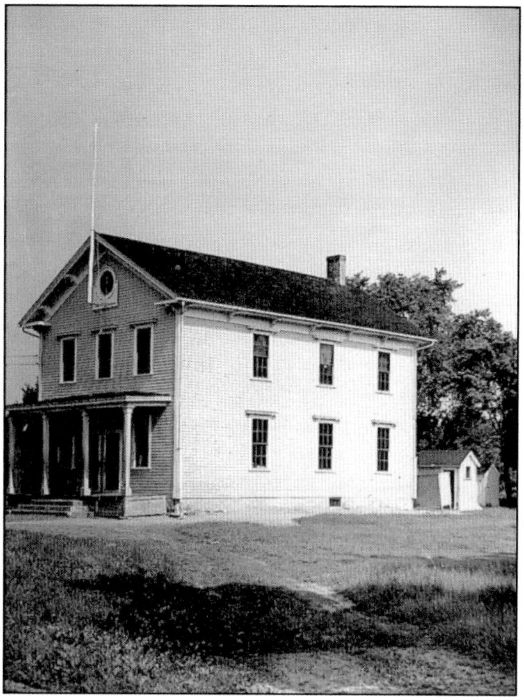

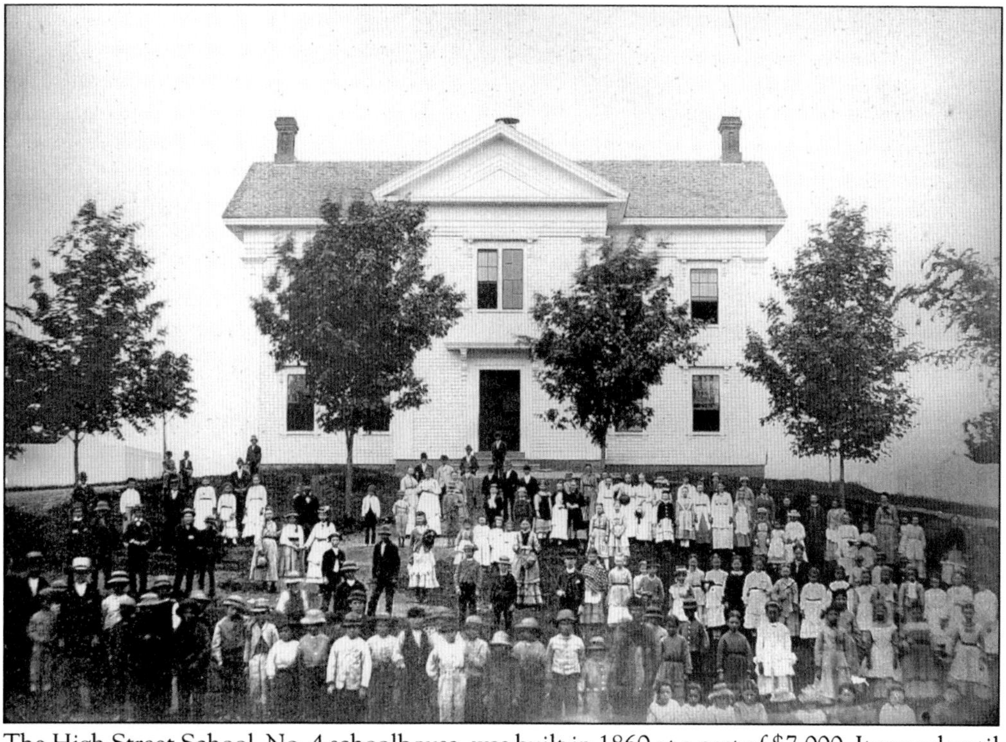

The High Street School, No. 4 schoolhouse, was built in 1860 at a cost of $7,000. It served until a new brick schoolhouse was built on the site *c.* 1939 with Works Progress Administration (WPA) funds. The brick building is now the Medway Public Library. This photograph was taken *c.* 1895.

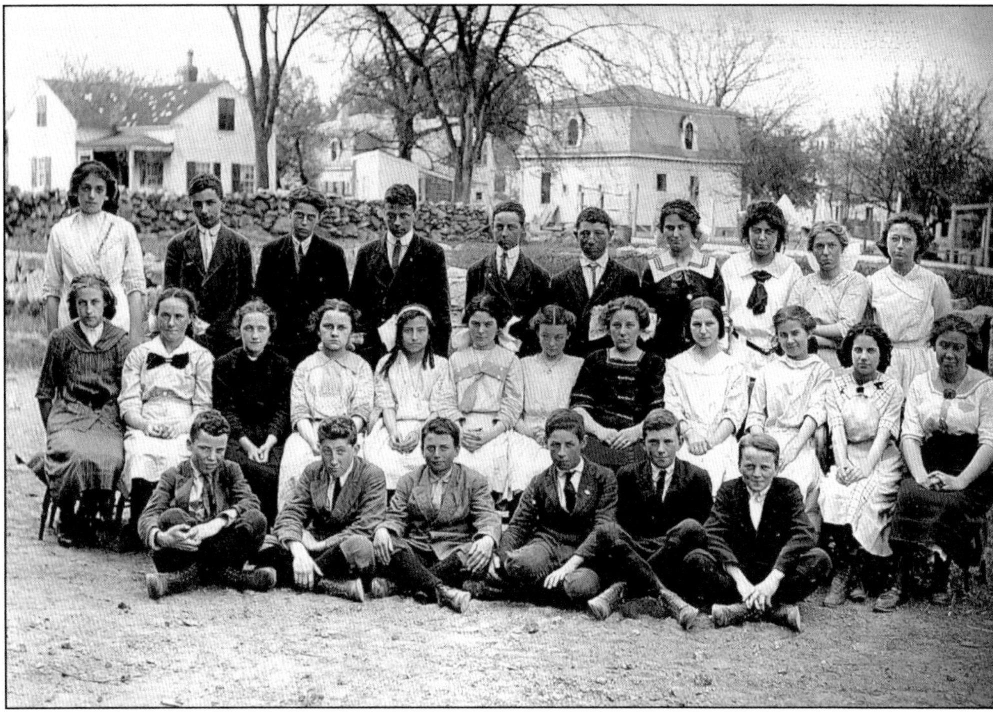

Students at the High Street School in 1913 are pictured at the rear of the school. Buildings at 181 and 183 Main Street can be seen in the background.

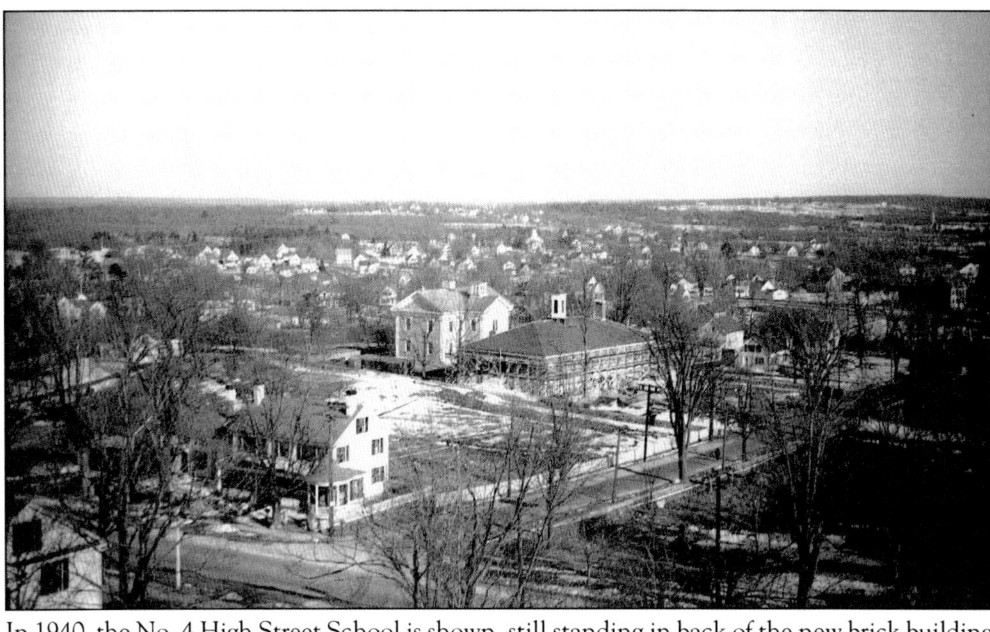

In 1940, the No. 4 High Street School is shown, still standing in back of the new brick building. The old schoolhouse was used until the new one was ready for occupancy; then the old building was razed. (Courtesy Priscilla Robertson.)

A debate on the need for a new high school was held in 1916 and featured music and entertainment by high school students.

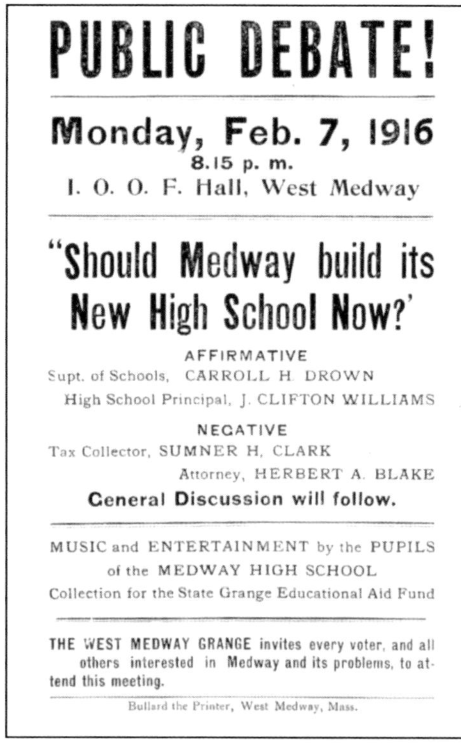

PUBLIC DEBATE!

Monday, Feb. 7, 1916
8.15 p. m.
I. O. O. F. Hall, West Medway

"Should Medway build its New High School Now?'

AFFIRMATIVE
Supt. of Schools, CARROLL H. DROWN
High School Principal, J. CLIFTON WILLIAMS

NEGATIVE
Tax Collector, SUMNER H. CLARK
Attorney, HERBERT A. BLAKE

General Discussion will follow.

MUSIC and ENTERTAINMENT by the PUPILS of the MEDWAY HIGH SCHOOL
Collection for the State Grange Educational Aid Fund

THE WEST MEDWAY GRANGE invites every voter, and all others interested in Medway and its problems, to attend this meeting.

Bullard the Printer, West Medway, Mass.

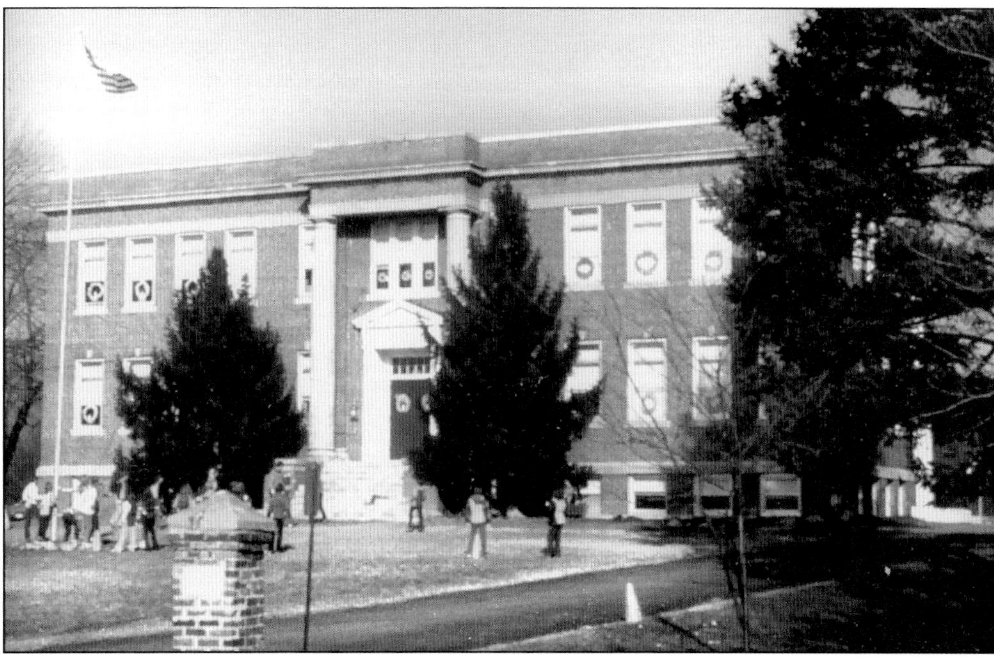

After further debate, the new high school was built on Village Street. Dedicated in 1928, this school served the town for 50 years—first as a high school and then as a middle school. Named the James G. Anderson School after a long-serving high school principal, this building now houses the Anderson Village condominiums. This view shows it in 1977, shortly before its schoolhouse days ended.

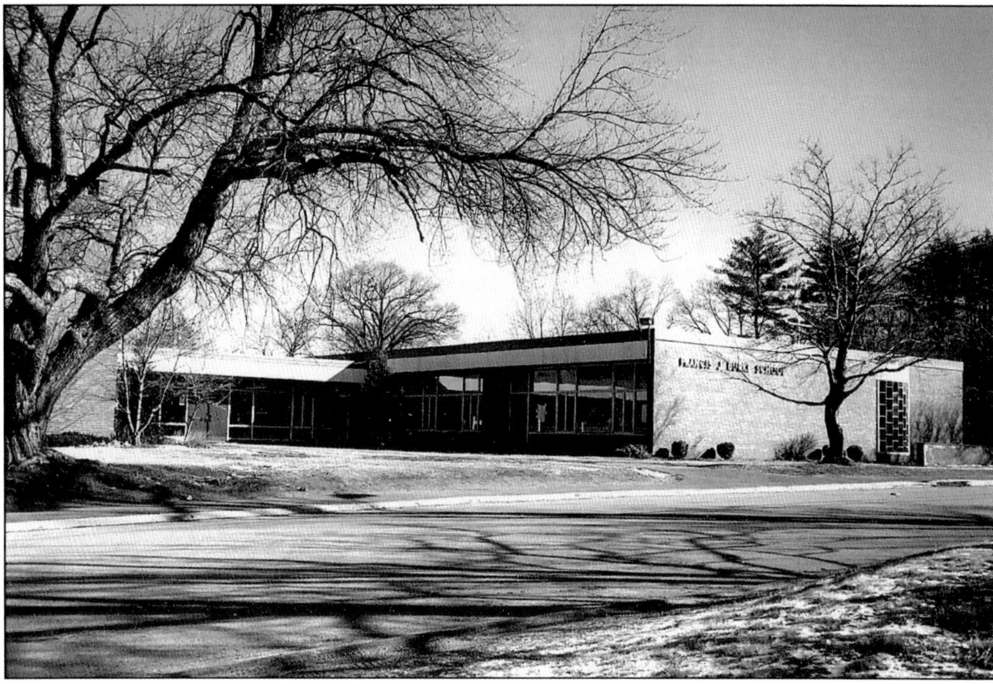

The Legion Avenue School, later named the Francis J. Burke School, was built in 1953 to accommodate the increase in elementary school students that came with the building and population boom following World War II.

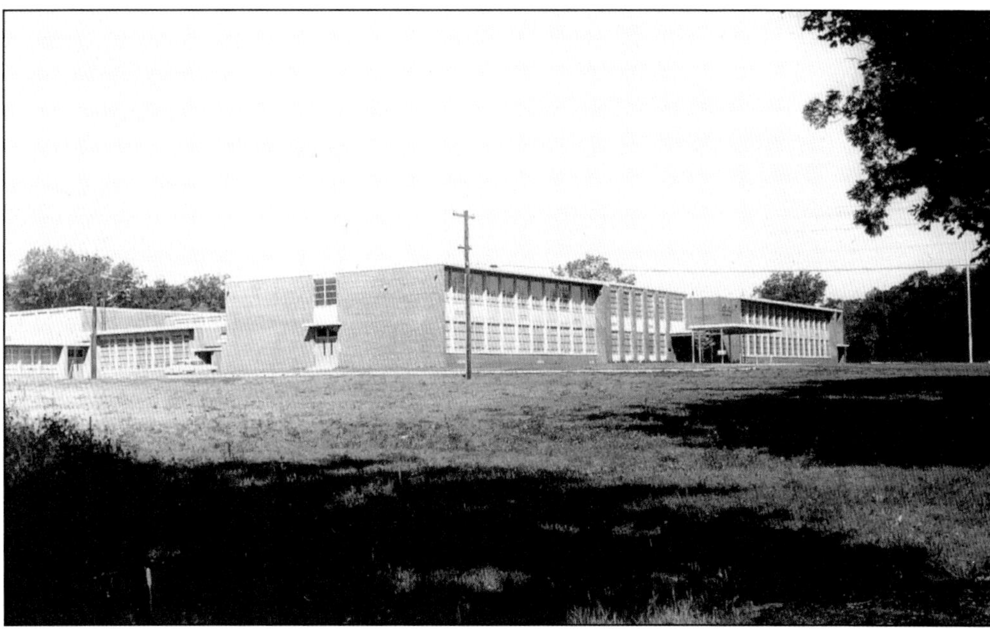

Shown here is Medway Junior-Senior High School, on Holliston Street, as it opened in 1962, when Medway's population was slightly over 5,000. With increasing enrollments, a town meeting in 1970 approved an addition on the right side of the building to accommodate middle school students.

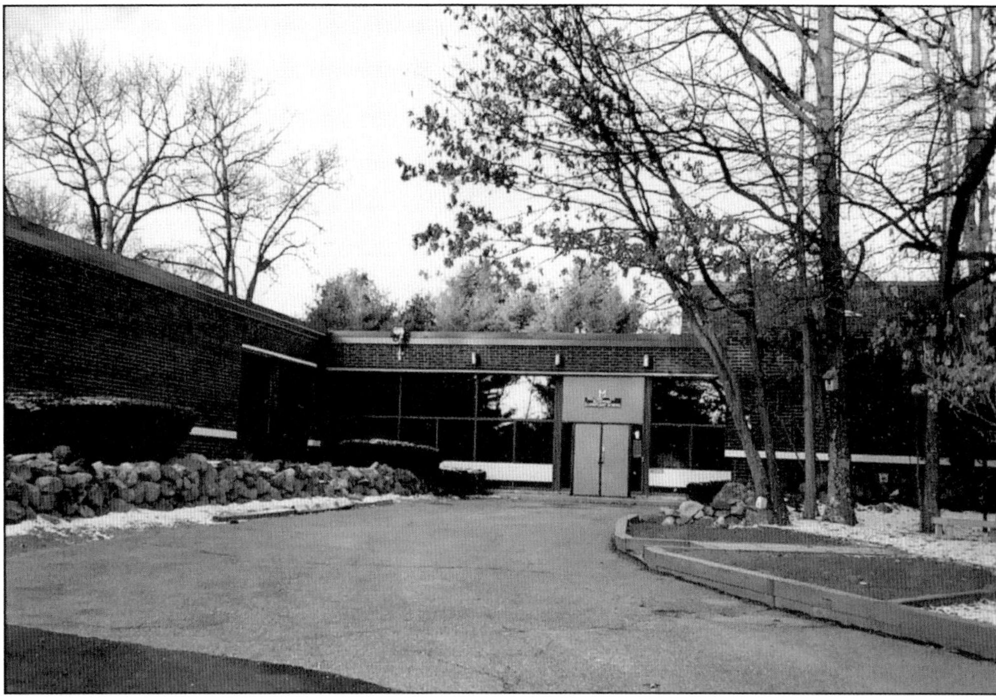

The North School, later named the John McGovern School, was opened on Lovering Street for elementary school students in 1967.

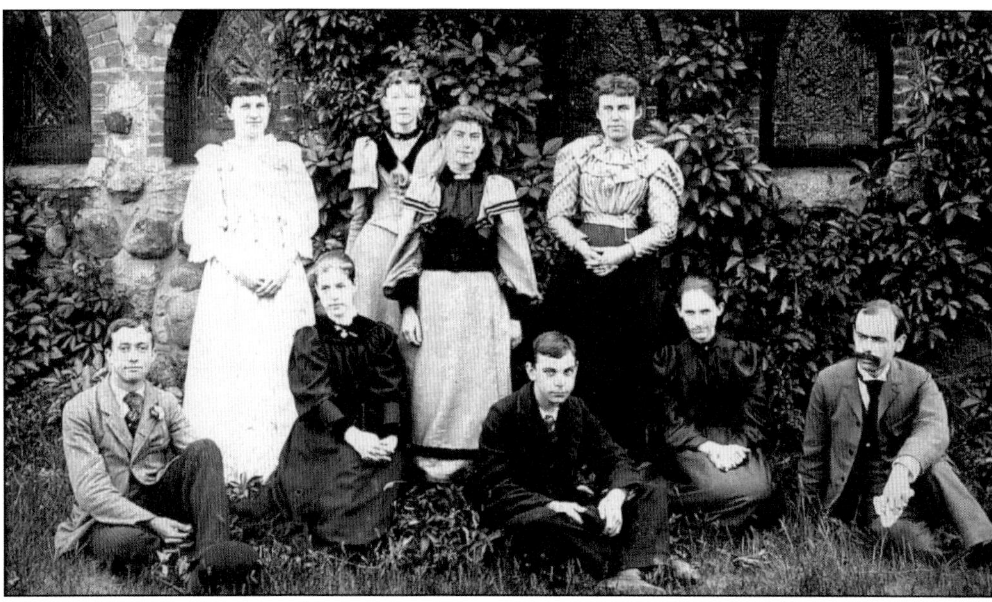

The graduates of Medway High School in 1894 are pictured in front of Christ Episcopal Church, on School Street, with their principal. From left to right are the following: (first row) Almon Lawrence Fales, Hannah Boyd Ware, George Samuel Grant, Annie Frances Foley, and W. J. Fisher, principal; (second row) Edith Lydia Cook, Nina Francis Ide, Edna Mabel Norton, and Edna F. Grant, assistant teacher.

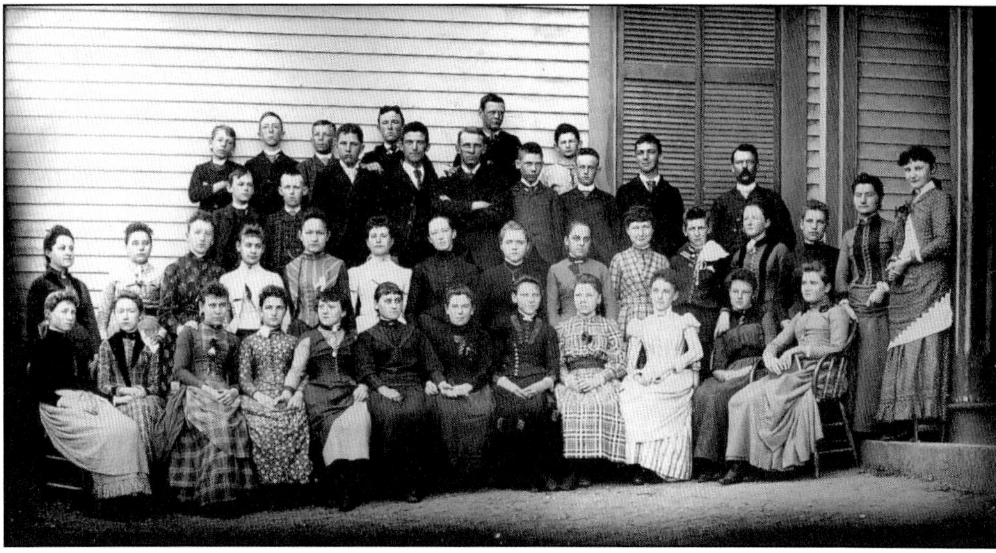

Shown here in 1889, the entire student body and faculty of the high school numbered 42. Medway's population at the time was just under 3,000.

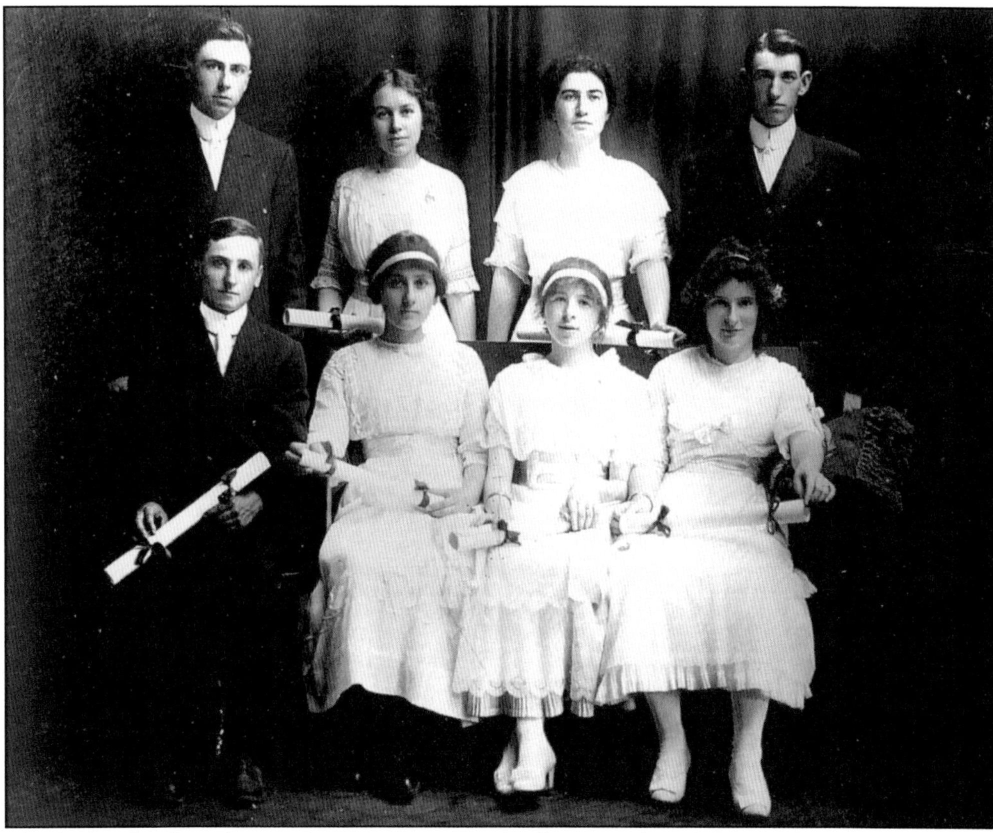

The high school graduates of 1913 are pictured. They are, from left to right, as follows: (first row) Philip Slepian, Gertrude Greenberg, Bessie Pinsky, and Esther Dewire; (second row) John Reardon, Mary Touhey, Mae Theresa Mooney, and Morris Stutman.

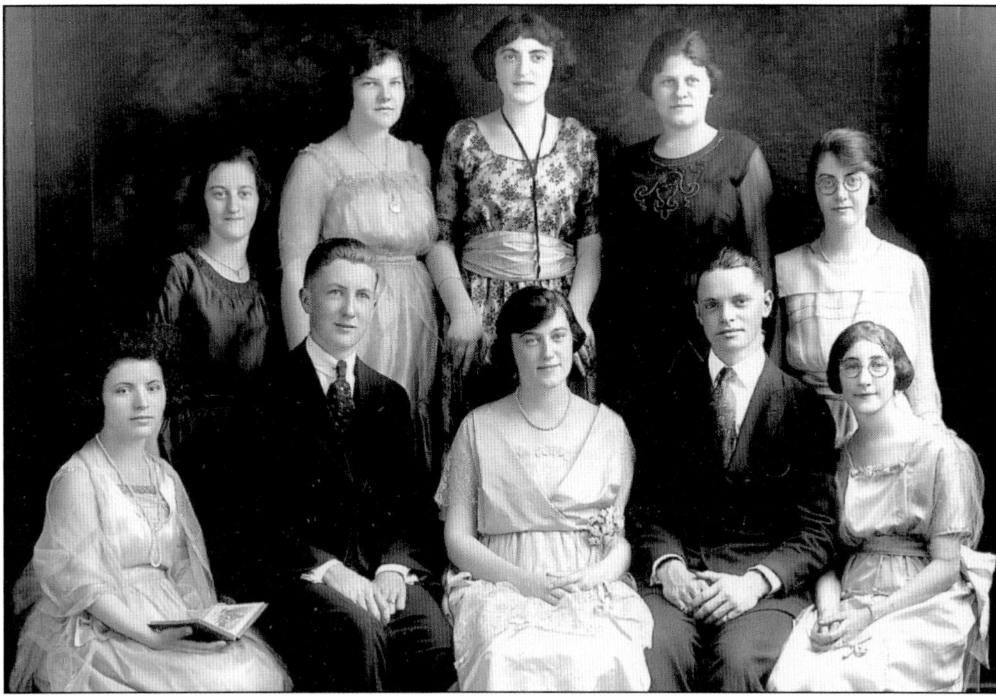

The class of 1921 included these students. They are, from left to right, as follows: (first row) Clara Popovsky, Trask Wilkinson, Alice Ollendorff, Arthur King, and Mary Small; (second row) Rebecca Stutman, Hope Clark, Sarah Katseff, Nellie Mae Stearns, and Madeline O'Donnell.

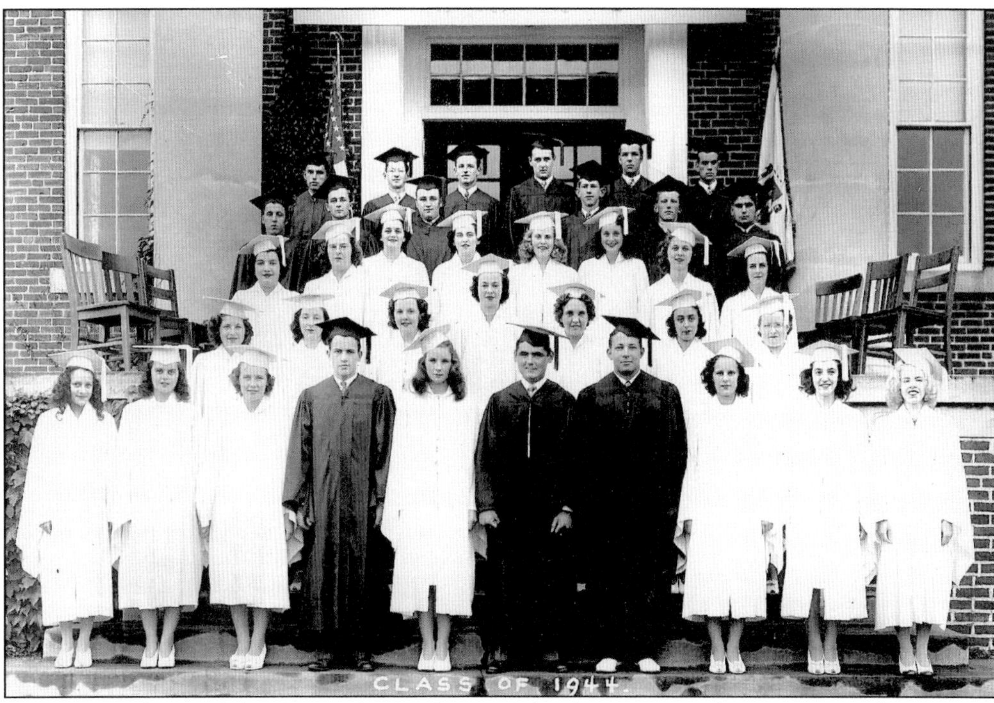

Pictured in front of the James G. Anderson School in caps and gowns is Medway's 1944 graduating class, which was considerably larger than earlier classes.

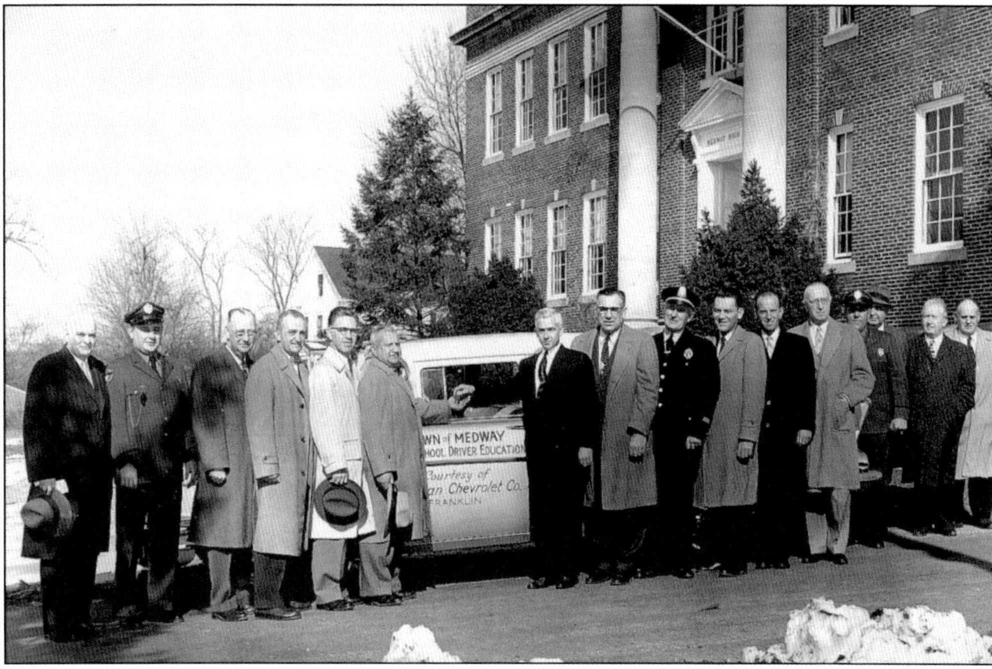

In 1957, Sherman Chevrolet of Franklin donated an automobile to the town of Medway for use in driver education classes. Pictured from left to right are Rudolph King, registrar of motor vehicles; Carl Catalano, registry inspector; unidentified; Jim Kelley; Francis J. Burke, school superintendent; Edward Handverger, school committee chairman; Herb Sherman; Ed Charland, high school principal; Leo Cassidy, police chief; Bill Kenney, selectman; and unidentified people.

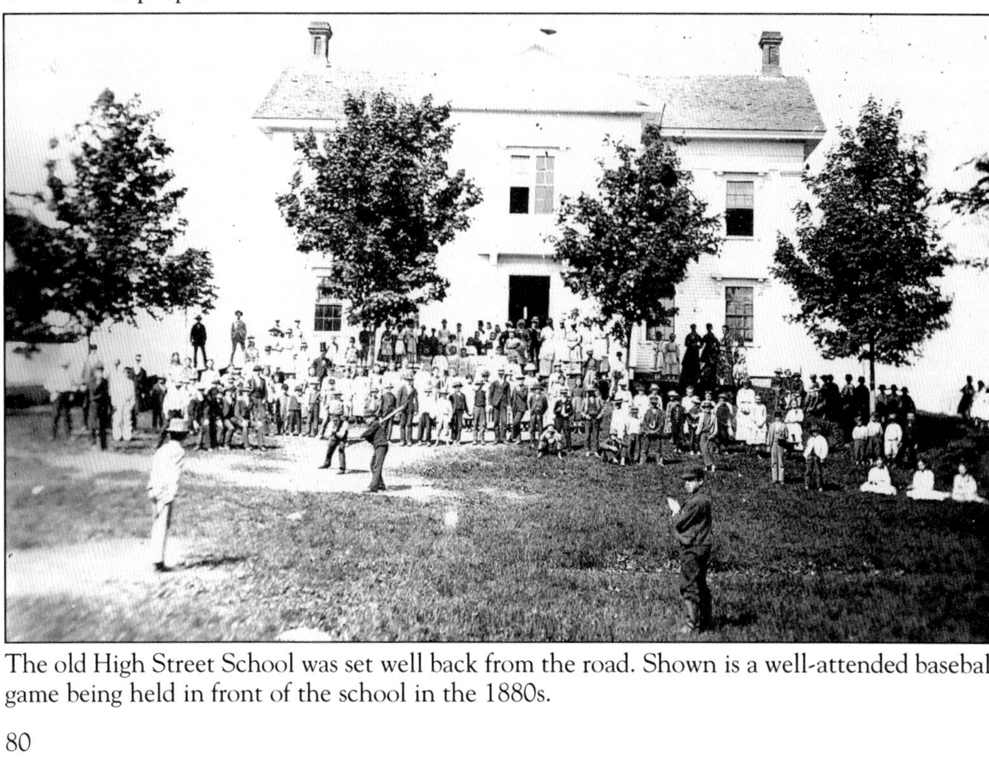

The old High Street School was set well back from the road. Shown is a well-attended baseball game being held in front of the school in the 1880s.

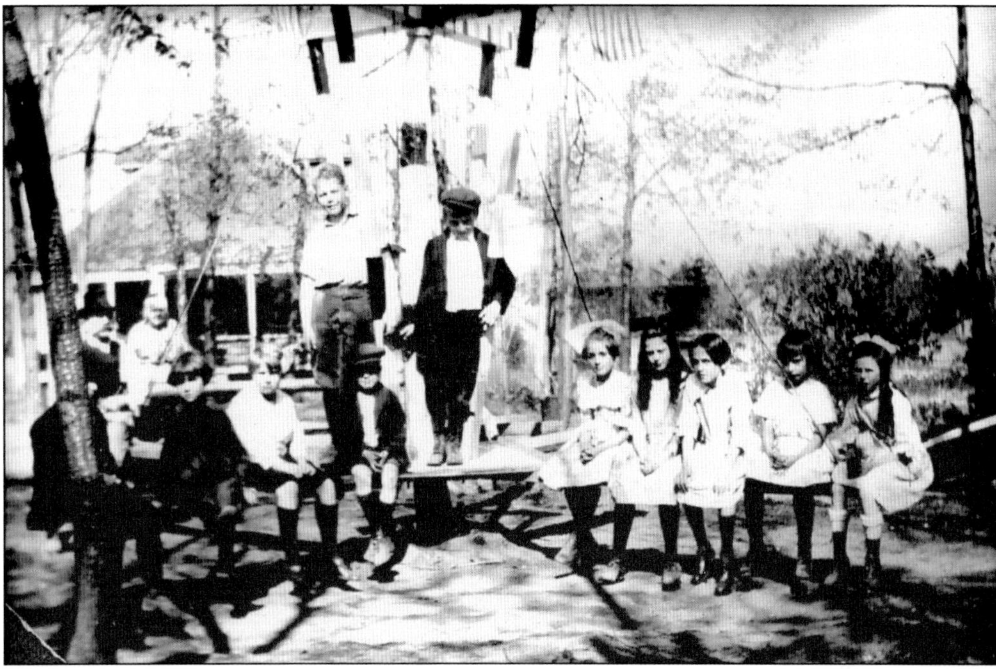

Students are pictured at recess on a self-propelled playground carousel *c.* 1910. The dark-haired girl with the big bow in her hair is Marion Ollendorff.

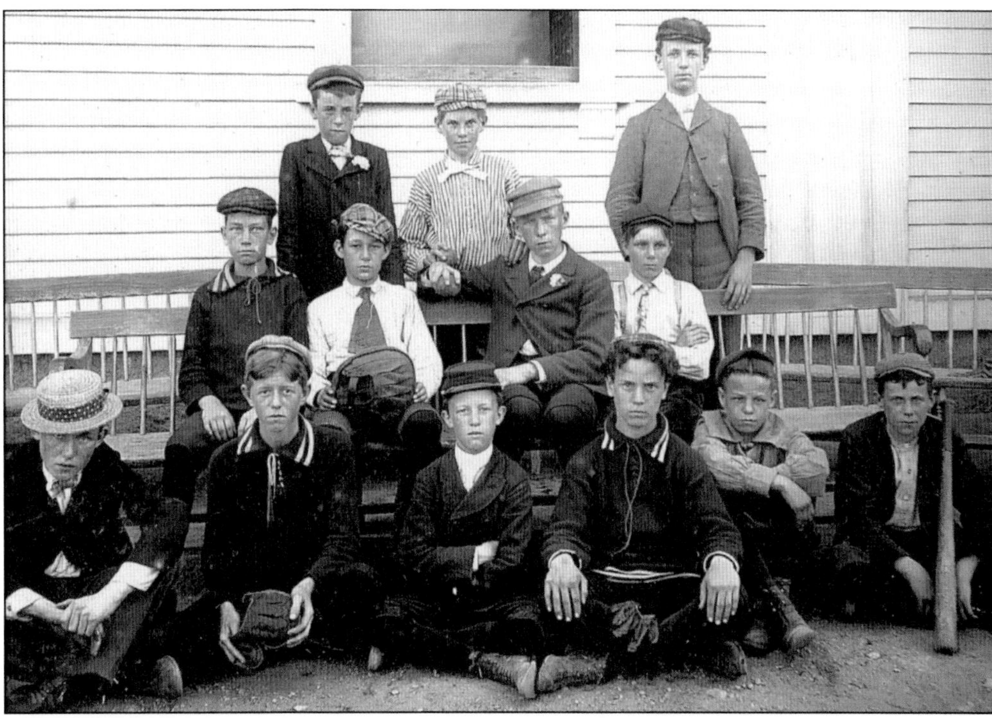

This undated photograph shows a group resigned to sitting for a picture before they can take the field and play ball. The *Medway Gazette* reported in May 1882 that "Base ball is just the latest to captivate local sportsmen, and amateur clubs are numerous."

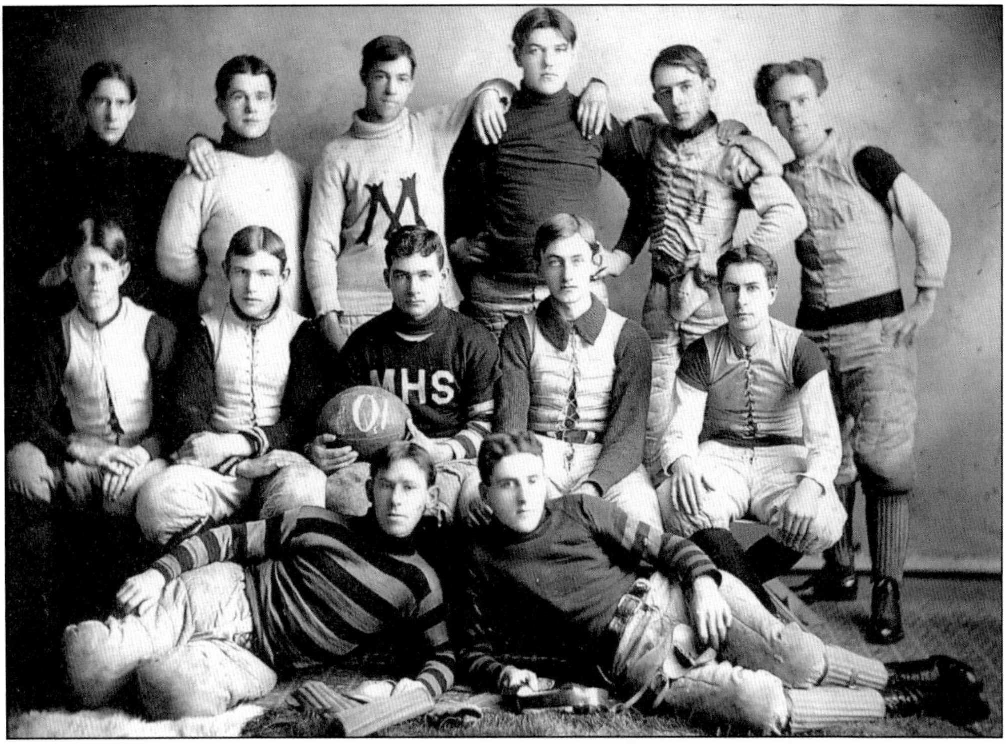

Pictured are members of the 1901 Medway High football team. From left to right are the following: (first row) Clark, right end; and McGinnis, left end; (second row) Fish, right tackle; T. McGlauflin, right guard; Malloy, captain and right halfback; Hawks, left guard; and Collins, left tackle; (third row) Snow, left halfback; Boutelle, left halfback; Hitchcock, quarterback; Coleman, center; Connolly, fullback; and Durfee, substitute. These players were required to furnish their own uniforms.

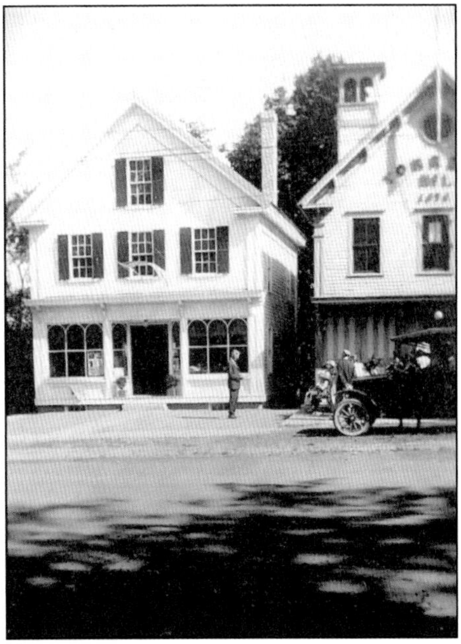

Originally a tailor's shop, this building was constructed in 1870. At the time the firehouse was built, this building was turned 90 degrees to make room. Located at 195 Main Street, the building was given to the town by the children of Addison and Lydia Thayer for use as a public library. It is pictured in 1918 as the Medway Free Public Library. The original three-pane windows with curved tops have been restored by the present owner.

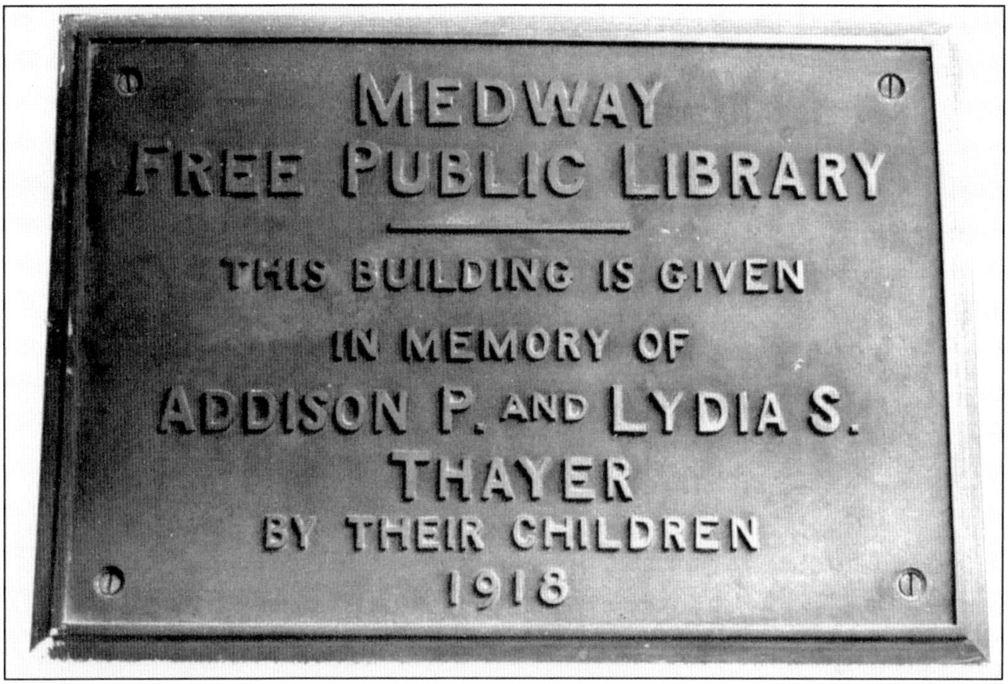

This bronze presentation plaque was mounted on the outside of the Medway Free Public Library, later the Cole Library. The plaque is now at the public library on High Street.

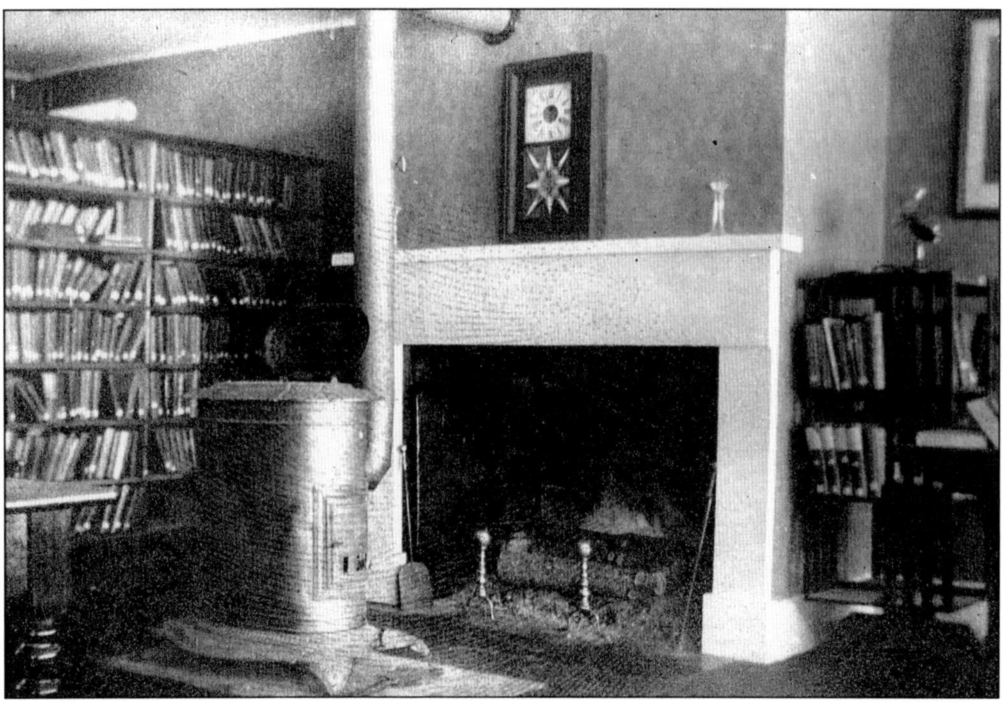

An interior view of the library when it opened in 1918 shows the heating system, later replaced with a hot-air furnace in the basement.

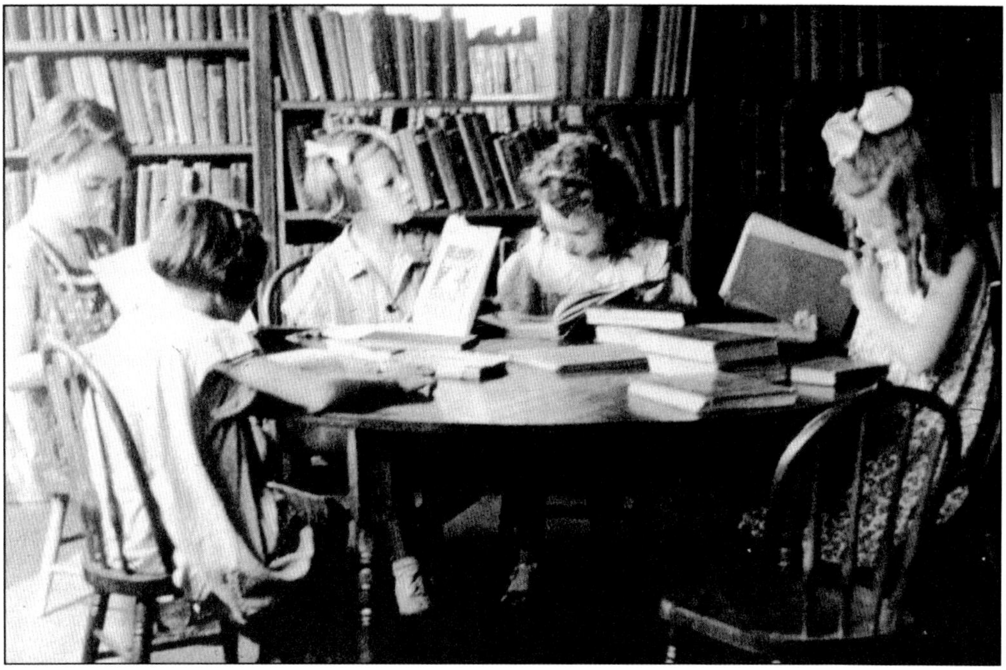

Pictured *c.* 1920, these children found plenty to interest them at the Medway Free Public Library. This table and these chairs are still in use in the library at High Street.

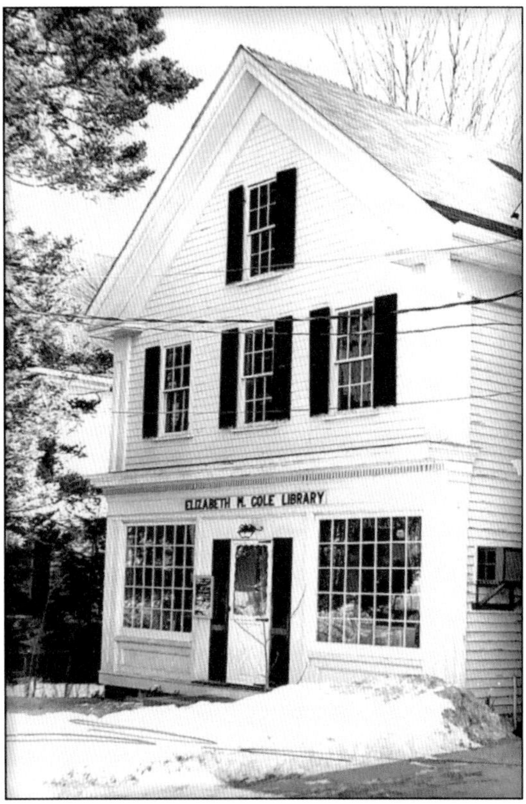

In 1962, the library was enlarged and a large picture window was added in the back. At that time, the name was changed to the Elizabeth Cole Library in honor of a much beloved librarian. It remained a library until 1980, when the books were moved to the former school on High Street. For a time, it was the home of the Medway Community Nursery School. It was threatened with demolition to build a larger fire station and later to become a parking lot for the church. Fortunately, it was saved and has become a residence.

Five

Homes, Hotels, and Taverns

Like all of the towns in Massachusetts, Medway has many beautiful and interesting homes. The selection in this book is somewhat random. Some of the photographs have people in them, making them more interesting. The Shumway and Garnsey houses represent the oldest houses in town. Neither still exists. Other homes were chosen because of their former occupants.

Medway was situated on the Middle Post Road (Village Street) and the Hartford and Dedham Turnpike (Main Street), where stagecoaches and later trolleys ran, meaning that there was a great need for hotels and taverns. Medway had many of those, and some are included in this chapter.

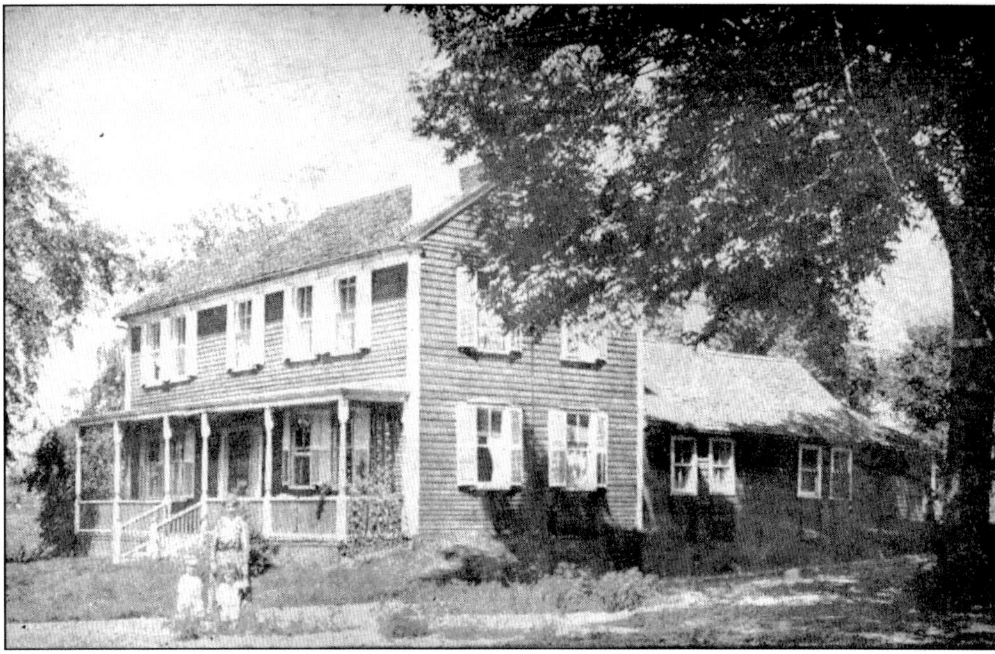

The ell of this building was built in 1737. It was known as the Midway Tavern in its early days and then as the Levi Adams Tavern. The main part of the building was constructed in 1823. The first meeting of the Masons was held here. Later on, it became a private home and Isaac Hixon was a resident. The building still stands at 260 Main Street.

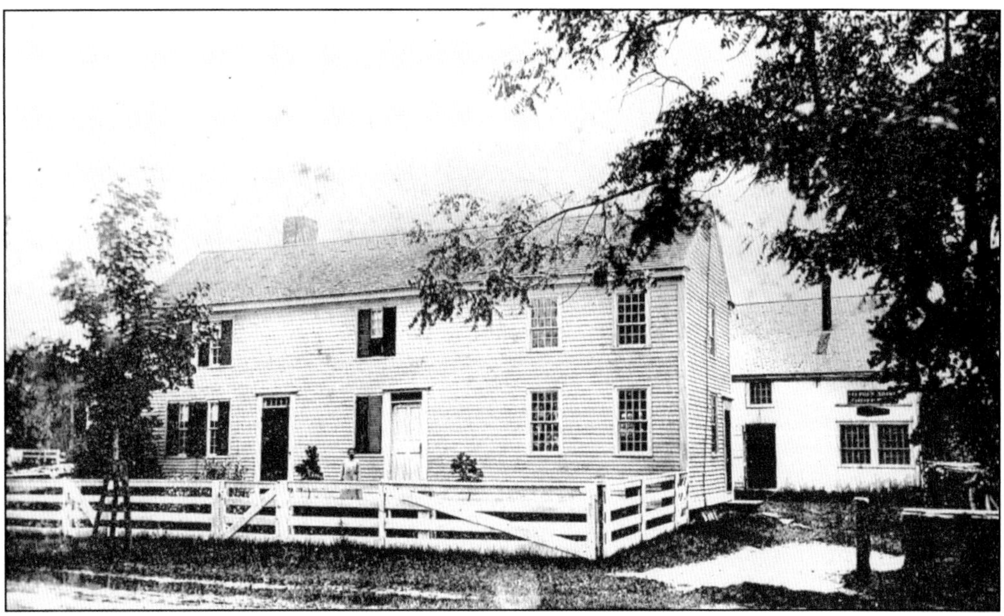

Stephen Adams, Medway's first cabinet and coffin maker, built this home at 207 Main Street in 1823. Adams conducted his business for 52 years from a shop in the west wing of the house. The living room was his coffin showplace, accessed by the right-entry door. Herbert Hixon, a later resident, added the summerhouse (background) in 1916. The second floor was expanded in 1984.

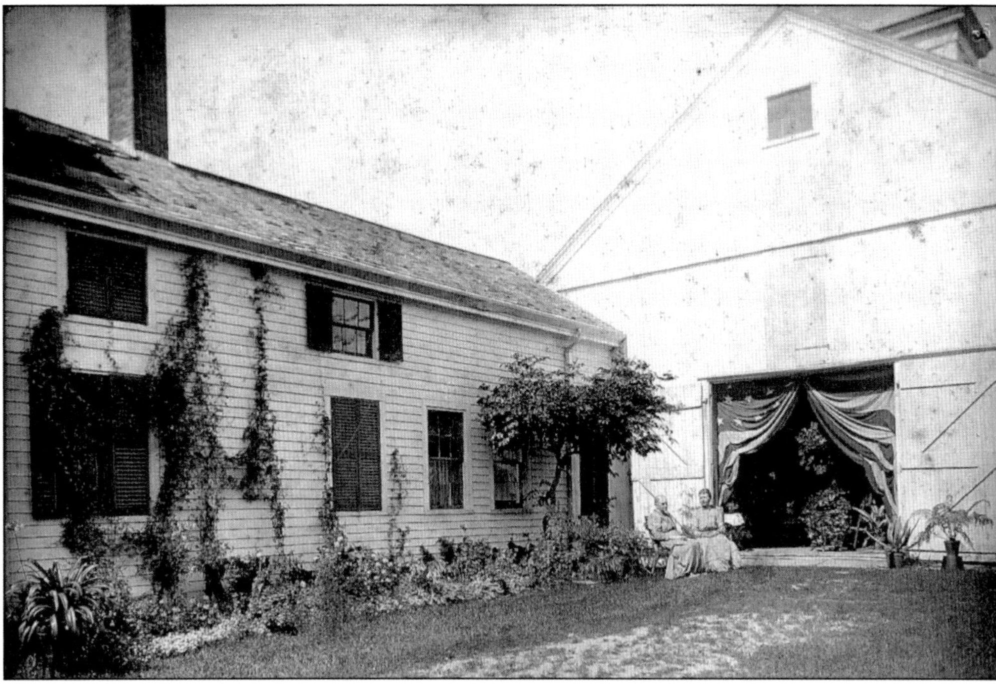

This home is one of two Greek Revival houses on Main Street. It was built at 204 Main Street by John Cushing *c.* 1838. Cushing was a merchant tailor who had a business there until he moved it to the Thayer office building, at 195 Main Street. The barn in the photograph is decorated for some occasion, and the two women are enjoying the fresh air.

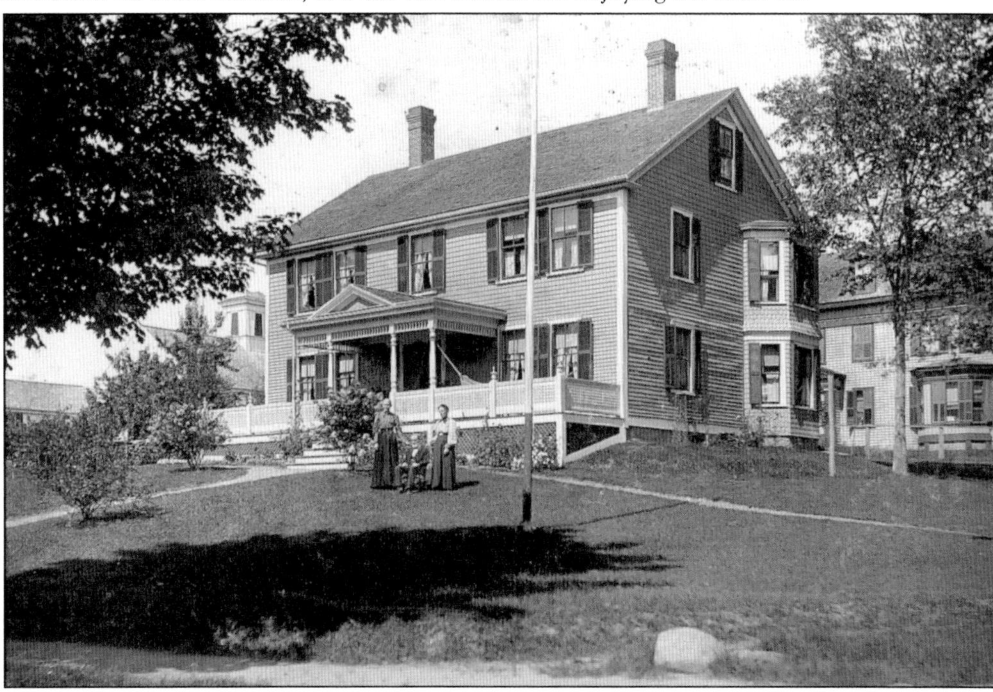

Standing at 200 Main Street, this house is the oldest in the Rabbit Hill area. It looks here much as it does today. A small store was located in the back of the house.

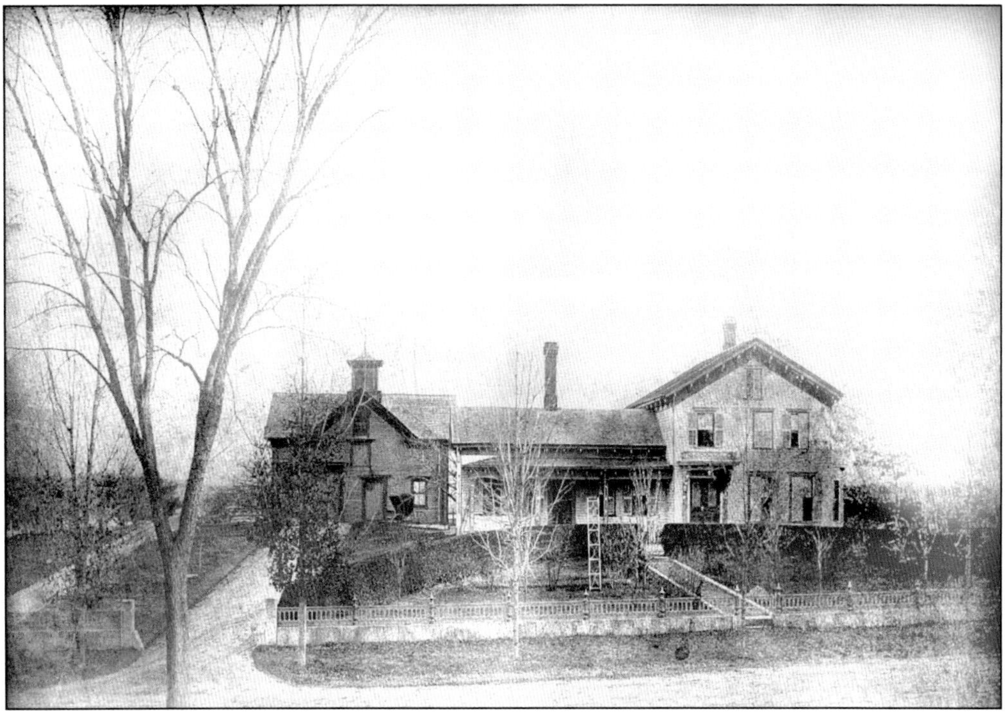

This house was the home of Leander S. Daniels, who owned the boot shop across the street at the corner of Main and Mechanic Streets. The house was built at 179 Main Street in 1862. At various times it was a doctor's office, a dentist's office, and a kindergarten.

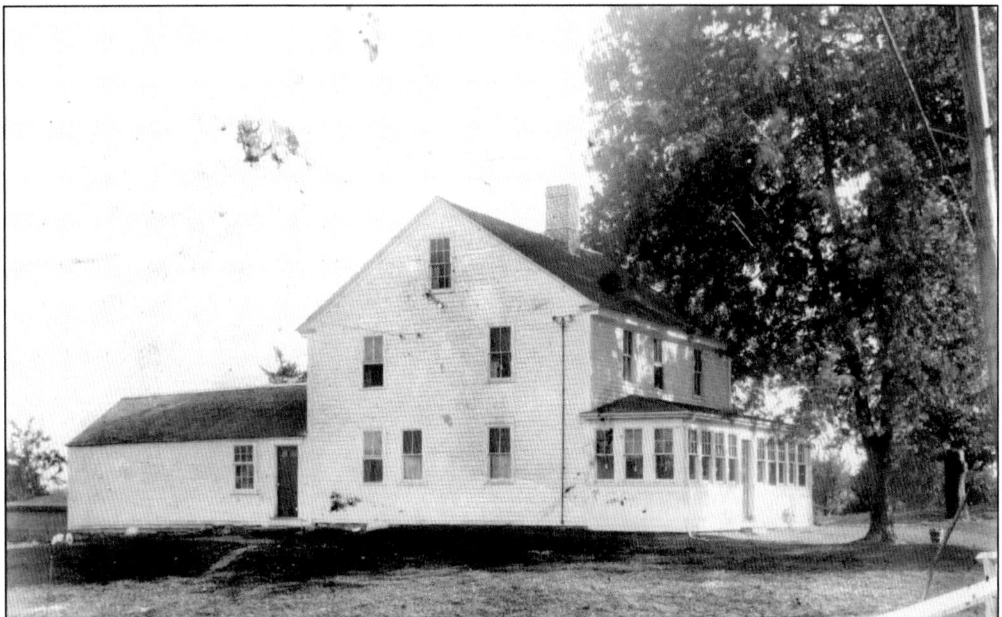

The Adams house, at 86 Holliston Street, dates to 1830 or earlier. By 1910, it was home to the Cassidys, three generations of whom farmed the large property. At present, much of the land is being developed for commercial use. (Courtesy Eileen Cassidy.)

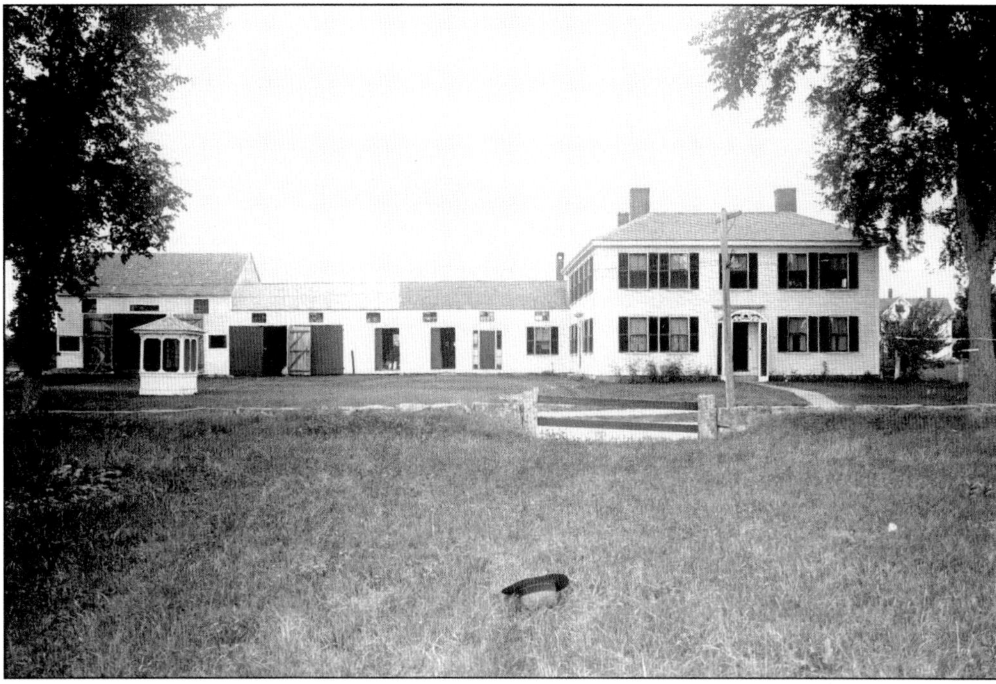

Jacob Ide, the pastor of the Second Church of Christ, lived at 158 Main Street. The house is located on the corner of Winthrop Street.

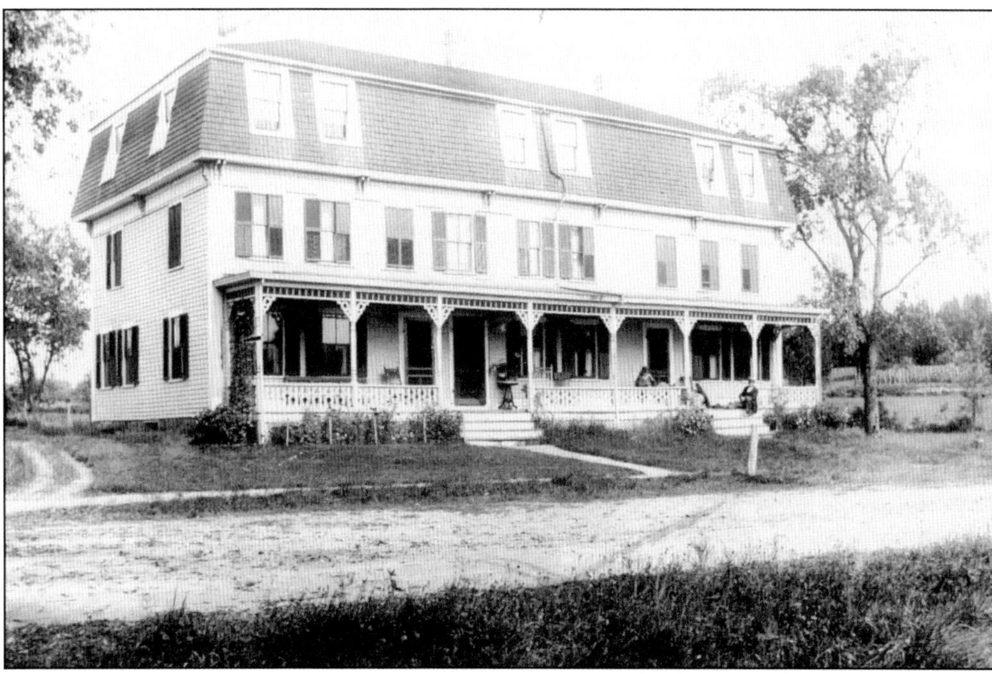

This house was once a boot shop. More recently it was the home of the Elder family. George Elder was the caretaker of many of the town buildings. His wife, Thelma, was a beloved teacher in the Medway schools and at the Medway Community Nursery School. The Elders had 12 children and dozens of grandchildren. This house on Main Street was demolished.

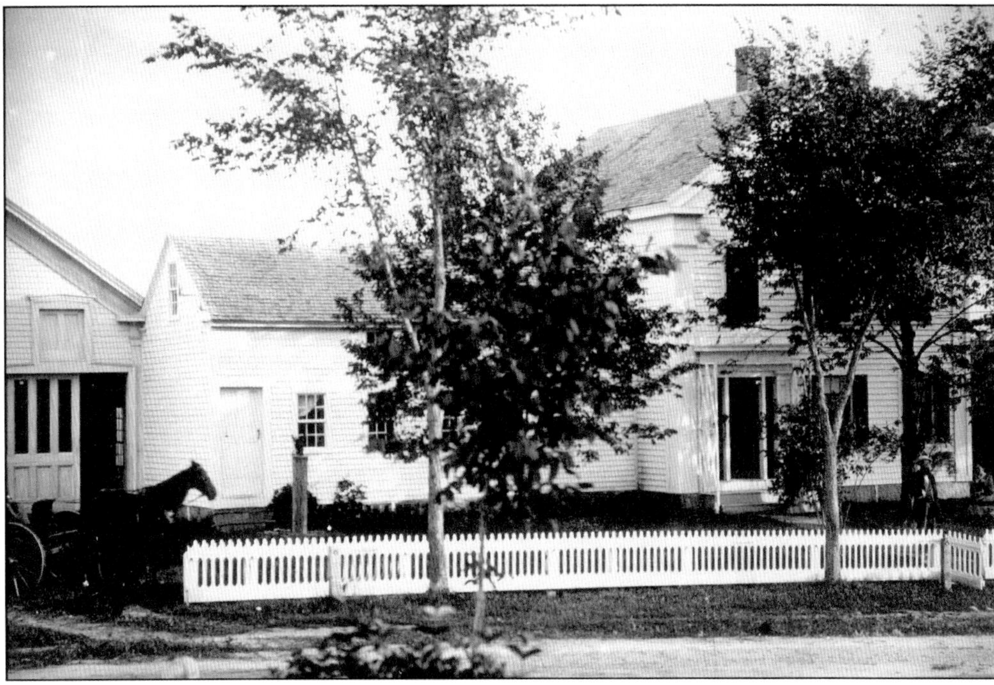

At one time, a bake shop was at the back of this house, the home of Eldridge Ware, at 127 Main Street. Most of the homes along this part of Main Street also had businesses in them. This photograph was taken in 1910.

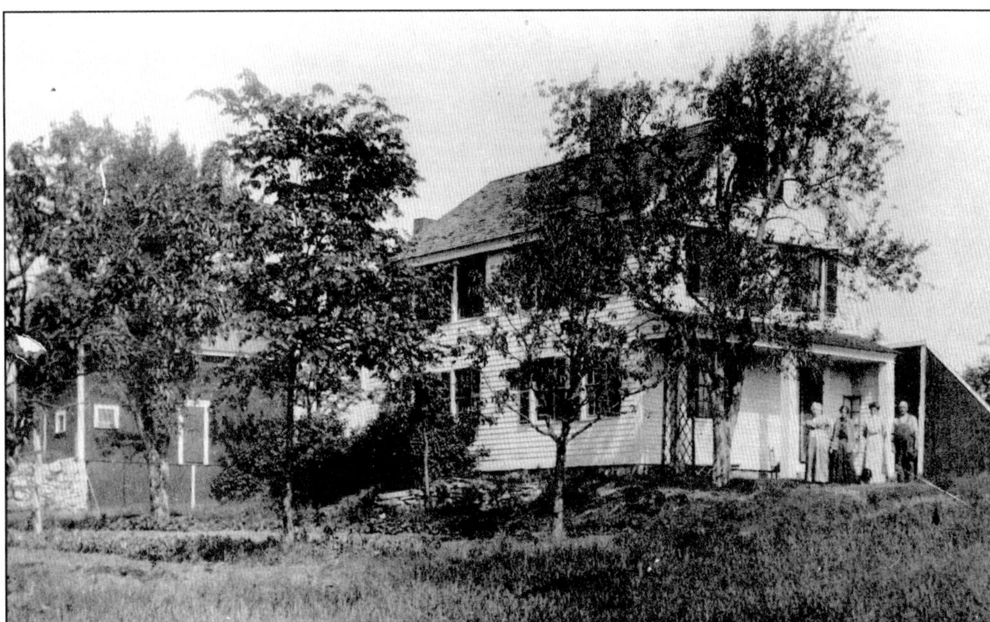

Located at 2B Oak Street, this house was the home of Addison and Lydia Thayer. The Thayers were prominent in Medway. They owned the Thayer Mill, across the street from Choate Park. After the death of Addison and Lydia, the children gave the Thayer Block at 195 Main Street to the town for a public library.

Emily Wardwell - Mowry

PRESENTS

Music of Queen Victoria's Day

If your club was among the many to hear Mrs. Mowry in "Vignettes of Parlor Music" you will find the same sparkling humor in this program. It consists of anecdotes of the Queen and dance music and ballads of that period. It is a revival of a program which Mrs. Mowry presented more than two thousand times.

"A DIFFERENT program but most delightful."

For further particulars address
~~10 VESPER STREET~~, WORCESTER, MASS.
Telephone PLeasant ~~3-3688~~ 5-1328
10 HACKFELD RD

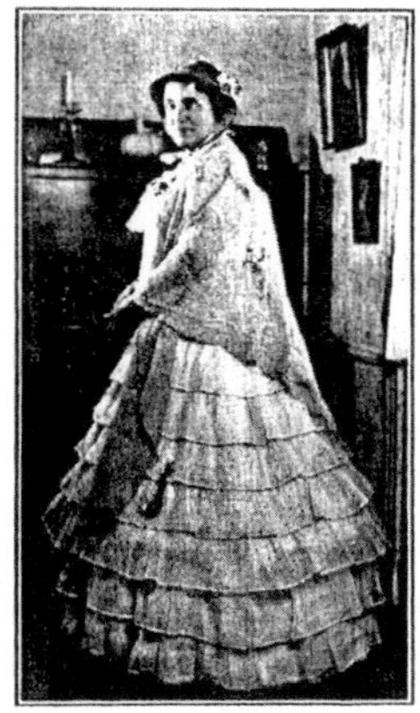

The Homeport Tea Room, located where the Cumberland Farms store is now, was a popular spot in the 1920s. Proprietor Emily Wardwell-Mowry was a performer. One of her programs was *Vignettes of Parlor Music*, consisting of anecdotes and music of Queen Victoria's day.

MENU

SANDWICHES

Sliced Ham	.20
Chopped Ham	.20
Chicken Salad	.40
Sliced Chicken	.35
Club	.65
Toasted Cheese	.20
Crab Meat Salad	.40
Egg Salad	.25
Egg and Pimento	.30
Toasted Bacon and Tomato	.35
Toasted Cheese and Bacon	.30
Nut Bread and Cream Cheese	.20
Nut Bread, Cream Cheese and Olives	.20
Sardine	.20

SALADS

Egg	.50
Crab Meat and F. F.	.75
Chicken and F. F.	.75
Tomato Stuffed with Chicken, F. F.	.70
Shrimp and Celery	.50
Fruit	.50
Pineapple and Cream Cheese	.40
Tomato	.50
Vegetable	.50

HOMEMADE NUT BREAD	.20
WAFFLES AND PURE MAPLE SYRUP	.40
CINNAMON TOAST	.25
CAKE	.20

ICE CREAM

Strawberry Sauce	.25
Pineapple Nut	.25
Hot Fudge	.25
Maple Nut	.25

BEVERAGES

Coffee with Cream Cup	.10
Tea, Pot .15 Cup	.10
Milk	.10
Iced Chocolate	.15
Iced Coffee	.15
Iced Tea	.15
Ginger Ale Pale Dry	
Orangeade	.15
Lemonade	.15

AFTERNOON TEA

Assorted Sandwiches, Cake, Tea-Coffee	.50

.75 if Bridge is to be played.

This is a sample menu from the Homeport Tea Room.

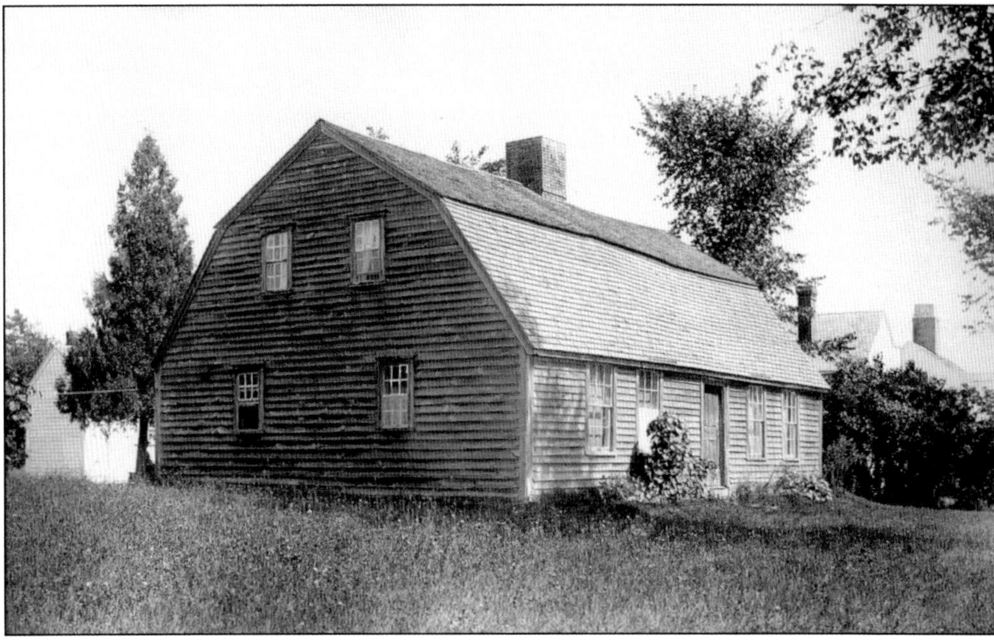

The Shumway house on Village Street was one of the older homes in town. At one time Jabez Shumway owned most of the Rabbit Hill district. In 1814, he deeded part of the district land for a church. This building was demolished in 1914.

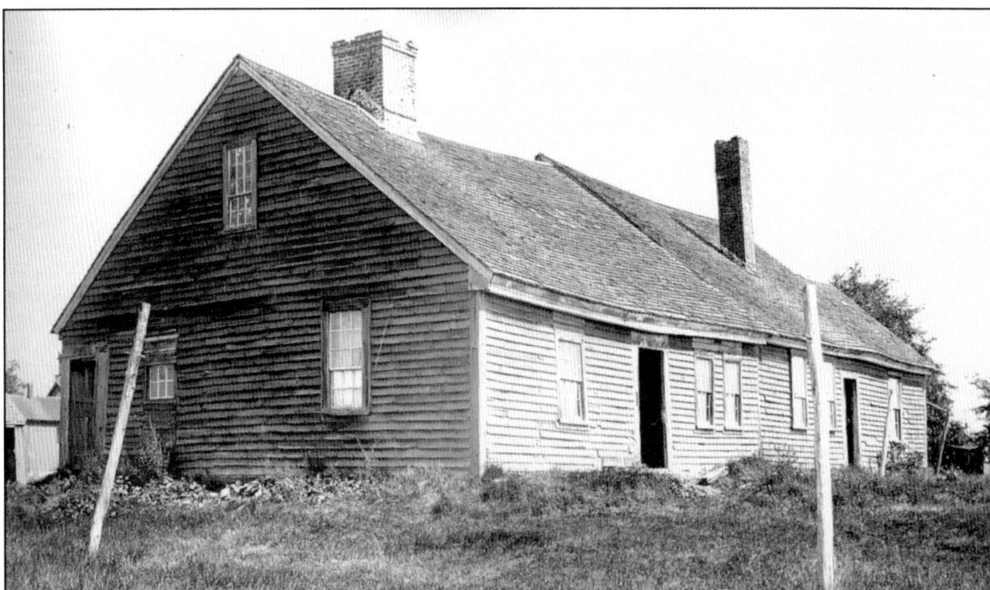

This is the home of Henry Garnsey, the first settler in the New Grant. It was used as a dwelling and, later, as a shop. It was torn down in 1923. Today, a dog park surrounds the remains of the building's foundation on Village Street.

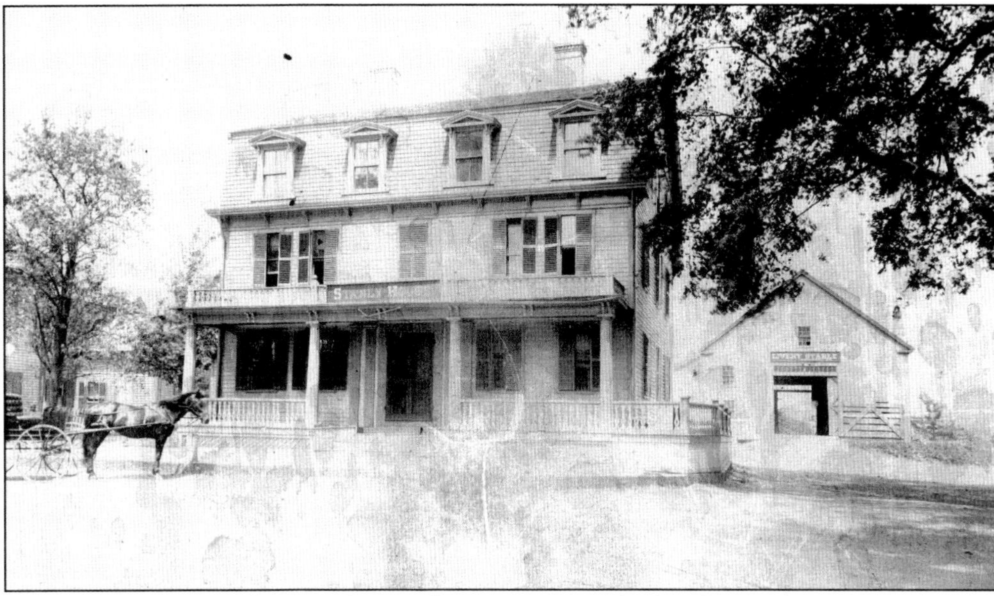

This c. 1890 photograph shows the Stanley House, a popular hotel in its day. At one time, the house was known as the Old Hunt Homestead. The property stretched all the way to the Charles River. The ell of this building is now part of Galante's Restaurant, at 320 Village Street.

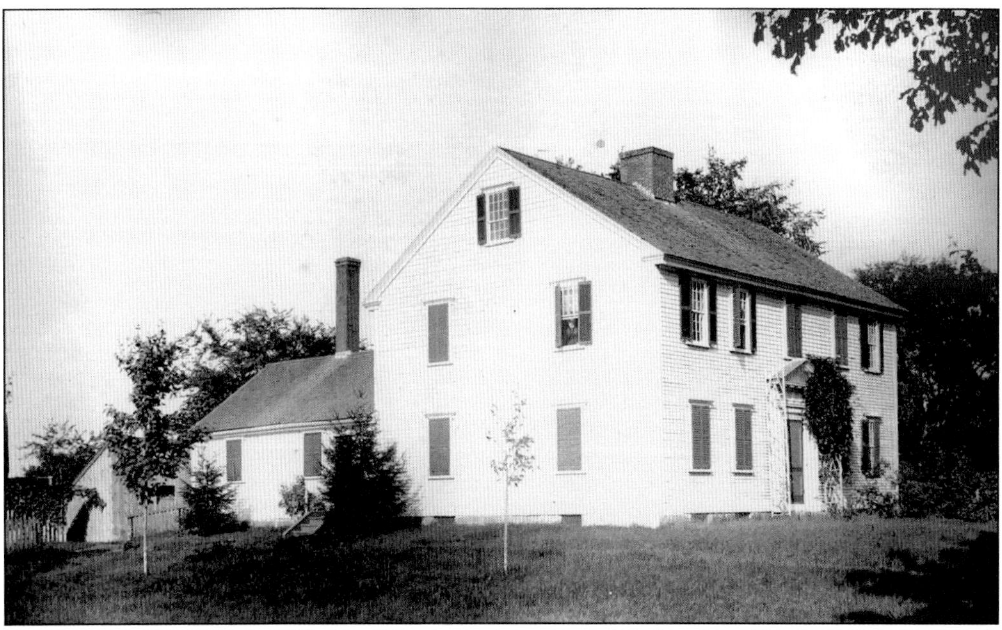

In 1779, Maj. Luther Metcalf started a cabinet business in Medway on this site. He built a small homestead, which was moved to 119 Village Street in 1792. At that time, he built the present building at 194 Village Street as a dwelling and shop. After he died in 1838, his son Luther Metcalf Jr. lived in the house. The son was a prominent cotton manufacturer in Medway. In 1898, the Metcalf family sold the building to be used as a boardinghouse. It is now the Village Inn. The original small house was demolished in 2003.

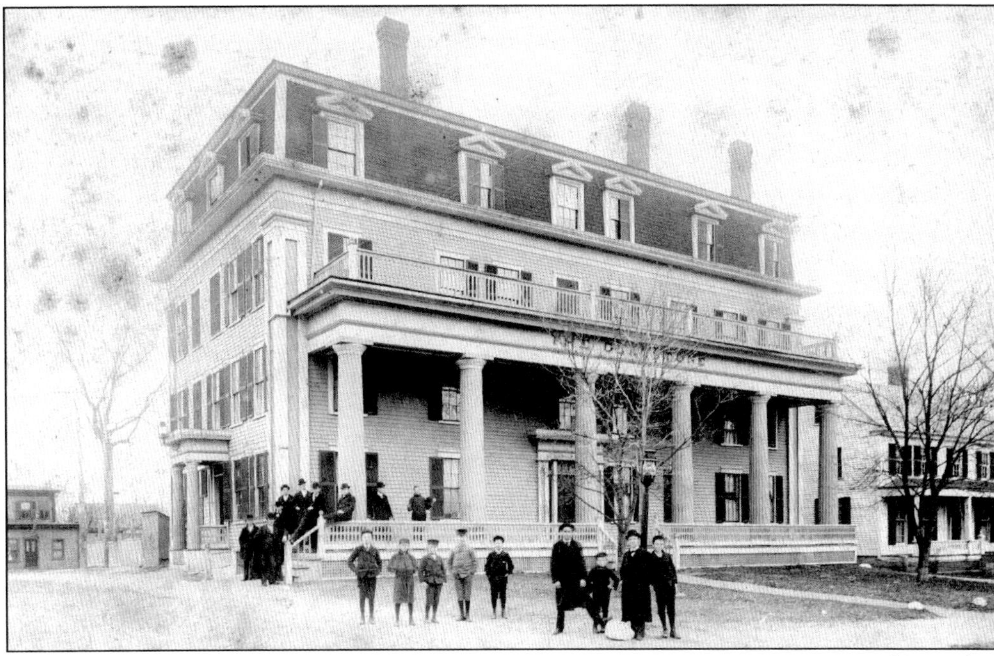

Job Harding built a tavern and store at this site in 1780. It was at one time owned by Laban Adams, the father of William Taylor Adams, the well-known, Medway-born author who wrote under the name Oliver Optic. The tavern was cut in half in 1853 and moved to Peach and North Streets. The Quinobequin Hotel was built on the site. The hotel burned to the ground in 1899 and a new hotel with twin towers was built to replace it. At various times, it was called the Gladstone Hotel, the New Medway Hotel, and the Gladstone House.

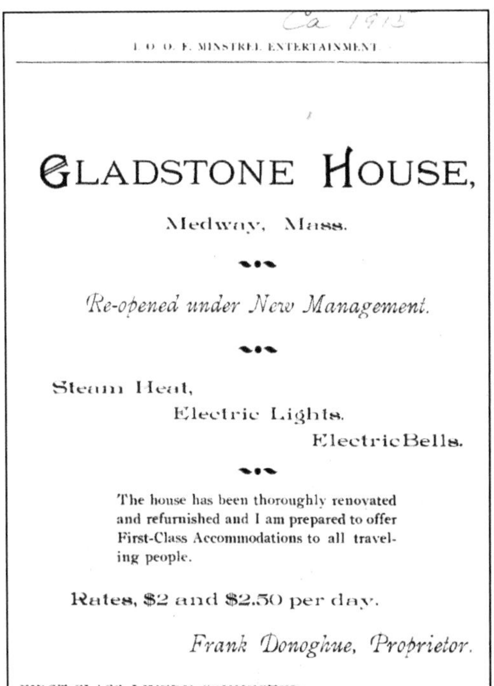

Ca 1915

I. O. O. F. MINSTREL ENTERTAINMENT

GLADSTONE HOUSE,

Medway, Mass.

Re-opened under New Management.

Steam Heat,
Electric Lights,
Electric Bells.

The house has been thoroughly renovated and refurnished and I am prepared to offer First-Class Accommodations to all traveling people.

Rates, $2 and $2.50 per day.

Frank Donoghue, Proprietor.

FIRST-CLASS LIVERY CONNECTED.

The Gladstone House, at Village and Broad Streets, hosted a minstrel show for the Odd Fellows in 1915. The event provided an opportunity to promote the hotel, which was under new management and offered steam heat, electric lights, and electric bells, all for $2.50 a day. This flyer gives the program, along with advertisements, including ads for Baker's cocoa and King Arthur flour.

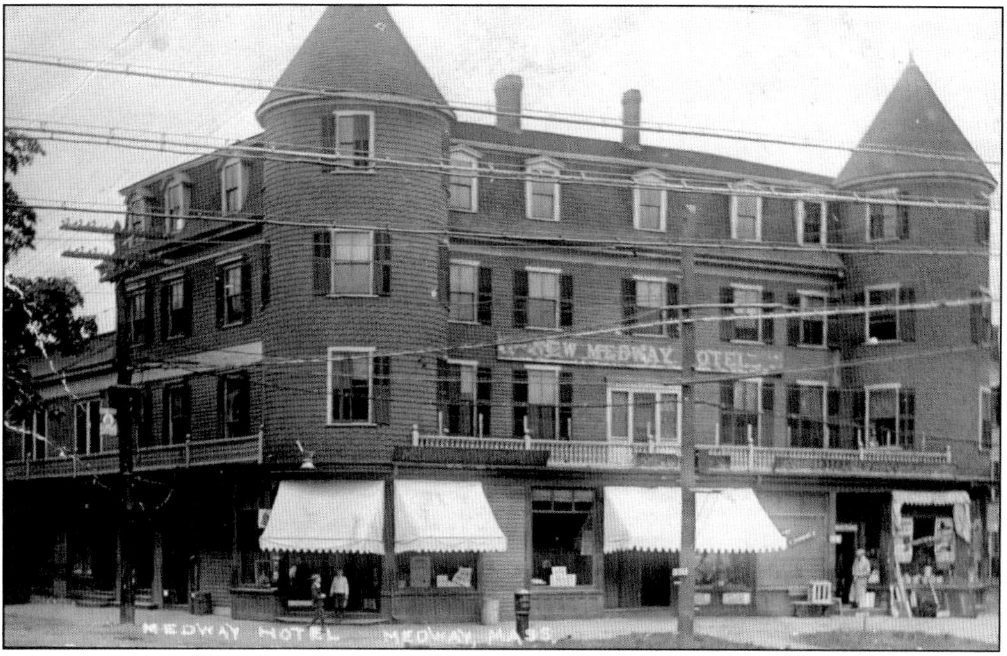

After the fire in 1899, this elegant building with towers was built. It was a center of activity, with fashionable dances and parties held here. There were several fires and other changes until a major fire in the 1990s destroyed the building. It has been replaced with apartments.

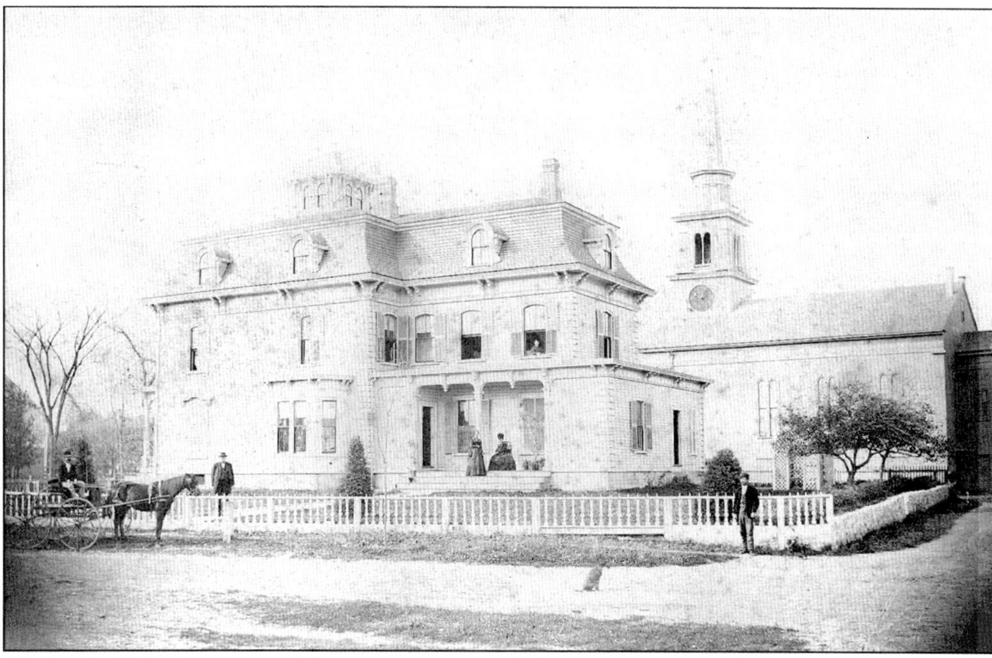

Clark Partridge, a successful businessman and state representative, built this impressive residence in 1869 at the northwest corner of Village and Broad Streets. Partridge, an energetic entrepreneur, started the first boot factory in town at age 28. Taken in 1873, this view from Broad Street shows the Village Church (beyond). The residence, opposite town hall, has recently undergone renovation.

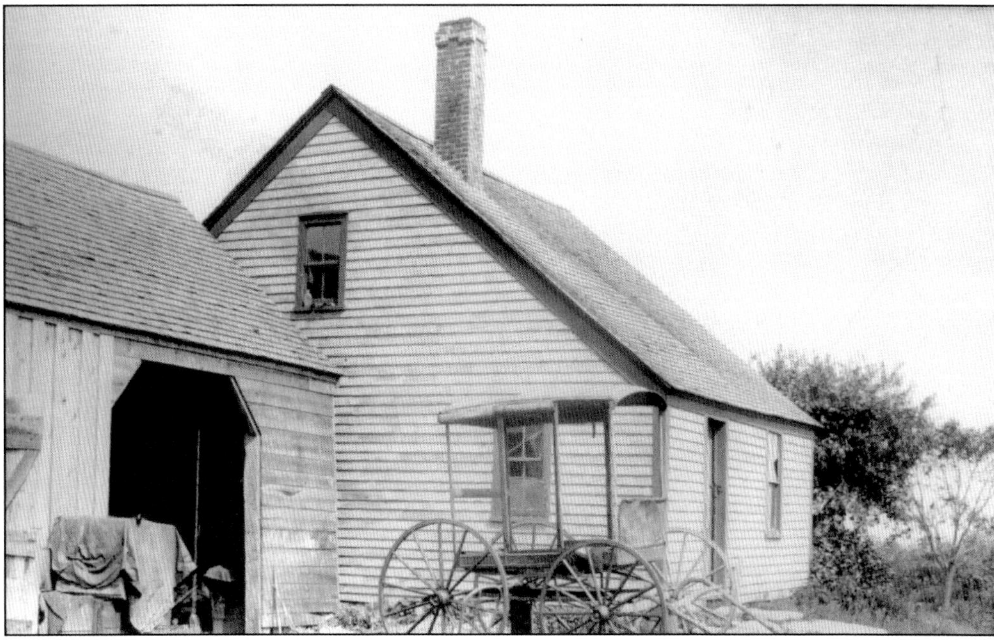

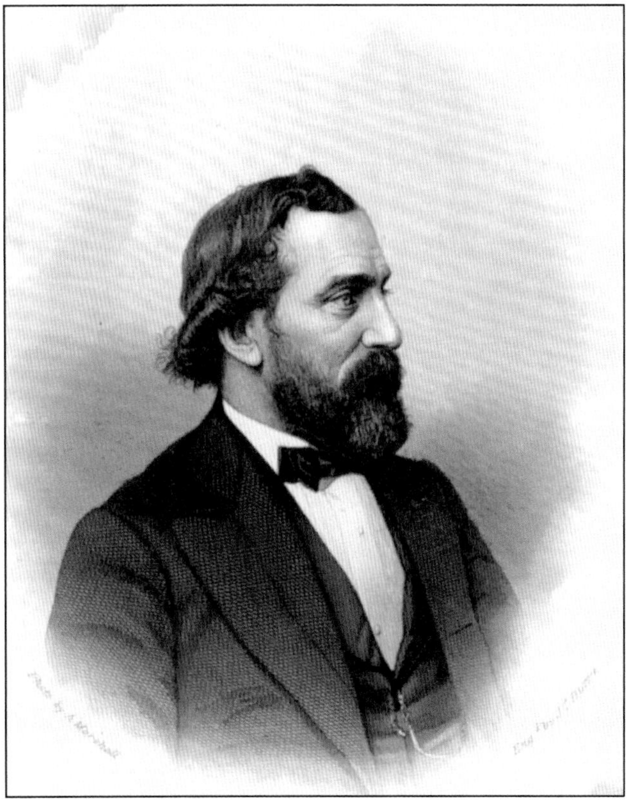

This is the house on Ellis Street where William Taylor Adams, who wrote under the name Oliver Optic, was born in 1822. The house burned in 1893. Adams (left) was an educator and legislator but was best known for his children's books, which made him quite famous. Many of these books are at the Medway Public Library.

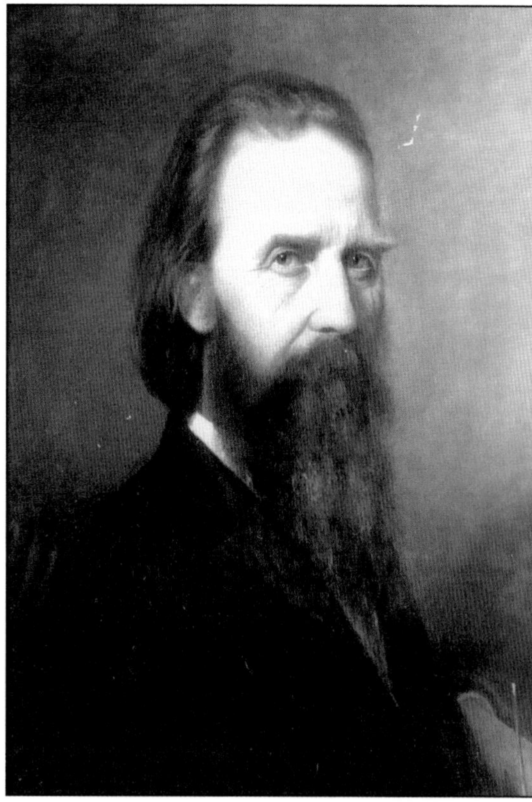

Shown is a self-portrait of Medway artist Anson Daniels, who was born in East Medway in 1813 and lived here all his life. In demand for his portraits, he also painted landscapes and still lifes. Several of his paintings are at the historical society, and his portrait of Dr. Jacob Ide can be seen at the Community Church. A teacher in early life, he later served 25 years on the school committee. The Anson Daniels house (below) still stands at the corner of Lovering and Winthrop Streets.

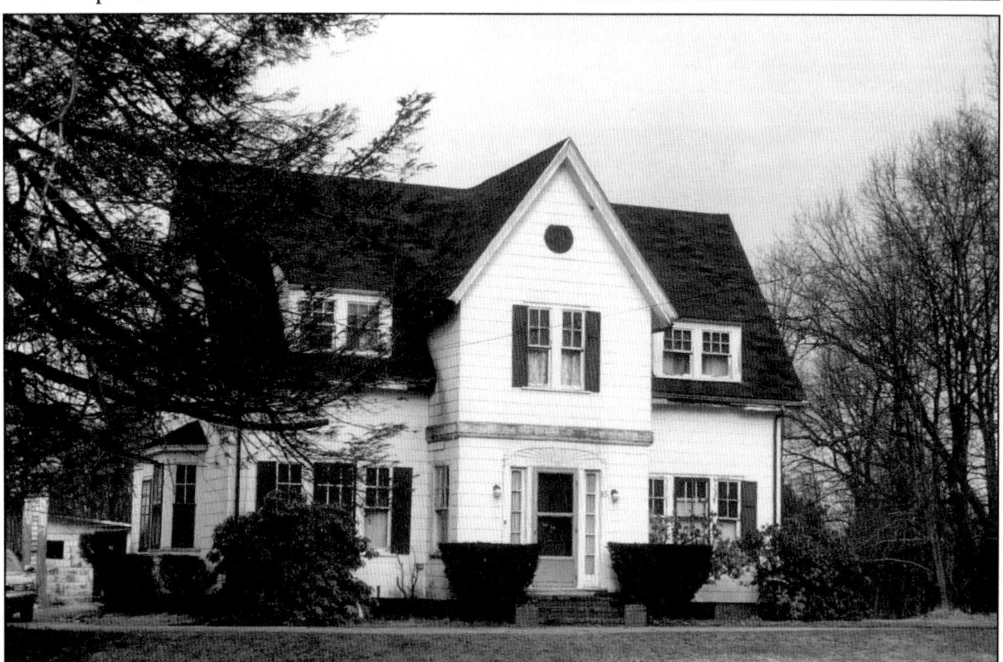

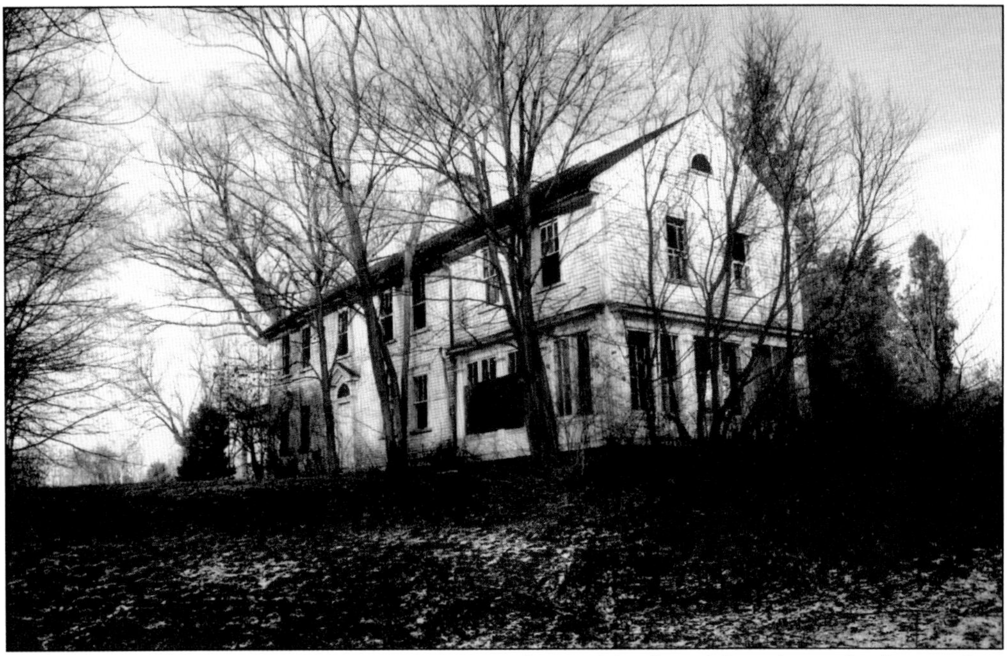

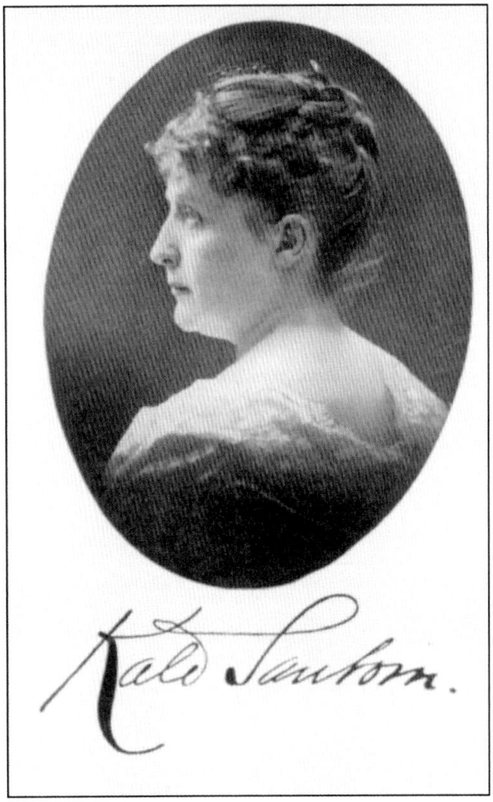

Breezy Meadows (above) was the home of Kate Sanborn (left), an author and interesting personality. It was at one time a beautiful home with unusual outbuildings and ponds and gardens. Sanborn entertained well-known personages at her farm. Later, the property served as a summer camp for city children. Then, it was sold as a religious center and, unfortunately, the house and other buildings were demolished.

Six

RECREATION

Photographs from the century covered in these pages show how people, even with long working hours, found the time to enjoy life. A handmade checkerboard and hand-carved children's toys at the historical society bear witness to the universal need for occasional escape from daily cares.

The early settlers were able to use the Charles River and Chicken Brook for boating, fishing, skating, and swimming. The dyes from the textile manufacturing plants colored the water of the Charles, as well as the swimmers who emerged from the river, with the tint of the week. The bank of the river was a great place for picnicking and socializing.

The southeast corner of Medway became a recreation center with its access to Populatic Pond, a popular spot for locals and summer visitors. Also, visitors traveled by train to the West Medway depot (near the present police station) for daily excursions across the river to Woodland Park for picnicking, dancing, and sports and to visit the zoo.

By the late 19th century, streetcars and better roads made it easier to get together for social occasions, as well as Sunday services. A small library was established at Medway Village in 1860 and another *c.* 1890 in West Medway. From outings at Woodland Park and swimming or canoeing on the Charles to lawn parties and dances, the choices for leisure time grew during the 20th century.

Today, the Lions Club, the Odd Fellows and Masons, the Veterans of Foreign Wars, and American Legion, as well as church-, park-, and school-affiliated groups, provide opportunities for a wide range of recreational and social activities.

The Charles, now cleared of industrial waste, is still there to enjoy. Among the many places to find natural beauty in Medway are the walking trail at Choate Park, the playgrounds at the park and Oakland Street, and the sports fields at Idylbrook, Oakland, Choate, and the schools.

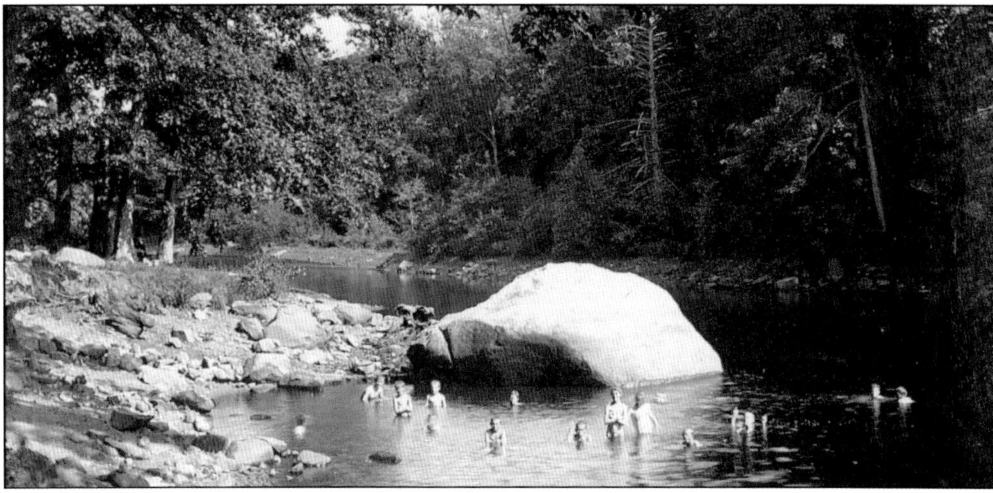

"The Big Rock" was a landmark in the Charles River, high water or low. A few hundred feet upriver from the Sanford Mill dam, it was a favorite swimming place. These pictures date from *c.* 1895, with Sanford Mill seen in the distance in the picture below.

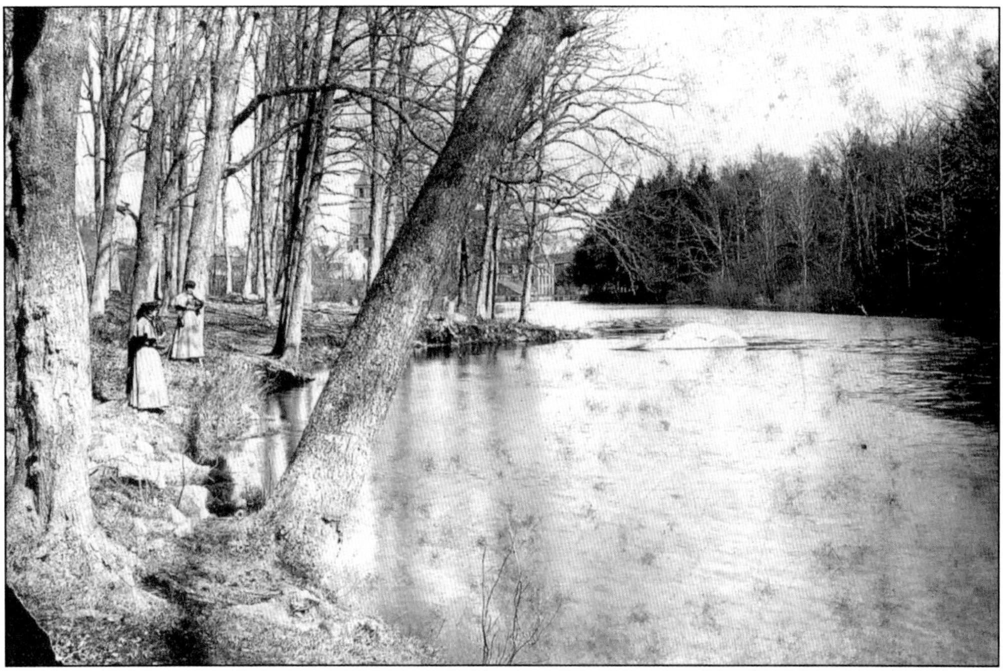

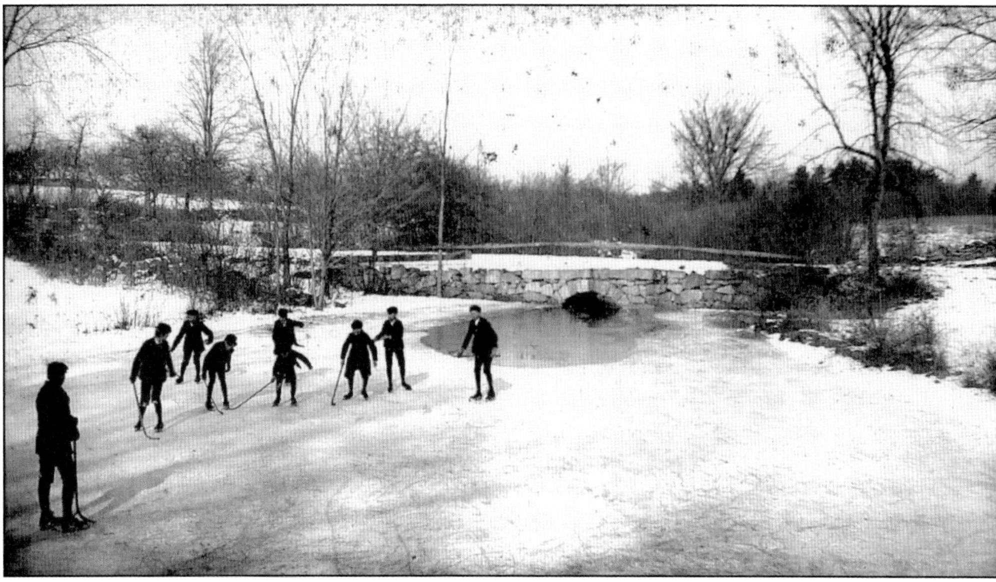

This photograph of a hockey game on the Thayer Mill pond was taken *c.* 1895. This pond was created by a dam at the old stone mill on Main Street. Notice the Oak Street bridge in the center background.

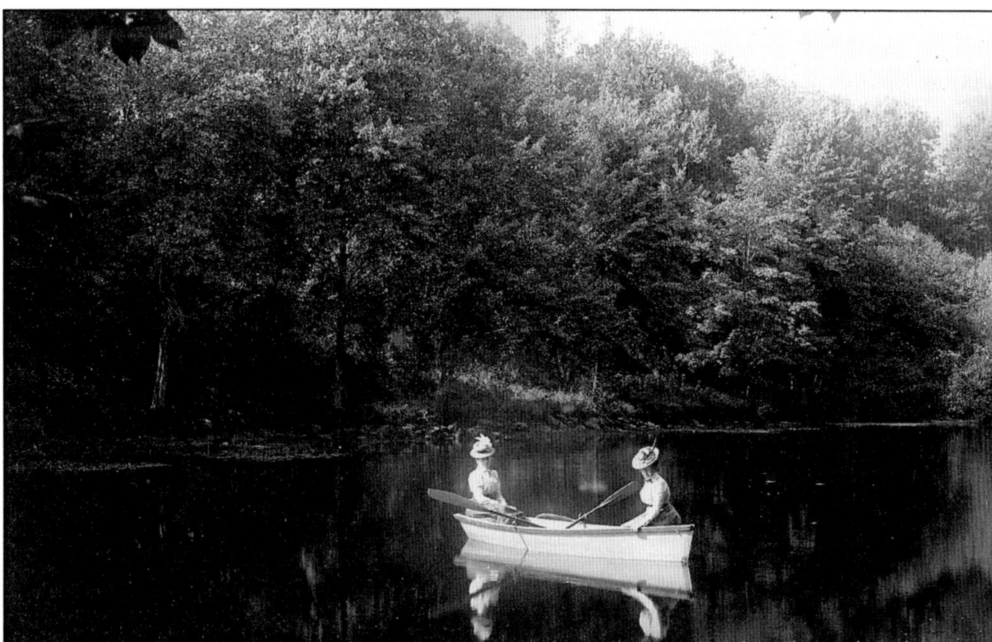

Even with the pressures of everyday chores in the early 20th century, an occasional afternoon was available for canoeing on the Charles.

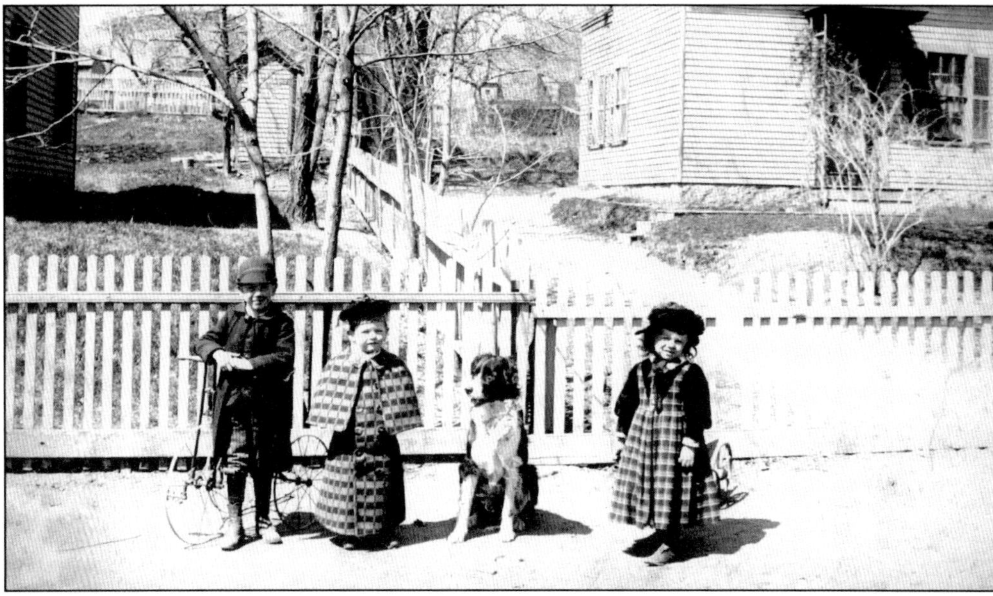

For three youngsters and their dog, a fine spring morning in 1892 opens a lot of possibilities. This photograph was taken on Barber Street in Medway Village.

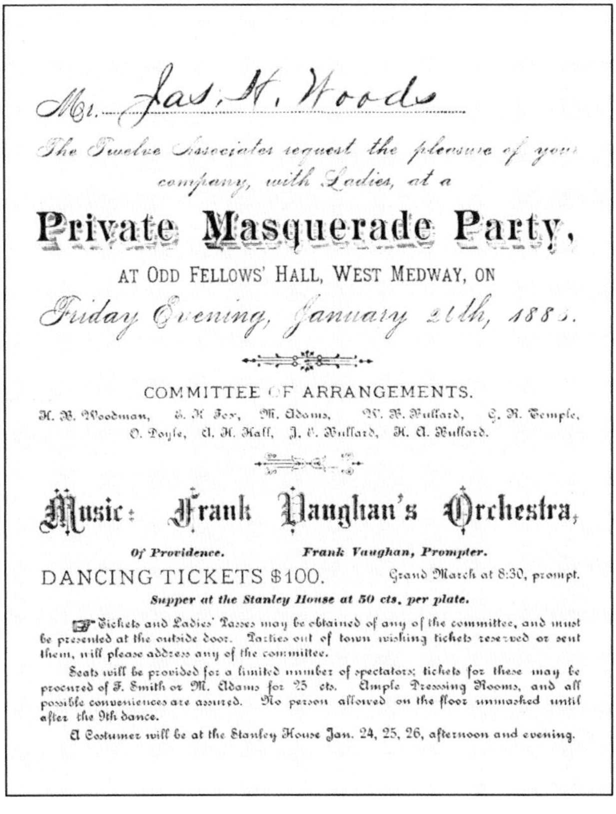

Mr. Jas. H. Woods

The Twelve Associates request the pleasure of your company, with Ladies, at a

Private Masquerade Party,

AT ODD FELLOWS' HALL, WEST MEDWAY, ON

Friday Evening, January 26th, 1885.

COMMITTEE OF ARRANGEMENTS.

H. B. Woodman, E. H. Fox, M. Adams, W. B. Bullard, G. R. Temple,
O. Doyle, A. H. Hall, J. E. Bullard, H. A. Bullard.

Music: Frank Vaughan's Orchestra,

Of Providence. **Frank Vaughan, Prompter.**

DANCING TICKETS $100. Grand March at 8:30, prompt.

Supper at the Stanley House at 50 cts. per plate.

Tickets and Ladies' Passes may be obtained of any of the committee, and must be presented at the outside door. Parties out of town wishing tickets reserved or sent them, will please address any of the committee.

Seats will be provided for a limited number of spectators; tickets for these may be procured of F. Smith or M. Adams for 25 cts. Ample Dressing Rooms, and all possible conveniences are assured. No person allowed on the floor unmasked until after the 9th dance.

A Costumer will be at the Stanley House Jan. 24, 25, 26, afternoon and evening.

This invitation to a masquerade party, with instructions that "No one is allowed on the floor unmasked until after the 9th dance," is evidence of a lively social life in Medway in 1885. However, with supper offered at 50¢, the price of a ticket to the party was most likely $1 rather than the $100 that is printed.

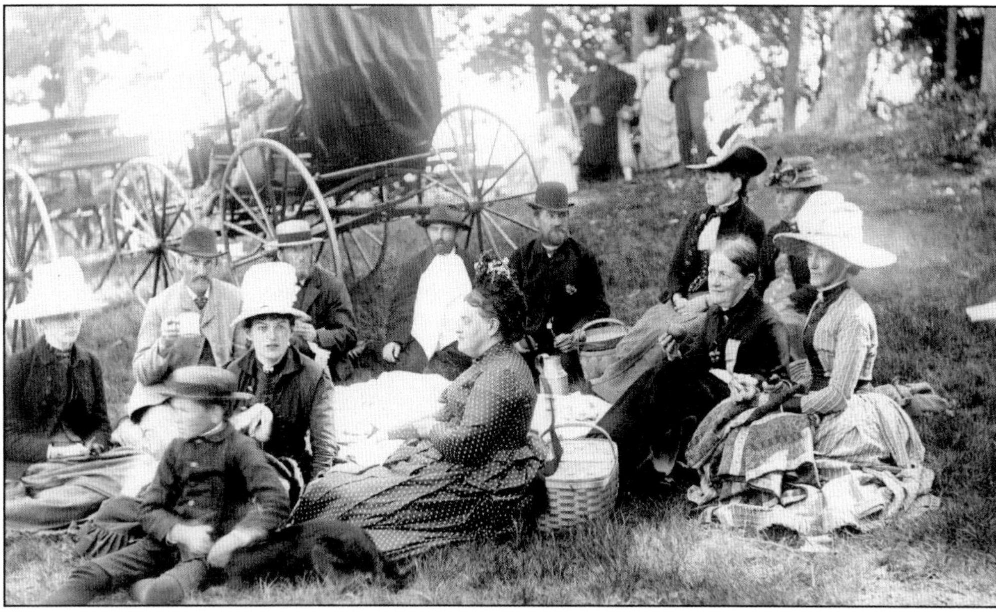

This unidentified group was able to take advantage of a warm summer afternoon for a picnic on the banks of the Charles sometime in the 1880s.

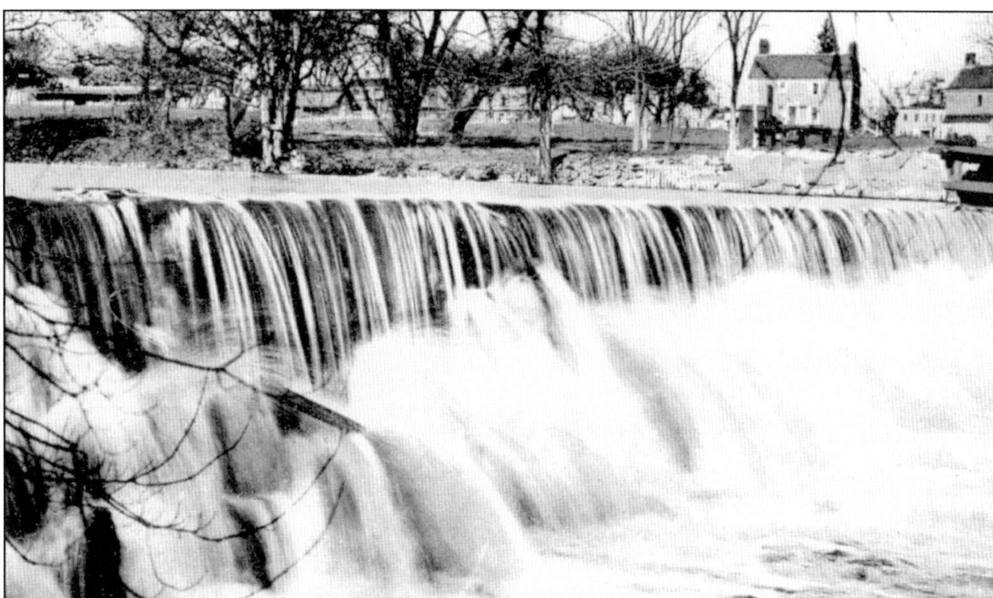

Woodland Park, across the Charles River in West Medway, was a favorite spot for dances, picnics, ball games, and outings *c.* 1900. Taken from below the park, this image looking toward Medway shows the two houses (right) built for Campbell paper mill workers. The Cephas Thayer house, at 314 Village Street, is also visible in the distance (between the mill houses).

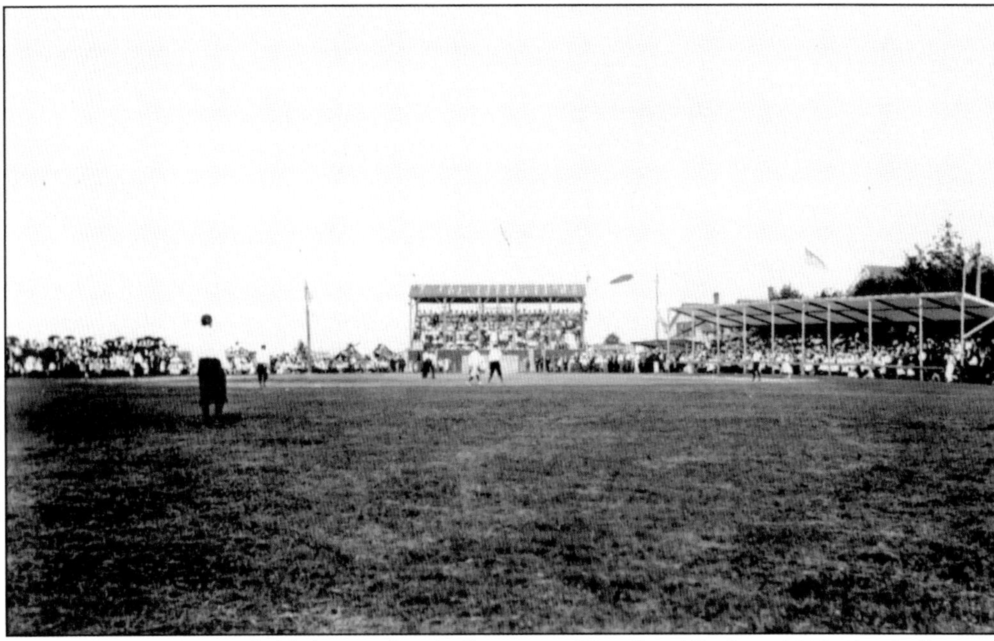

This view from the outfield shows a baseball game at Woodland Park in 1902. Baseball games drew a large crowd. Teams were regional, and competition keen. It is said that Ty Cobb played here.

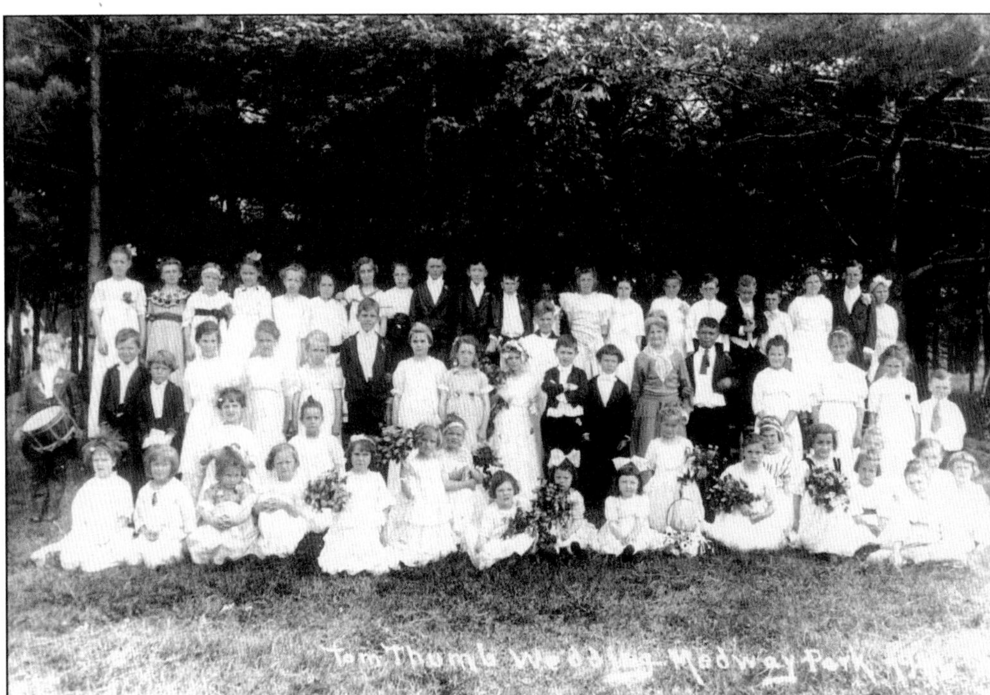

The *Tom Thumb Wedding* was one of the productions staged at Woodland Park in 1916. Among those in the cast are Marion Ollendorff, Bob Butler, Janet Russell, Dick Wilkinson, Hope Clark, Marjorie Ollendorff, Dick George, and Marion Clark.

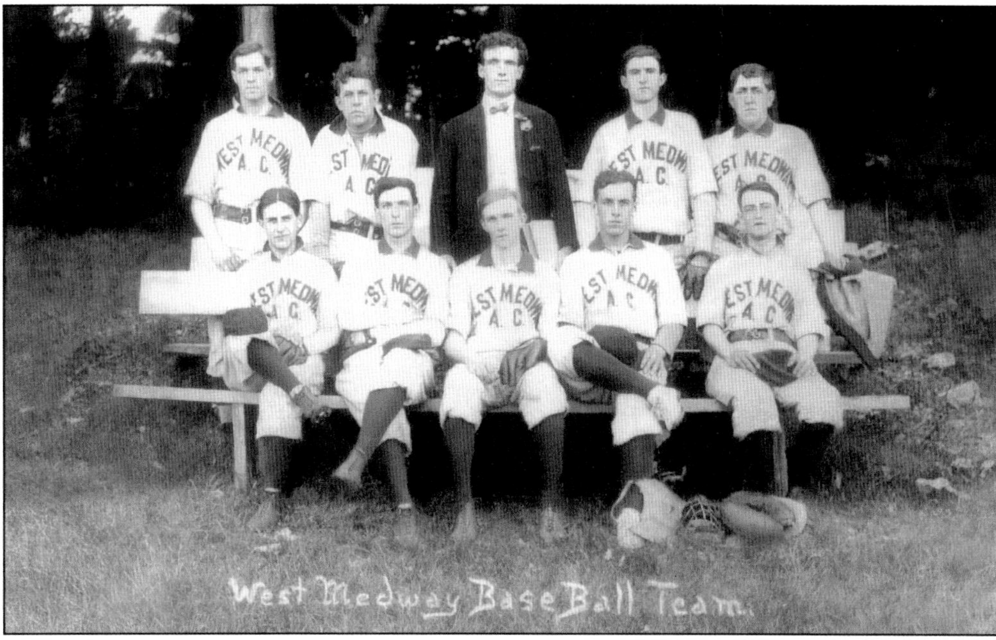

A baseball team sponsored by the Medway Athletic Club competes at Woodland Park in 1908. This club was one of several regional teams of the early 1900s. Among those pictured is Leon Hitchcock (far left, standing). (Courtesy Stephen Malloy.)

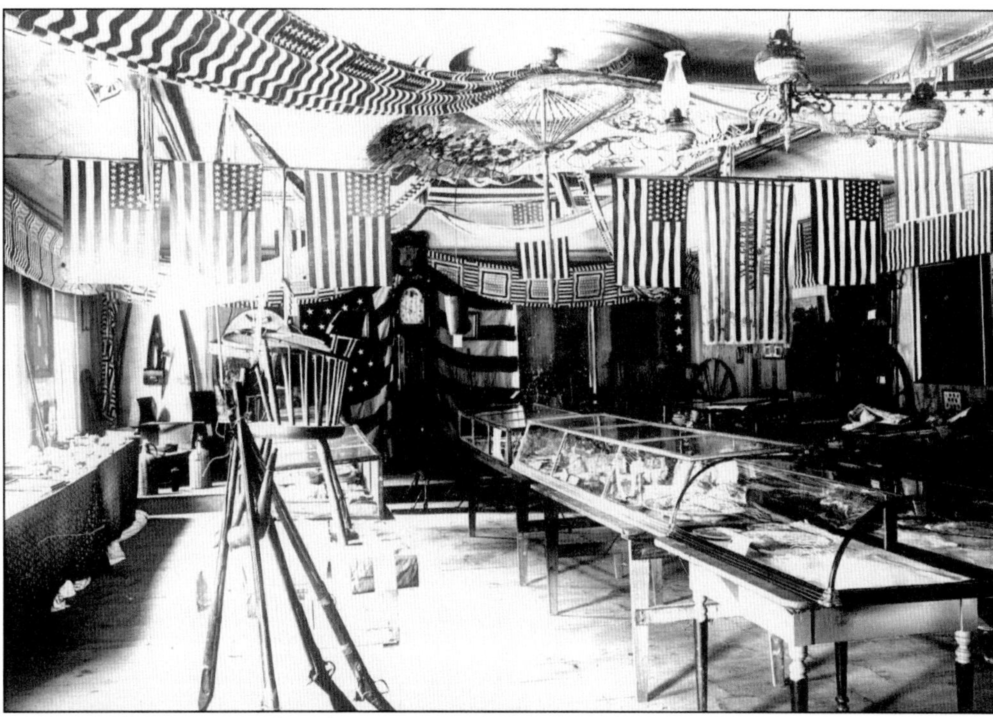

In 1903, the newly formed Medway Historical Society organized this exhibit for Old Home Day at the Old Parish House in West Medway. Although the Edison Electric Illuminating Company installed streetlights in 1898, it was several years before all residences were electrified.

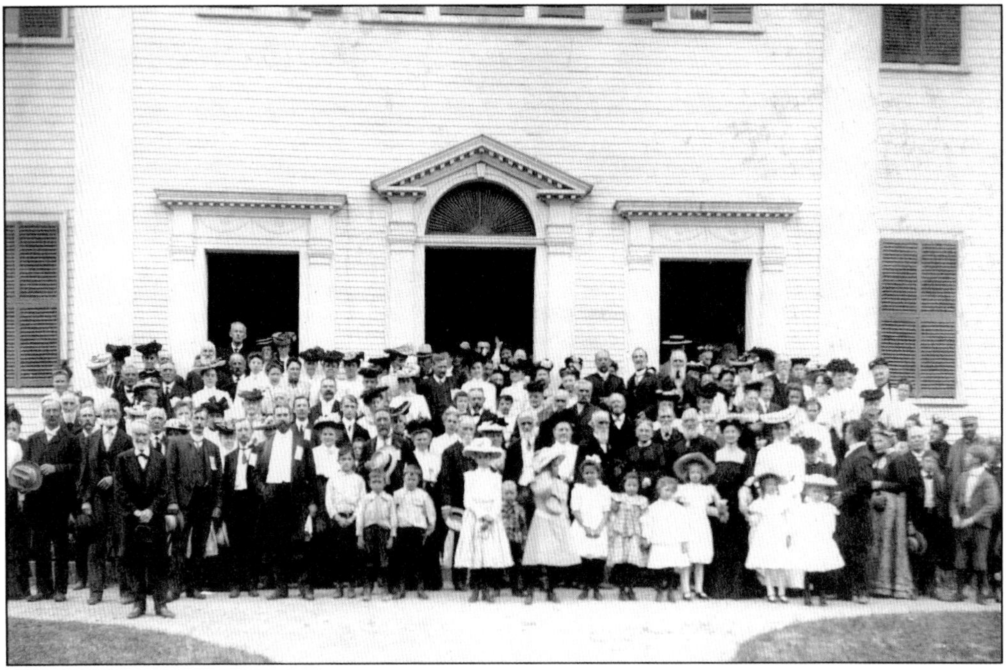

The Old Home Day observances, sponsored by the Medway Historical Society, brought together many people from Millis, as well as Medway. Pictured here in front of the Second Congregational Church, now the Community Church, are costumed characters who participated in the second Old Home Day, in 1904.

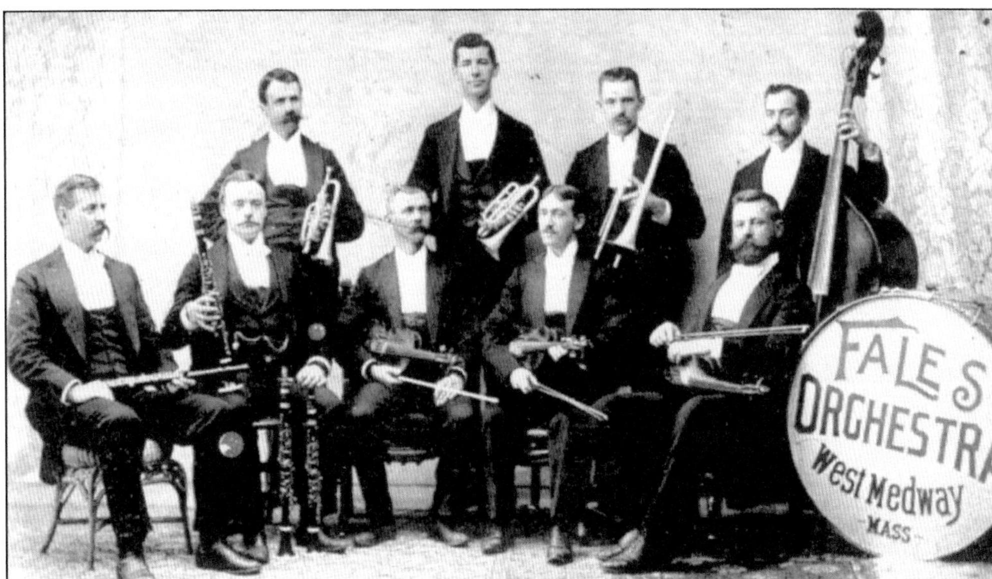

Fales Orchestra of West Medway was a popular choice for special occasions. From left to right are the following: (first row) two unidentified members, Allie Vose, and two unidentified members; (second row) Frank Adams, Jim Allen, Imlah ?, and William Fales. This photograph was taken in 1895.

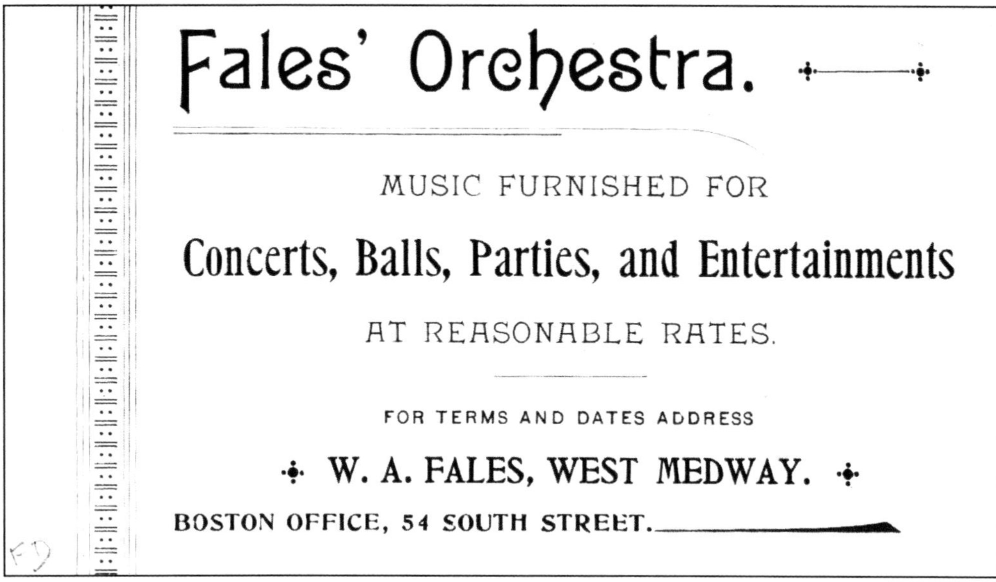

The booking card shows that the Fales company of strings, woodwinds, and brass could adapt to many different gatherings.

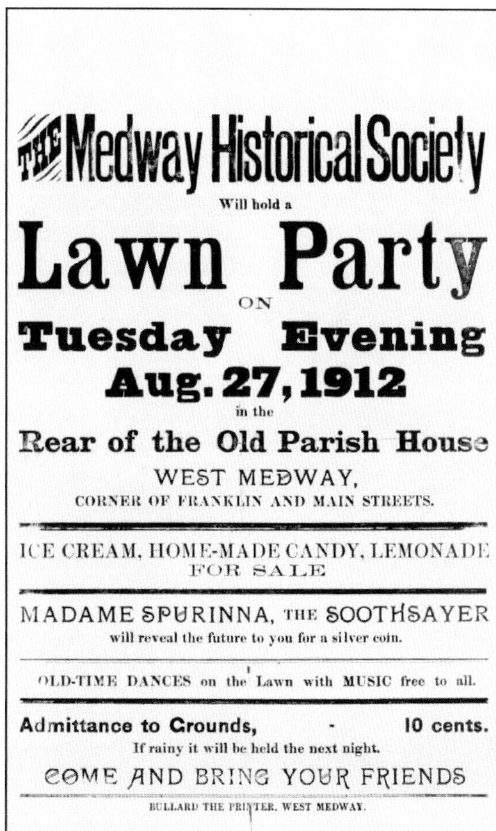

Before movies were available, a lawn party was a welcome outing on a warm summer evening. Probably Madame Spurinna the Soothsayer was an added attraction.

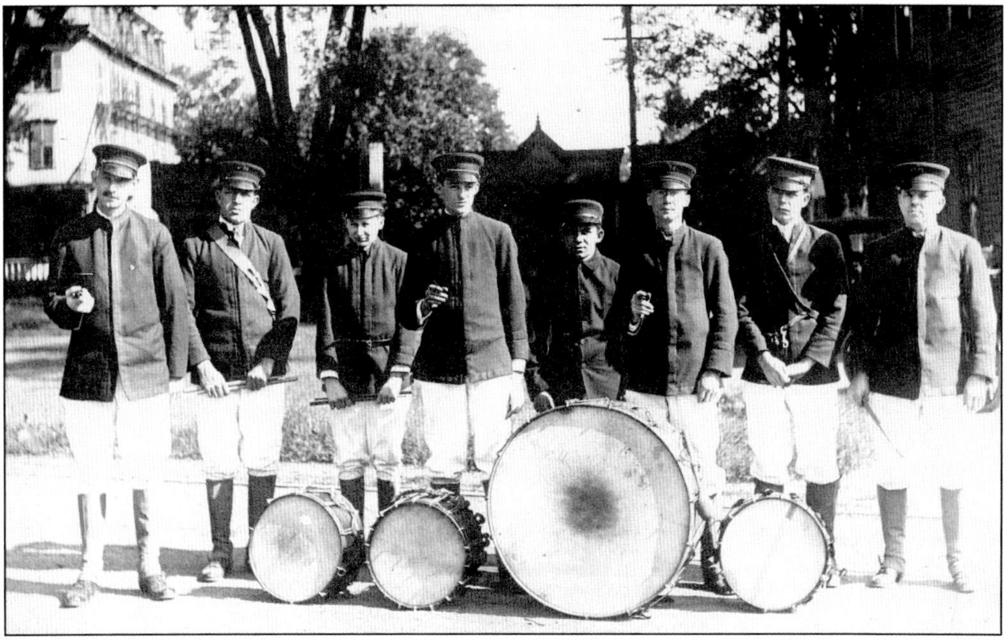

The Fales Band is shown ready for the Memorial Day parade *c.* 1910. Visible are Smith's Block (center background) in profile on Main Street, and the side of the original Odd Fellows building (left).

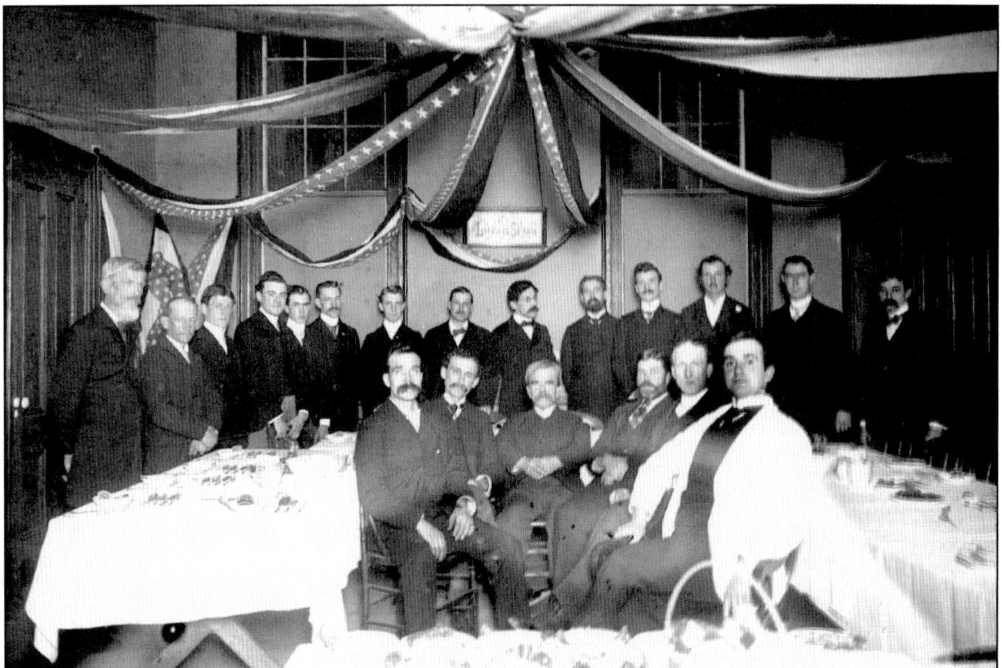

The Men's League was one of several groups that met to socialize and support civic projects in the early 20th century. Among those pictured is Alonzo Hixon (front center).

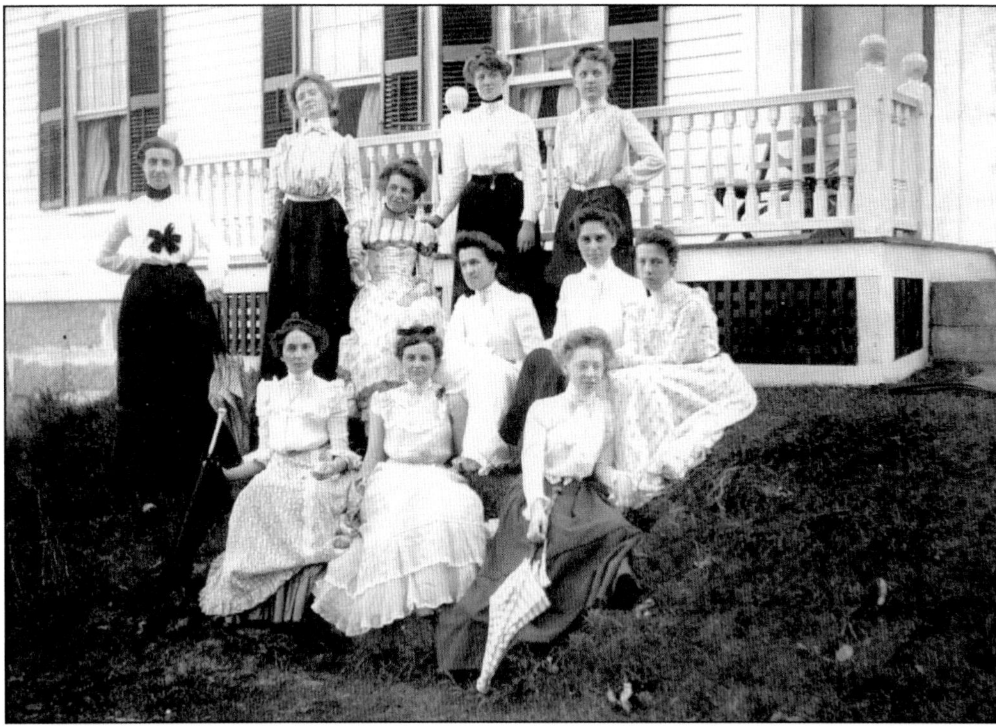

The Phyllyne Club is pictured in front of the porch at the side of the Second Church parsonage, a porch the club had raised funds to build. Among those pictured are Eudora Treen, Alice Woodman, Hattie Coombs, Selma Pond, Marian Metcalf, and Alice Ollendorff.

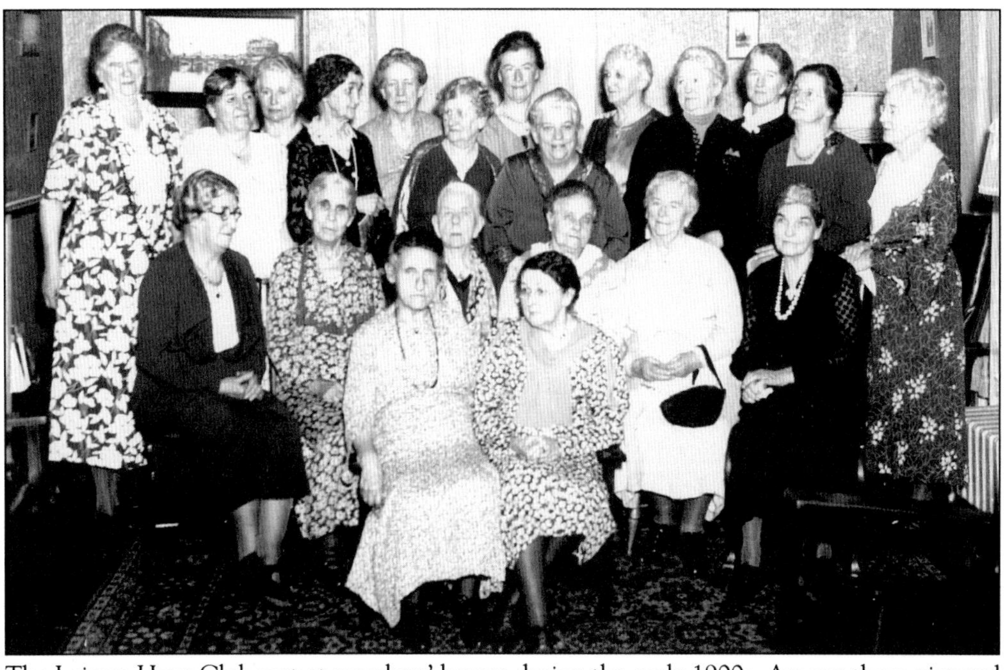

The Leisure Hour Club met at members' homes during the early 1900s. Among those pictured *c.* 1920 are Anna Fales, Mary Fairbanks, Rose Wood, Sarah Sparrow, and Lizzie Mann.

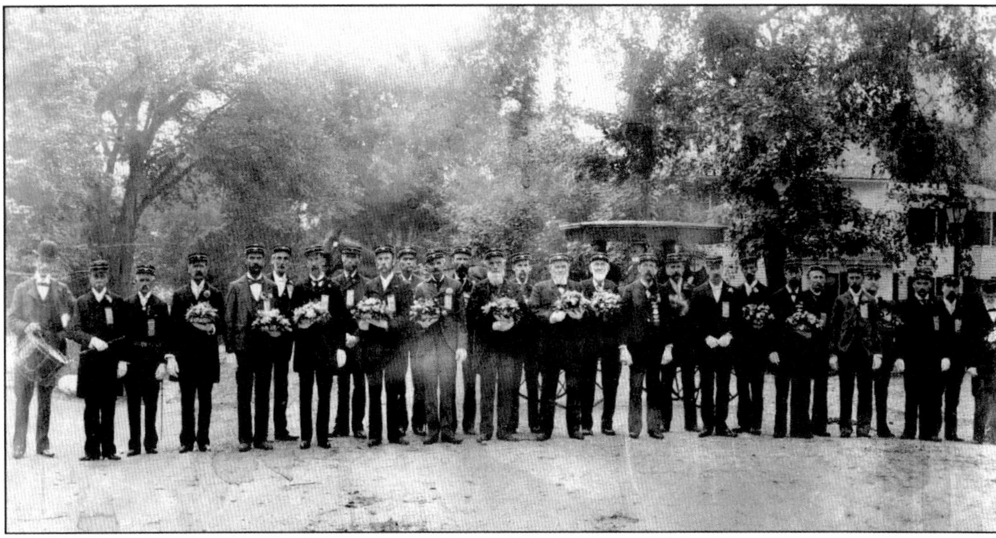

Members of Rising Sun Lodge, International Order of Odd Fellows, are pictured at their 50th anniversary. Organized in 1845, the Rising Sun Lodge is still active today. It sends one student each year to the United Nations to observe and learn. Odd Fellows organizations across Massachusetts have combined in this effort for the past 60 years.

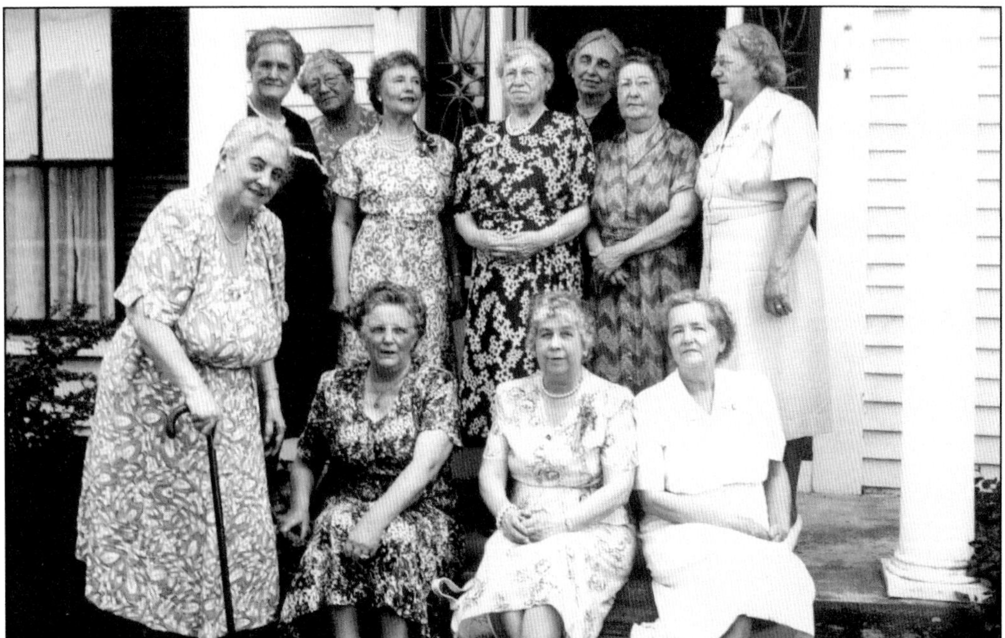

The UDAHLI Club, whose full name was a secret, was one of the longest-lasting social groups. From 1909 to 1958, members met at homes to talk, sew, and enjoy refreshments. Over the years, they made costumes for the 1913 pageant, supported the war effort in World Wars I and II, and worked on relief projects during the Great Depression. Shown in 1951, from left to right, are the following: (first row) Lillian Fales, Alice Albee, Ethel Rogerson, and Marguerite Labaree; (second row) Carrie Hodgson, Alice Ollendorff, Olive Mason, Mabel Wilkinson, Florence Metcalf, Lillian Ramsey, and Agnes Hobart. (Courtesy Priscilla Robertson.)

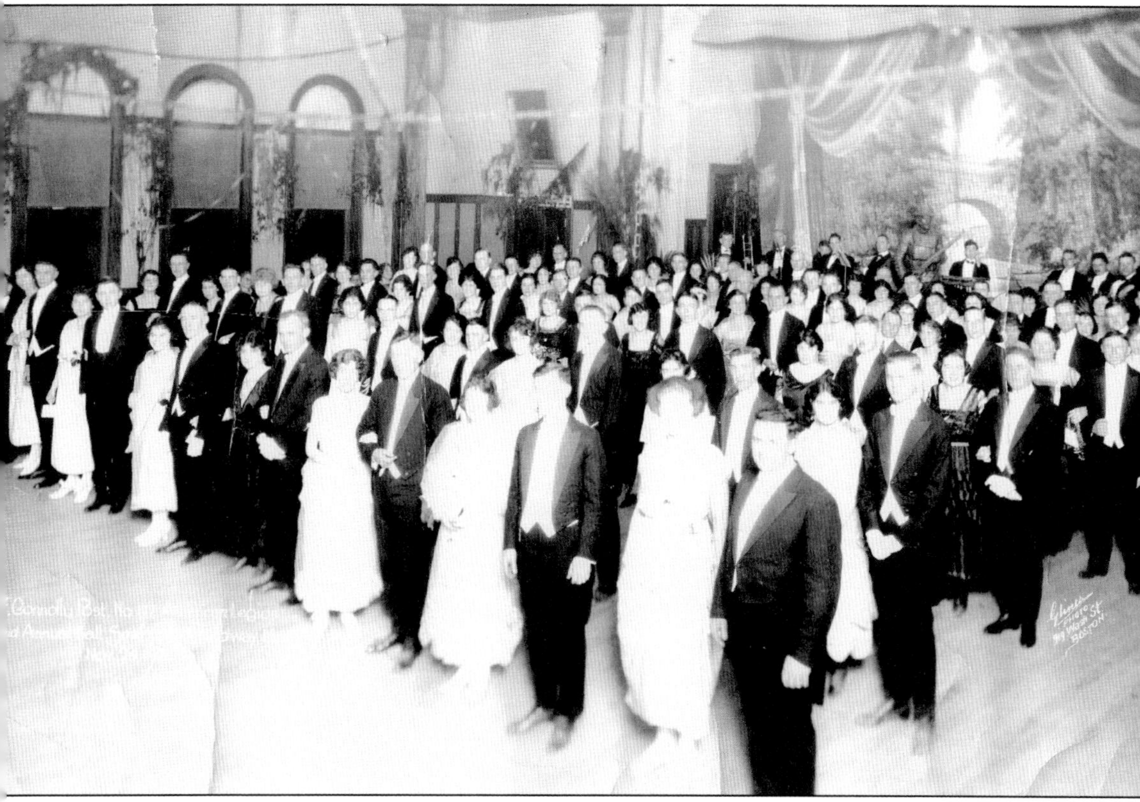

The John Connolly Post No. 177 of the American Legion has a good turnout for its dance in November 1920. The upper floor in Sanford Hall was used for dances, plays, high school graduations, and even as a movie theater. This hall had an ornamental tin ceiling, which was very attractive. It was lost to view when the space was converted for office use and a suspended ceiling was installed.

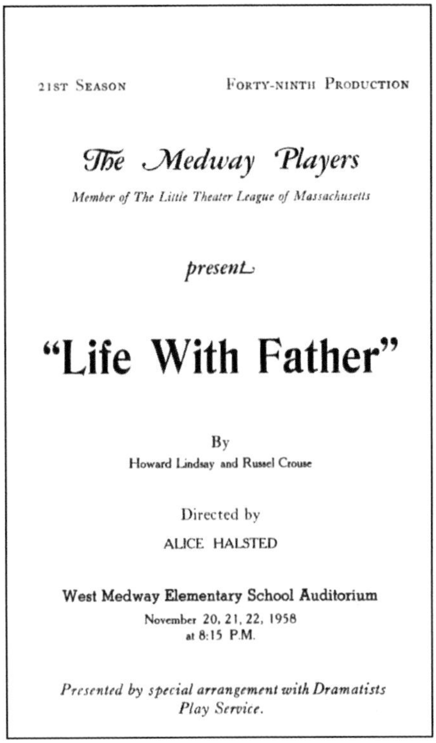

21st Season	Forty-ninth Production

The Medway Players

Member of The Little Theater League of Massachusetts

present

"Life With Father"

By

Howard Lindsay and Russel Crouse

Directed by

ALICE HALSTED

West Medway Elementary School Auditorium

November 20, 21, 22, 1958
at 8:15 P.M.

Presented by special arrangement with Dramatists Play Service.

The Medway Players, an amateur theater group, organized in 1935 and staged *Lady Windermere's Fan*. Thereafter, the troupe produced one or more plays annually through *Life with Father* in 1958. Reorganized as the Medway Community Players c. 1995, the group continues to stage productions twice a year at the Medway Public Library.

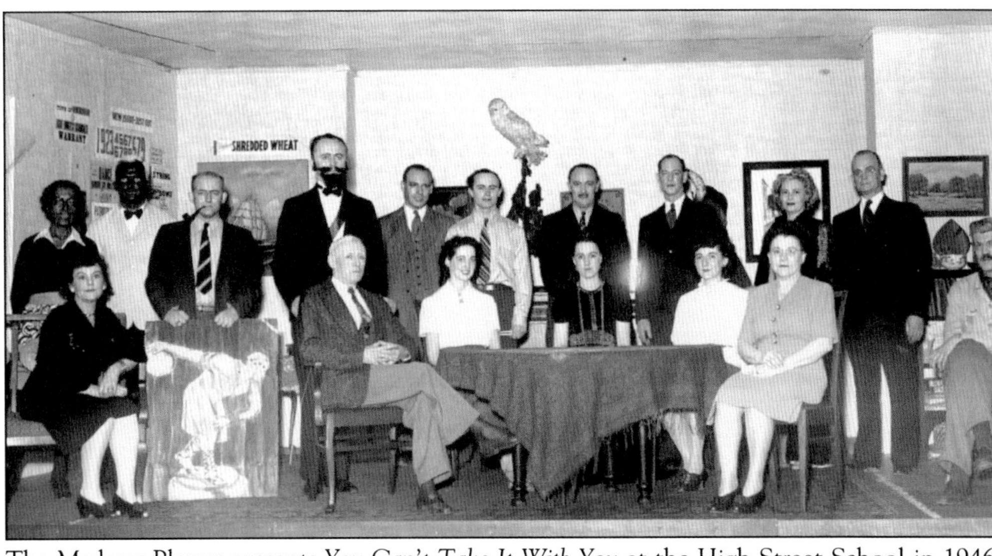

The Medway Players presents *You Can't Take It With You* at the High Street School in 1946. Cast members are, from left to right, as follows: (first row) Nadine Anderson, Shelley Richardson, Audrey Thomas, Ruth Ellis, Lenore Beers, Nellie Rotzel, and Ted Ellis; (second row) Cathleen Knowlton, Howard Ayer, Bob Milligan, Gil Grove, Allen Richardson, Clarence Esten, Stewart Smith, Shaw Hudson, Mildred Youman, and Andy Tillberg.

Seven

CELEBRATIONS

Many different occasions call for a celebration, among them family events, sporting activities, special honors, and national holidays. The celebrations covered in this chapter are uniquely local: two special anniversary celebrations marking milestones in the history of Medway.

The first of these, in 1913, was the bicentennial celebration of the incorporation of Medway as a town. One of the events listed in the schedule was an automobile parade, which must have been impressive. Unfortunately, no photographs of this early-20th-century parade were immediately available.

In 1963, Medway organized a second town-wide celebration marking 250 years since founding. Many residents of today remember this observance; indeed, they took part in it. Both these commemorations not only paid tribute to the past but also took note of present accomplishments and future prospects.

1713 1913

THE TOWN OF MEDWAY

(Medway — Millis)

MASSACHUSETTS

Will Celebrate Its

BI-CENTENNIAL

You are cordially invited to be present

Friday, Saturday and Sunday, July 4, 5 and 6, 1913

PROGRAM

FRIDAY, JULY 4th — Automobile and Trades Parade
Historical Pageant
Band Concert and Fireworks

SATURDAY, July 5th — Historical and Literary Exercises
Historical Pageant
Banquet and Band Concert

Sunday, July 6th — Millis — Special Religious Exercises
in Old First Church
Address and Band Concert

During entire Celebration there will be an Historic Exhibit

COMMITTEE

Millis	Medway
MELVIN J. WEST	HERBERT N. HIXON, Chairman
LOUIS LA CROIX	ORION T. MASON, Secretary
J. WARREN CLARK	WILLIAM W. OLLENDORFF
EVAN F. RICHARDSON	WALTER L. PALMER
	ROBERT M. O'DONNELL

In 1913, Medway pulled out all the stops for a three-day observance of the bicentennial of its founding. Most of the population took part in the events, including many residents of Millis, a part of Medway only 28 years earlier.

OFFICIAL PROGRAM FOR

Medway Bi-Centennial,

July 4, 5 and 6, 1913.

Friday, July Fourth.

4.00 A. M. Salute by Bells and Whistles.

6.00 A. M. Town Crier's Advent.

7.00 A. M. Automobile Parade Through Adjoining Towns, Starting at Millis.

8.00 A. M. Parade at West Medway by Fire Department, Sons of Veterans, Boy Scouts, Hand-Tub Contests and Coupling Contests.

3.00 P. M. Historical Pageant of Medway, on the Banks of Charles River at Medway.

7.00 P. M. Band Concert and Fireworks on Pageant Field, Medway.

Saturday, July Fifth.

10.00 A. M. Historical Exercises under Auspices of Historical Society in Meeting House of Second Church, West Medway.
Hon. Robert Luce, Orator.
Historical Address by Orion T. Mason.

10.30 A. M. Band Concert on Pageant Field, Medway.

3.00 P. M. Pageant on Pageant Field, Medway.

7.00 P. M. Banquet in Sanford Hall, Medway, Henry T. Richardson, Esq., Toastmaster.

7.00 P. M. Band Concert in Depot Square, West Medway.

Sunday, July Sixth.

10.30 A. M. Historical Exercises in Meeting House of First Church, Millis. Speakers: Rev. Alexander B. McLeod, Hon. Fred H. Williams.

2.00 P. M. Band Concert on Common, Millis.

7.00 P. M. Vesper Service in First Church, Millis. Lieut.-Governor David I. Walsh, Orator.

Parking for Automobiles for the accommodation of those touring to the Pageant, close by the Pageant Field.

Admission and Reserved Seats to Pageant, 35c, 50c, 75c, $1.00.

Banquet Tickets, $1.50.

Tickets for all on sale at Adams' Pharmacy, West Medway, Medway Pharmacy, Medway, Rice's Pharmacy, Milford, Harry Holbrook's, Millis.

Should either day prove stormy, reserved seats will be good for Monday, July 7th.

H. N. HIXON, CHAIRMAN,
O. T. MASON, SECRETARY,
General Committee.

Perhaps recalling that in 1813 the only notice of the first 100 years of incorporation as a town was a special sermon by Rev. Luther Bailey at the First Church in Millis, residents decided that 1913 should be celebrated with pomp and circumstance.

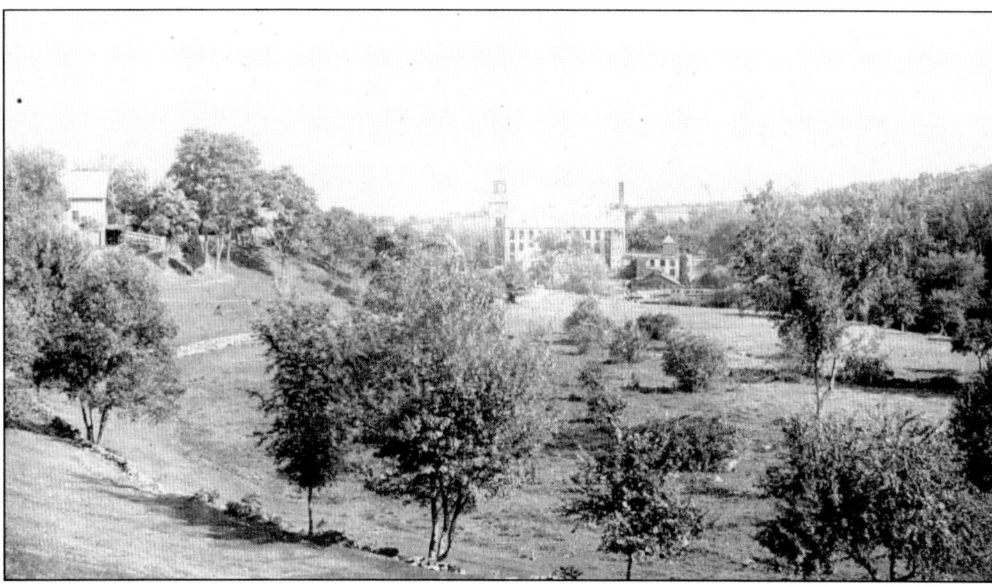

This 1894 view shows the natural amphitheater in which the 1913 bicentennial pageant was held. Pictured are buildings on Village Street (upper left), the Charles River (right), and Sanford Mills (center distance).

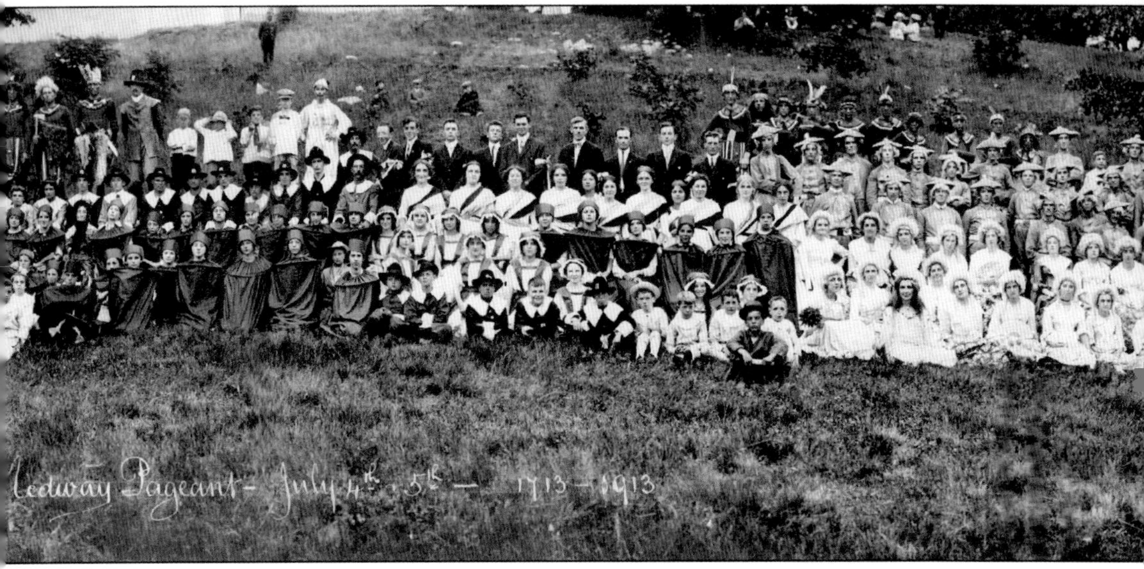

The pageant was an elaborate affair dramatizing events in town history. The "red menne" came down the river in canoes and attacked the settlement, burning homes. Village life, schools, and town meetings were portrayed. The drama was long; the first acts were staged on Friday. On

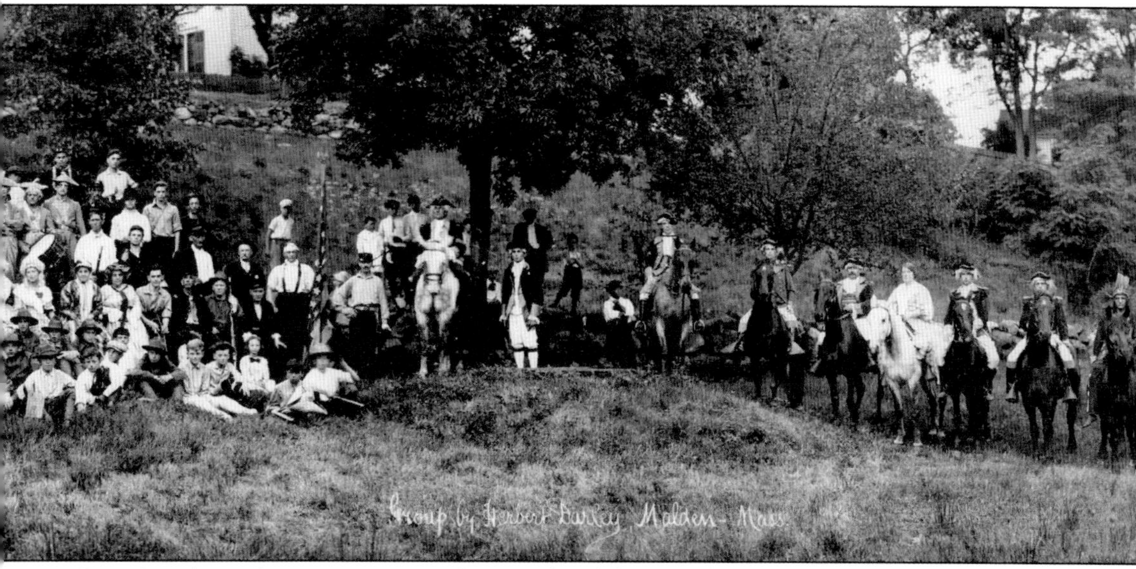

Saturday, the earlier portions were shortened and the complete play performed. For the finale, the whole cast assembled—"red menne," Puritans, soldiers, and townspeople—to join in singing "The Star-Spangled Banner."

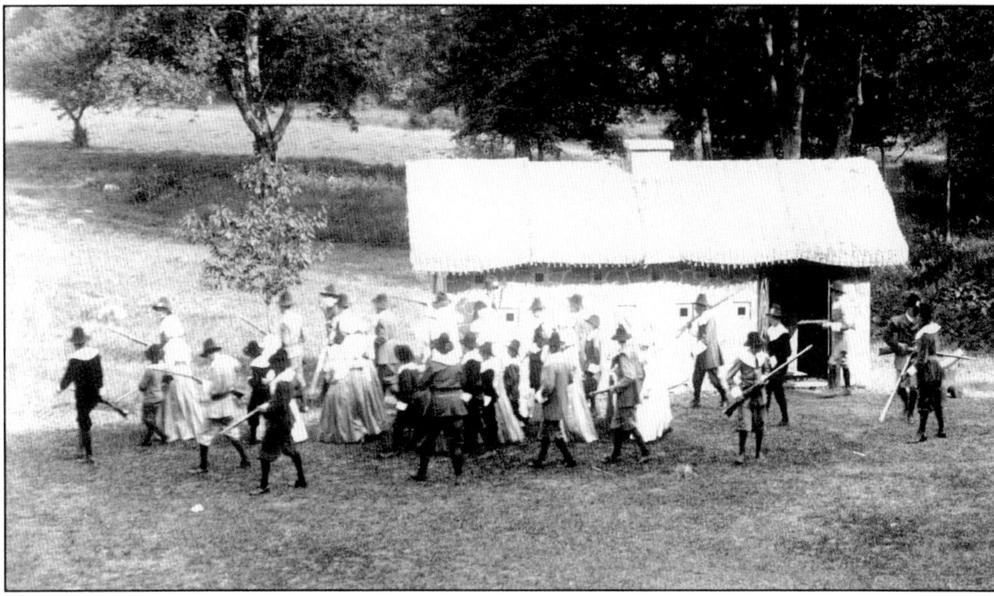

An early scene in the pageant showed the settlers under Indian attack during King Philip's War, hurrying to the stone fort for cover.

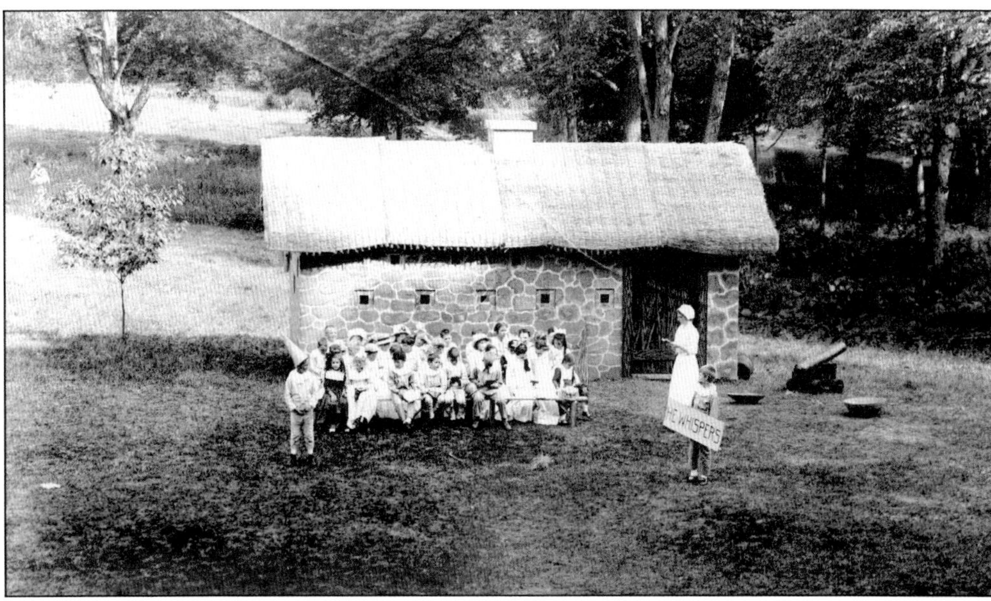

In this view of the pageant, the student wearing a dunce cap was singled out for discipline in the early school with the signed explanation "He whispers."

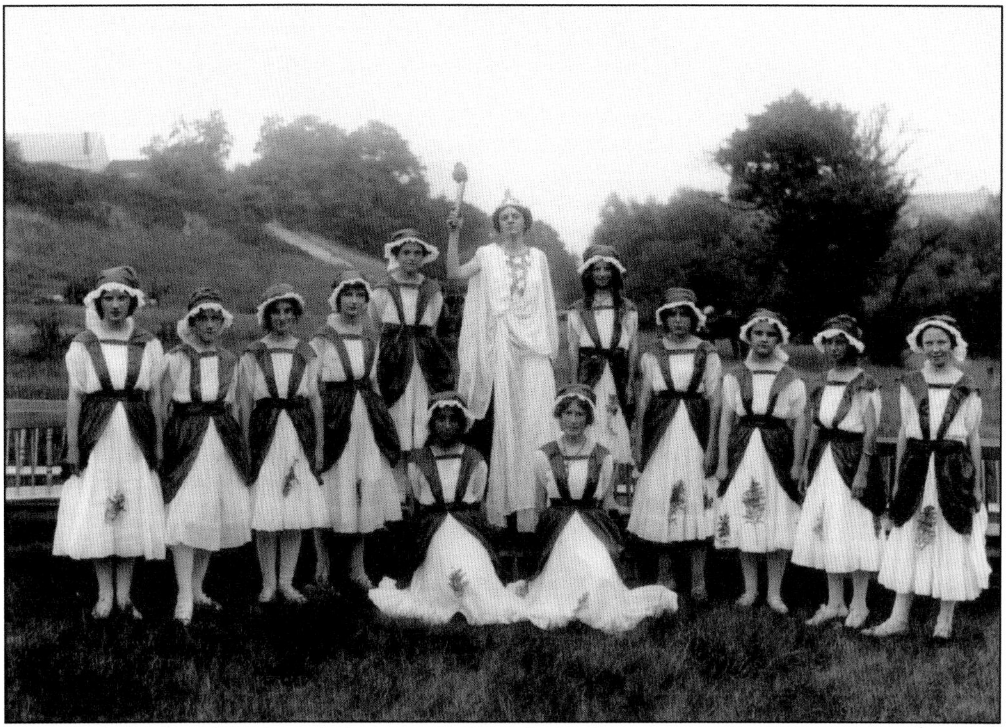

The Goldenrods (above) and the Firecrackers (below) were two groups taking part in the pageant. Costumes for both groups were made by the UDAHLI Club.

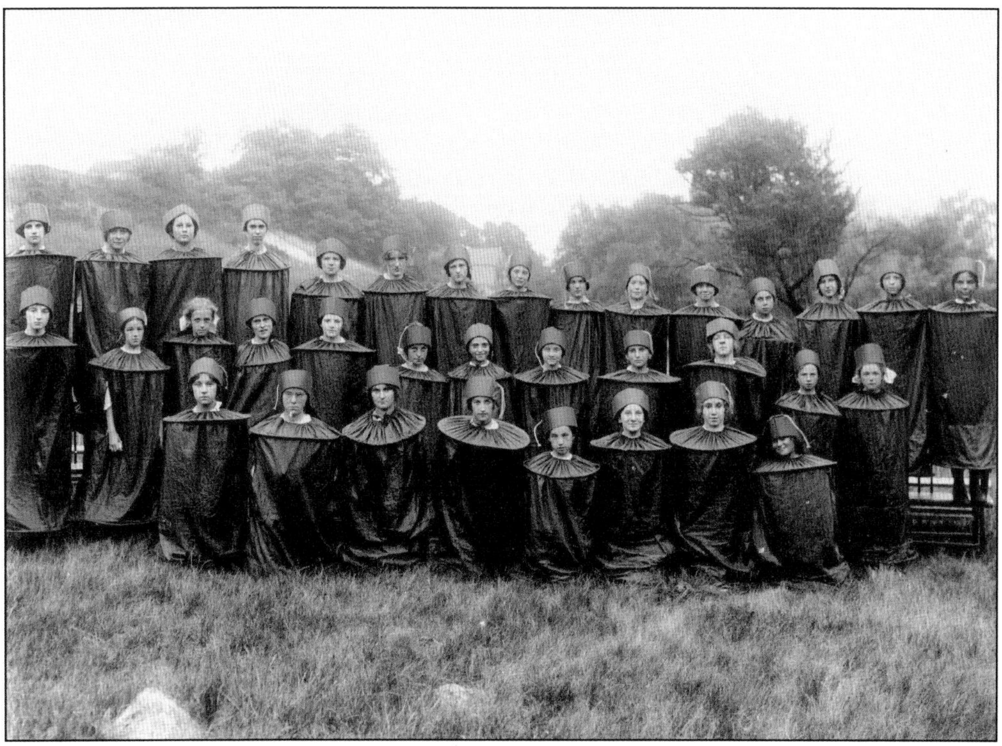

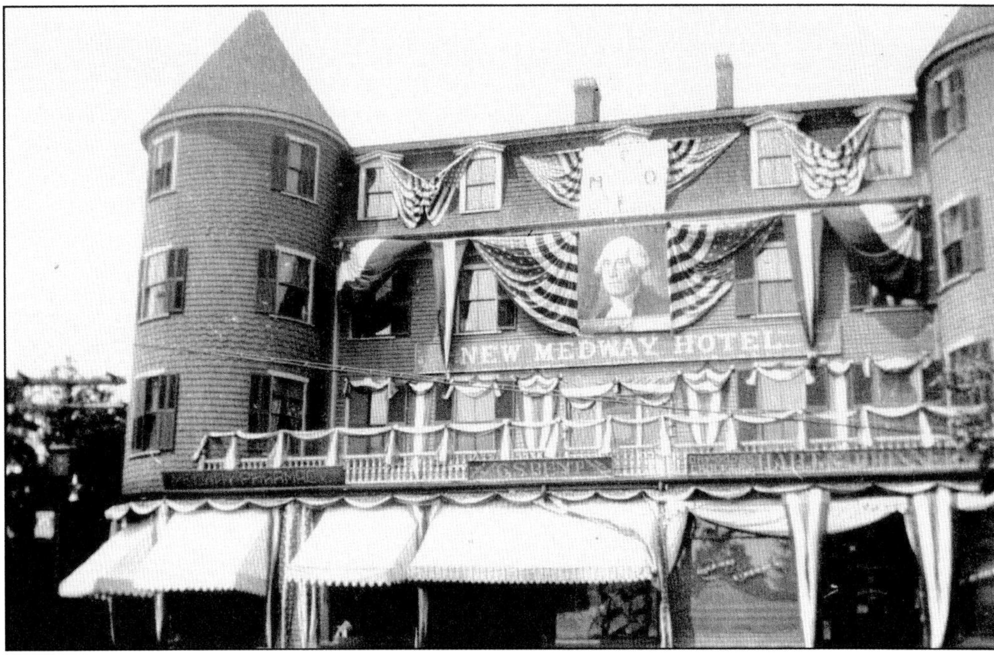

Known as the New Medway Hotel in 1913, this building stood at the northeast corner of Broad and Village Streets and is decorated for the bicentennial. Businesses on the street level at the time were, from left to right, Medway Pharmacy, G. S. Bent, and Hart and O'Donnell dry goods and grocery store. (Courtesy Priscilla Robertson.)

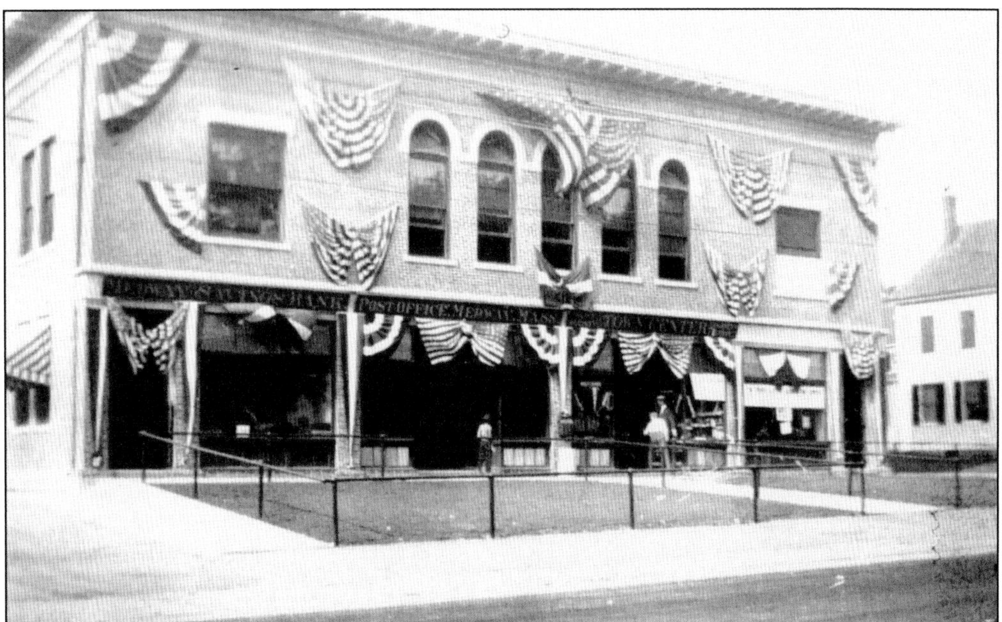

The new Sanford Hall, built after the first one burned in 1911, was ready to join the town celebration in July 1913. Occupants of the lower floor included the Medway Savings Bank, post office, and town center. (Courtesy Priscilla Robertson.)

The impressive Cowell-Fisher Block, at the corner of Village and Sanford Streets, was decorated in 1913. Home at the time to the Veteran Firemen's Association, the building was destroyed by a disastrous fire in 1930.

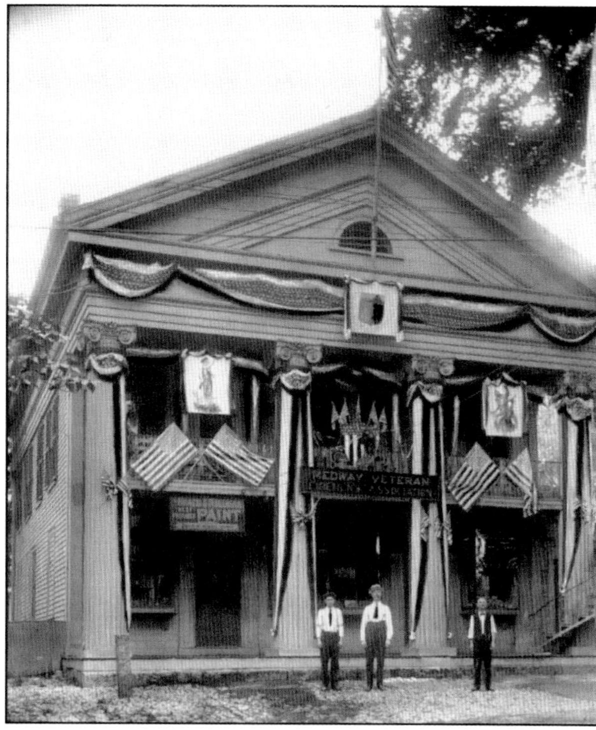

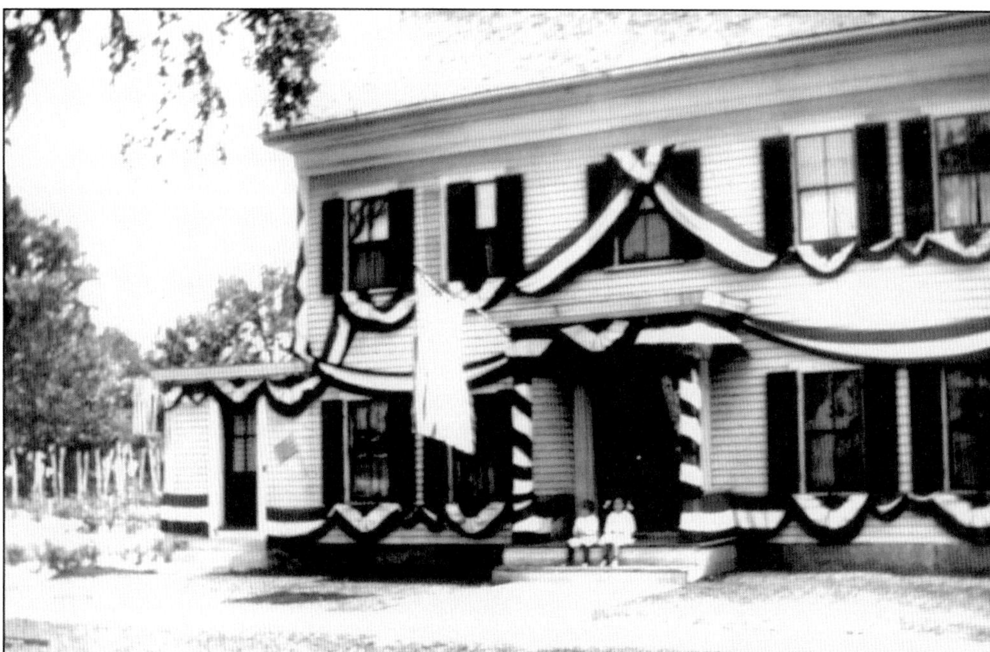

Many homes, as well as public buildings, were decorated for the celebration. Pictured is the Saunders residence, at 329 Village Street. Virginia and Elizabeth Saunders are on the steps, perhaps waiting for the parade. (Courtesy Priscilla Robertson.)

Schedule of Activities

WEEK OF JUNE 22 - JUNE 29

Saturday, June 22

FIREMAN'S DAY

Firemen's Parade, 10:00 A.M.

WATER POLO AND HAND TUB COMPETITION

Afternoon — Legion Field.

ANNIVERSARY BALL, JUNIOR, SENIOR HIGH SCHOOL

Presentation of Queen and her court.

Sunday, June 23

FAITH OF OUR FATHERS

All Faith Religious Service Legion Field 11:30 A.M. Historical address by F. D. Donovan.

CYO DRILL COMPETITION

Hundreds of units; Legion Field 2:00 P.M.

EXHIBITION TENNIS MATCHES

Charles River Tennis Court, 5:00 P.M. to 8:00 P.M.

Monday, June 24

YOUTH DAY

Events for 3rd and 4th grades 10:00 to 11:30 A.M. Events for 5th, 6th, 7th and 8th grades 1:30 to 4:00 P.M. Tug of War for Junior Belles and Junior Brothers of the Brush 4:00 P.M. to 5:15 P.M.

SENIOR CITIZENS PROGRAM, JUNIOR, SENIOR HIGH SCHOOL

6:30 P.M.

TEEN-AGE DANCE

Popular disc jockey; Fernandes Shopping Center 8:00 P.M. to 11:30 P.M.

FIREWORKS DISPLAY

11:00 P.M.

Tuesday, June 25

PIONEER DAY

Old Homes — Historical tours 1:30 P.M. to 4:30 P.M. — 7:00 P.M. to 10:00 P.M.

HOBBIES, ARTS, CRAFTS AND ORGANIZATIONS

Medway Elementary School 8:00 P.M.

PAGEANT SPECTACULAR

Legion Field 8:30 P.M. Crowning of Queen.

FIREWORKS DISPLAY

11:00 P.M.

Wednesday, June 26

PIONEER DAY

HOBBIES, ARTS, CRAFTS AND ORGANIZATIONS

Medway Elementary School 8:00 P.M.

PAGEANT SPECTACULAR

Legion Field 8:30 P.M.

FIREWORKS DISPLAY

11:00 P.M.

Thursday, June 27

LADIES DAY

Centennial Belle Activities; Merchants Carnival; Country Fair; Bargain Day; Luncheon.

FASHION SHOW

Lakeview Club, Mendon 8:00 P.M.

PAGEANT SPECTACULAR

Legion Field 8:30 P.M.

FIREWORKS DISPLAY

11:00 P.M.

Friday, June 28

INTER-RACIAL DAY

Ceremonies devoted to racial groups of Medway; merchants carnival; booths, rides, Legion Field.

PAGEANT SPECTACULAR

Legion Field 8:30 P.M.

FIREWORKS DISPLAY

11:00 P.M.

Saturday, June 29

GOVERNORS DAY

Parade — 5 divisions, 60 musical units, drill corps; antique cars 10:00 A.M. at Community Church.

DARING AERIAL MERCHANTS CARNIVAL

Afternoon at Legion Field.

DRAWING OF GRAND PRIZE

Cadillac Convertible.

The 1963 celebration marking 250 years of the town's founding was a week-long affair. Groups of Anniversary Belles and Brothers of the Brush organized, Catholic Youth Organization drum corps were popular at the time, and the Charles River Tennis Club was active. The week culminated in a grand parade on the final Saturday.

In front of Sanford Hall, selectmen pose with the birthday cake for the town. From left to right are Richard Coakley, William Kenney, Robert O'Donnell (chairman of the observance), and Charles Bresnahan.

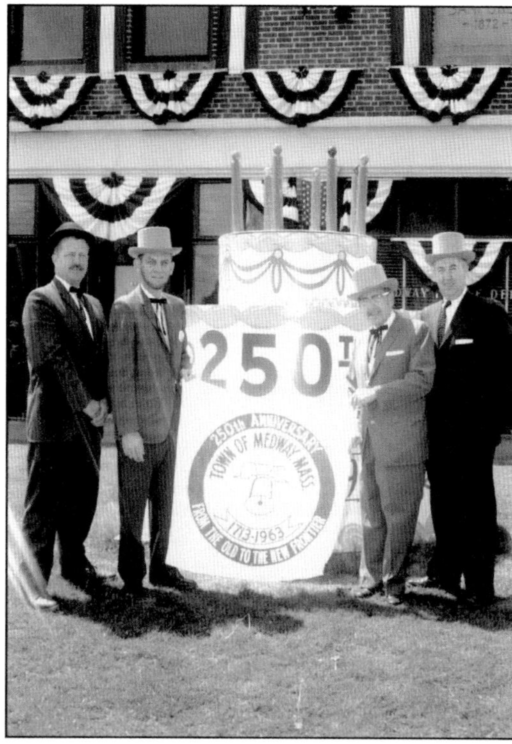

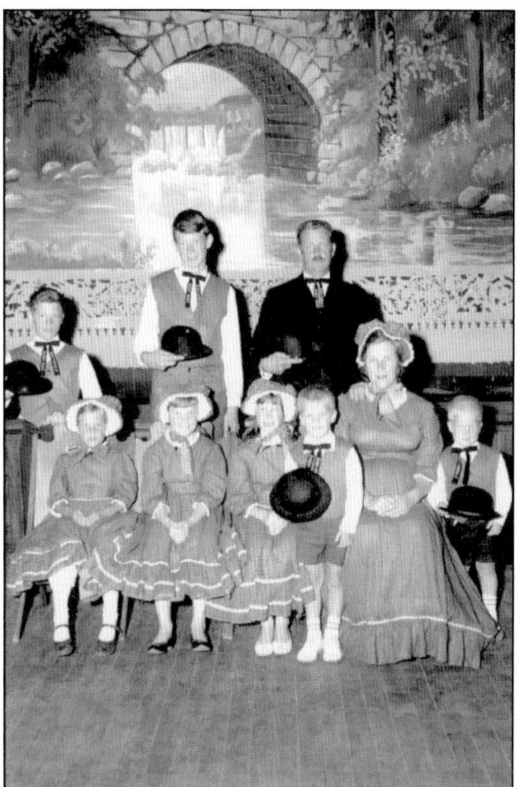

Selectman Richard Coakley and his wife, Doris, pose with their children in Sanford Hall. Doris Coakley made the costumes for herself and the children.

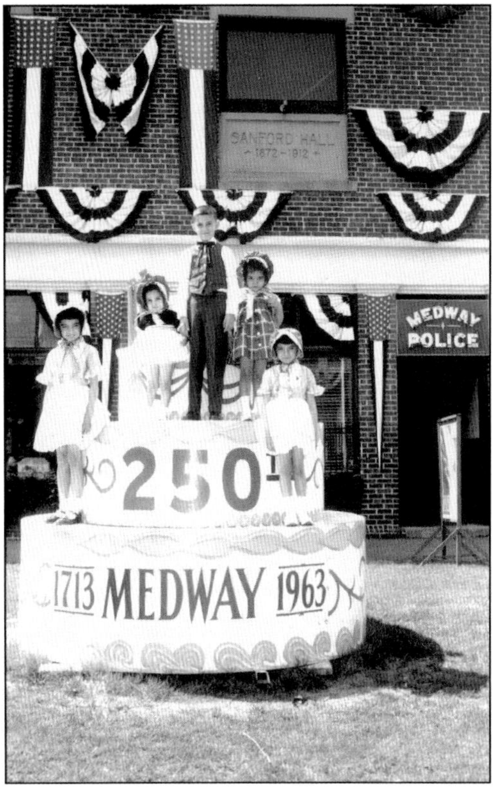

Pictured on top of the birthday cake are the Lewis children, from left to right, Barbara, Carol, Billy, Mary Jane, and Terry. The Rojee Decorating Company made the cake and decorated all town buildings in 1963.

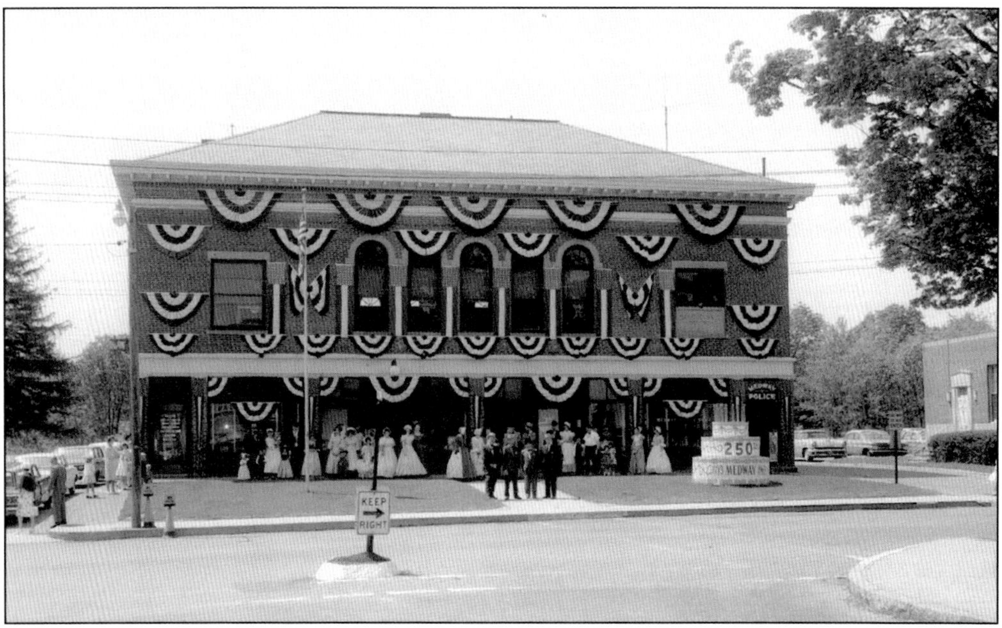

Shown are Sanford Hall and residents dressed up for the 250th anniversary. Decorations throughout the town and many of the parade floats were made by the Rojee Decorating Company, a family business started in the 1950s by Joseph Rojee and now operated by his sons. One of Rojee Decorating's latest projects was building a float for the movie *Mystic River*.

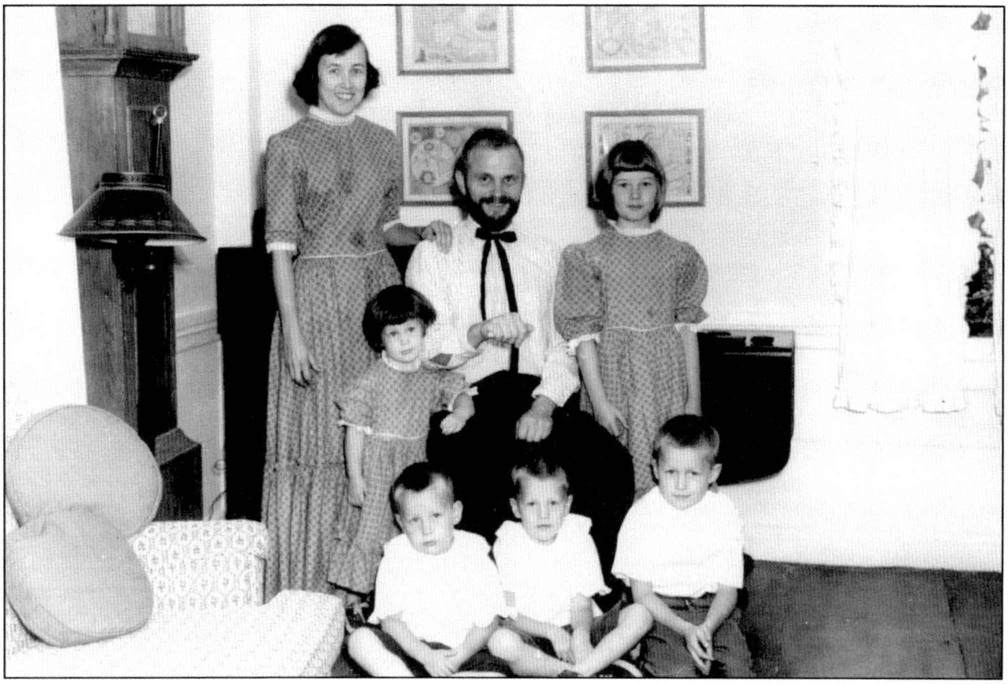

Members of the Hoag family join in the spirit of the celebration, donning period costumes and posing in the living room of their 1800 home. From left to right are the following: (first row) Nick, Jeff, and Peter; (second row) Grace, Lucy, David, and Becky.

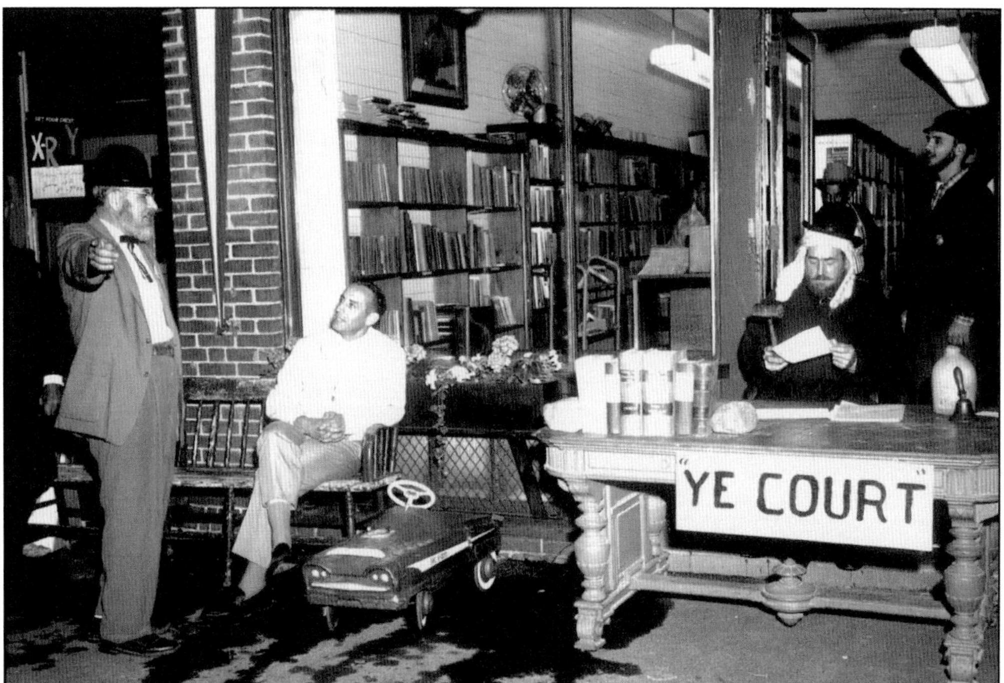

Prosecutor Sam Mushnick makes the case against Mike Matondi for being clean-shaven during the anniversary, while the judge seems disinterested. Visible is the Dean Library (background).

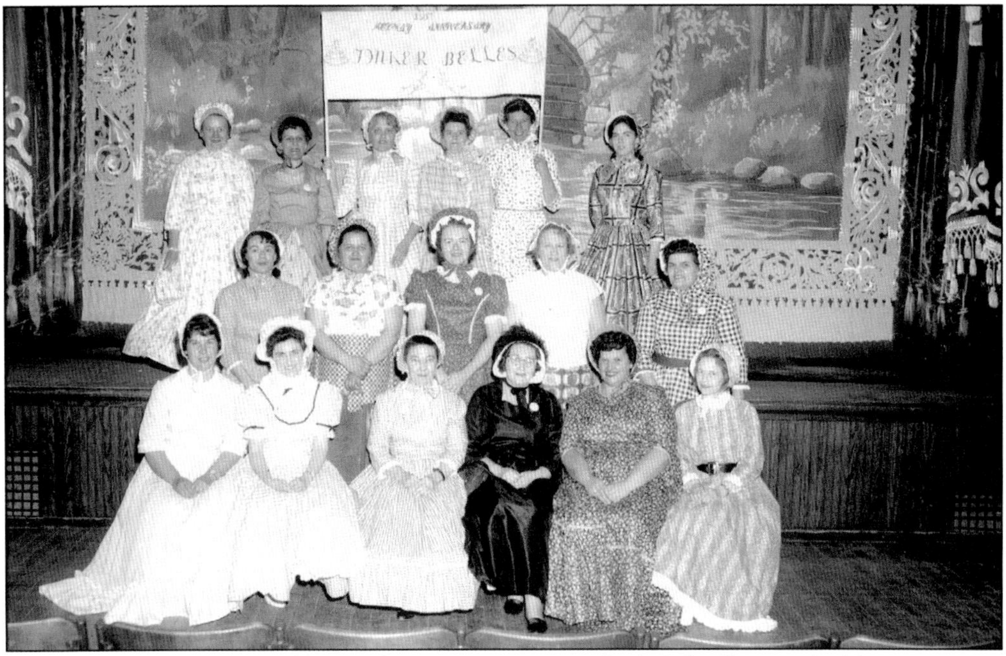

The Anniversary Tinker Belles are shown upstairs at Sanford Hall. The wonderful stage curtain was operated by a large roller at the top of the stage.

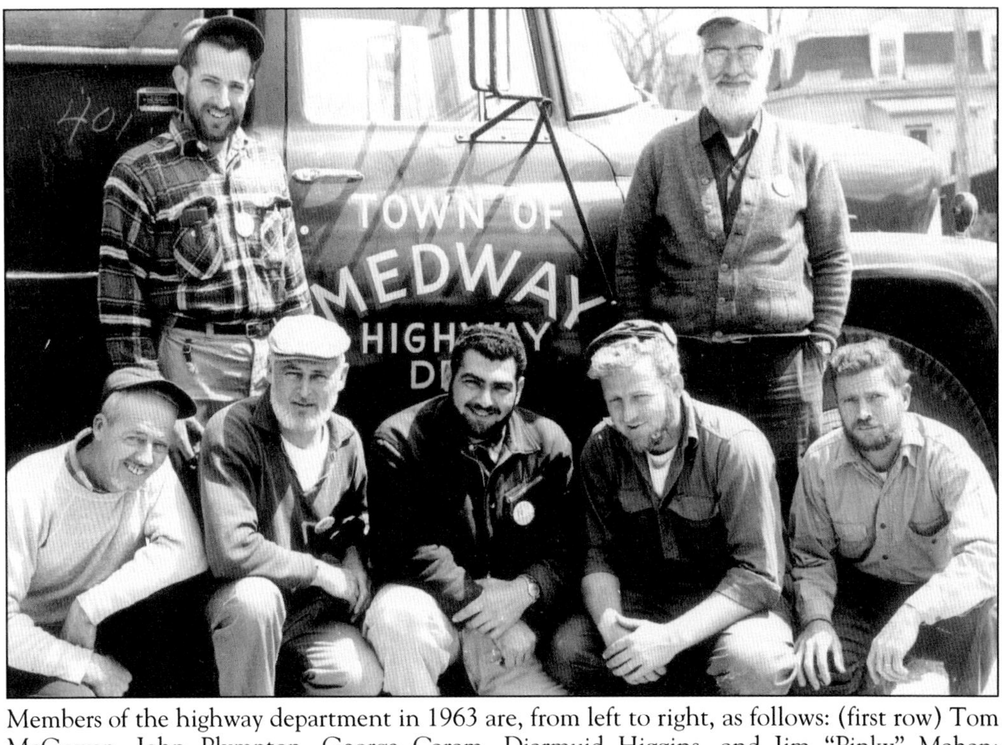

Members of the highway department in 1963 are, from left to right, as follows: (first row) Tom McGowan, John Plympton, George Caram, Diarmuid Higgins, and Jim "Pinky" Mahan; (second row) John Clark and Charlie Upton. Although most men wore the button for a shaving permit, these seven evidently decided not to use it.

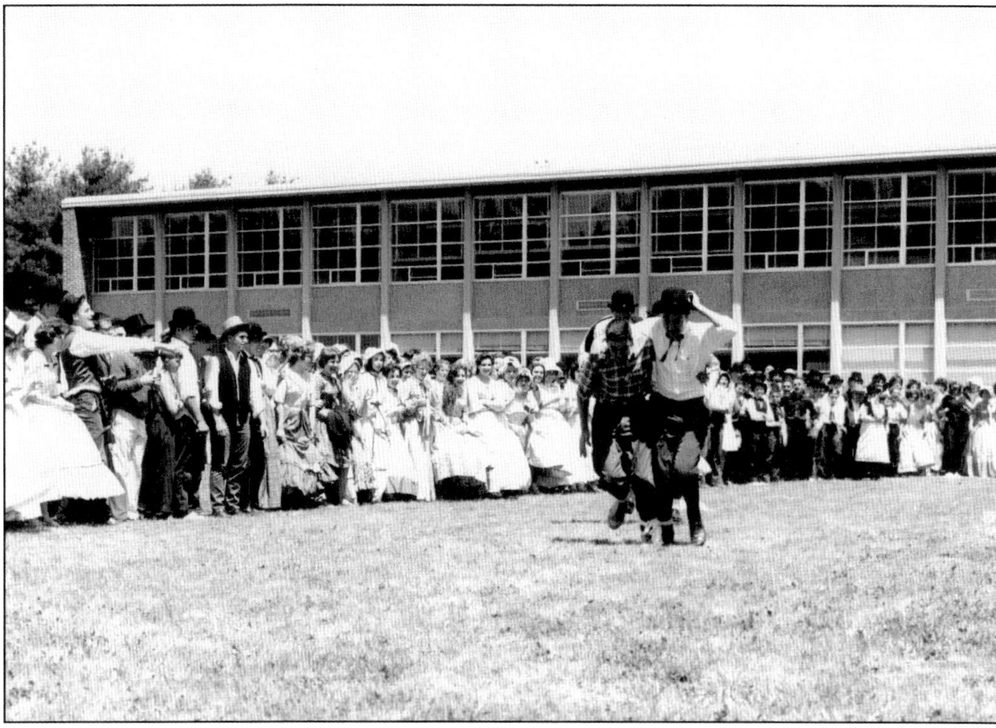

Field days scheduled during the anniversary included three-legged races at the high school (above) and watery tug-of-war competitions between Brothers of the Brush groups (below) on the lower Charles.

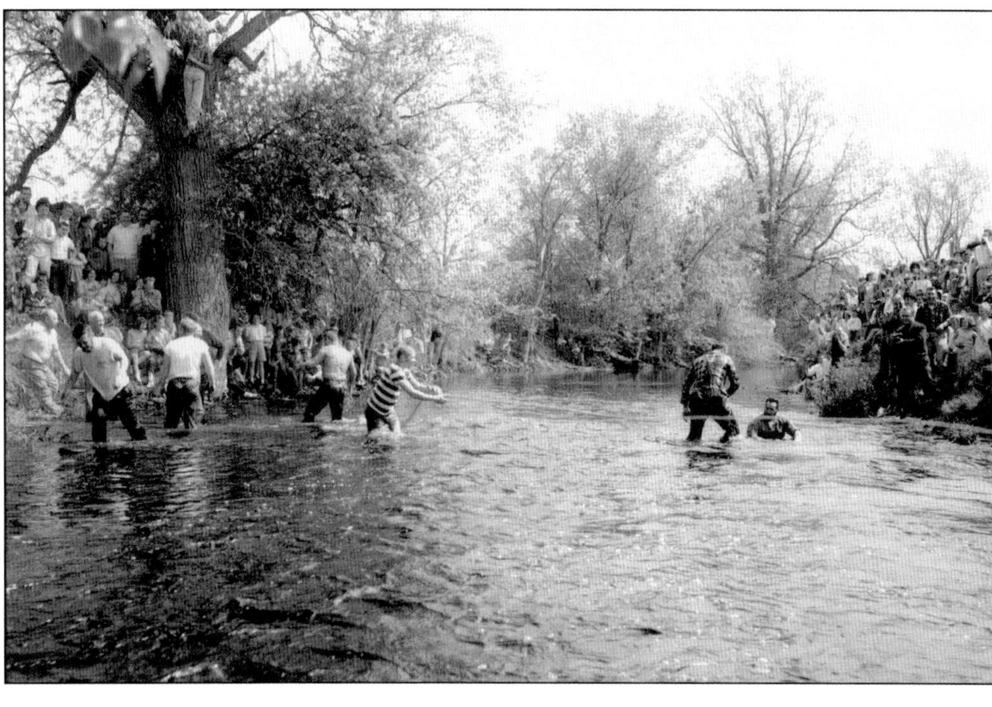

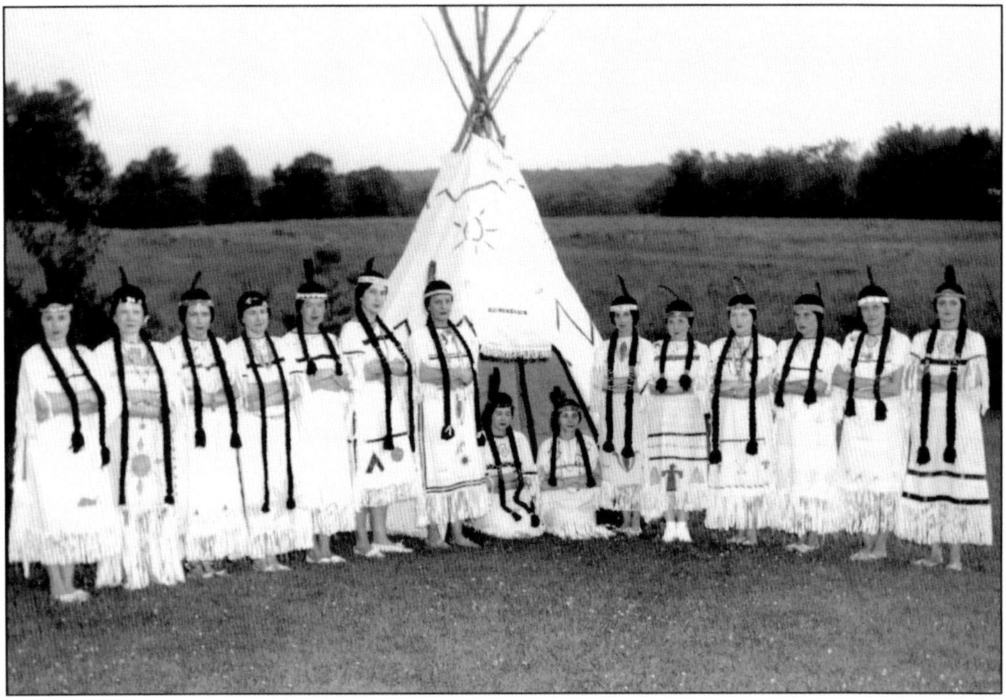

With fine weather during the week, most anniversary events were held outdoors. The Quinobequin Indian Belles (above) are, from left to right, Ann Reardon, Hester Kenney, Isabel Mann, Helena Wasnewsky, Louise Smith, Virginia Glennon, Helen Doyle, Shirley Cherry, June Hemsted, Rosemary Van Rye, Marilyn Bukis, Freda Jacobson, Kay Bates, Irene Hanlon, and Teresa Kenney. The queen and her court (below) attend the pageant spectacular.

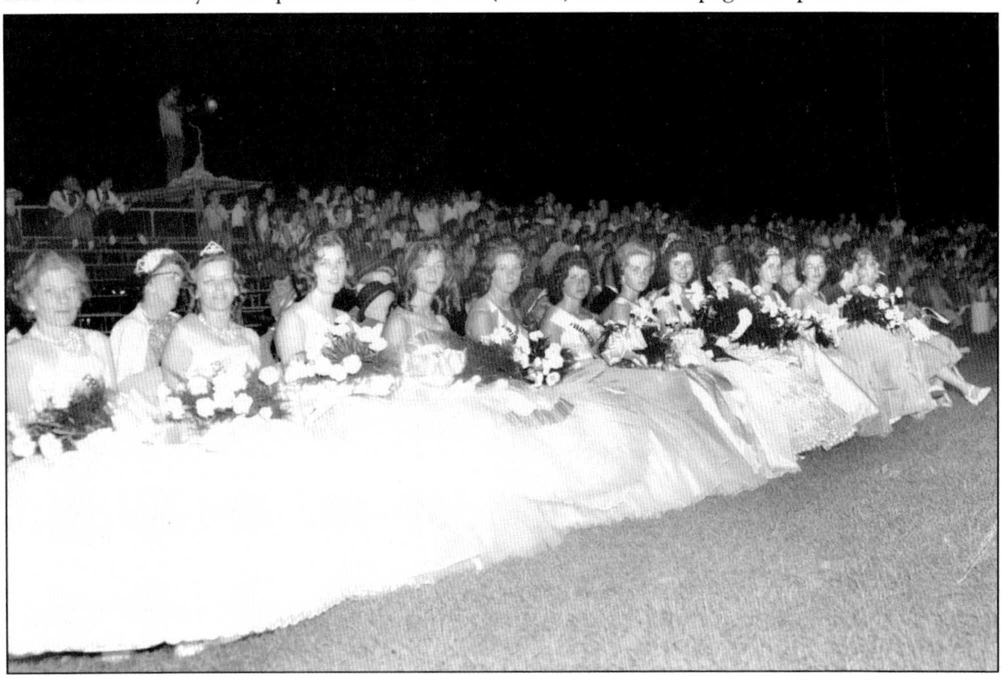